# SPACE AND STORAGE

TIME
LIFE
BOOKS

This volume is part of a series offering home
owners detailed instructions on repairs,
construction and improvements which they can
undertake themselves.

HOME REPAIR
AND IMPROVEMENT

# SPACE AND STORAGE

BY THE EDITORS OF
TIME-LIFE BOOKS

TIME-LIFE BOOKS
AMSTERDAM

**TIME-LIFE BOOKS**
EUROPEAN EDITOR: Kit van Tulleken
*Design Director:* Ed Skyner
*Photography Director:* Pamela Marke
*Chief of Research:* Vanessa Kramer
*Chief Sub-Editor:* Ilse Gray

**HOME REPAIR AND IMPROVEMENT**
EDITORIAL STAFF FOR SPACE AND STORAGE
*Editor:* William Frankel
*Picture Editors:* Adrian G. Allen, Kaye Neil Noble
*Designer:* Herbert H. Quarmby
*Associate Designer:* Robert McKee
*Text Editors:* Don Earnest, Anne Horan, Robert Tschirky
*Staff Writers:* Sally French, Kumait Jawdat, Ruth Kelton, Michael Luftman, Don Nelson
*Researchers:* Tom Lashnits, Brian McGinn, Scot Terrell, Henry Wiencek
*Art Associates:* Faye Eng, Kaye Sherry Hirsh, Richard Salcer
*Editorial Assistant:* Karen Z. Barnard

EUROPEAN EDITION
*Series Editor:* Gillian Moore
*Head Researcher:* Jackie Matthews
*Text Editor:* Christopher Farman
*Researcher:* Mark Karras
*Designer:* Michael Morey
*Design Assistant:* Paul Reeves
*Sub-Editors:* Sally Rowland, Charles Boyle
*Proofreader:* Judith Heaton
*Series Co-ordinator:* Elizabeth Jones

EDITORIAL PRODUCTION
*Chief:* Ellen Brush
*Production Assistants:* Stephanie Lee, Jane Lillicrap, Linda Mallett
*Picture Co-ordinator:* Rebecca Smith
*Art Department:* Janet Matthew
*Editorial Department:* Theresa John, Debra Lelliott

THE CONSULTANTS: Ernest Scott has had more than 50 years of woodworking experience, beginning with an apprenticeship under his father in a firm of quality English cabinet-makers. Following World War II, he worked for 18 months as a joiner in Buckingham Palace before he embarked on a teaching career, which culminated in his appointment as Advisory Teacher in Design and Technology for the Inner London Education Authority. He has been a regular contributor and consultant to the magazine *Practical Woodworking* and is the author of several craft books.

Alan Bayliss served his apprenticeship with a leading Sydney cabinet-making firm. He worked as a carpenter and cabinet-maker for 18 years, then took a Diploma in Teaching from Sydney College of Advanced Education. Since 1970 he has been a teacher of cabinet-making at Sydney Technical College.

Miron Waskiw, the general consultant for this book, is an architect and the founder of Skiltech, a New York centre that offers courses in home repair, woodworking and furniture design.

Don Boyce, a cabinet-maker specializing in custom-designed interior furniture, prepared the plans for and built the bunk bed and room divider project that begins on page 68.

Louis Potts, a practical master of carpentry and electrical work, has been engaged in construction projects for more than 40 years.

Eric Stand, a cabinet-maker who teaches classes in woodworking, prepared the plans for and built the wall storage units on page 6.

# Contents

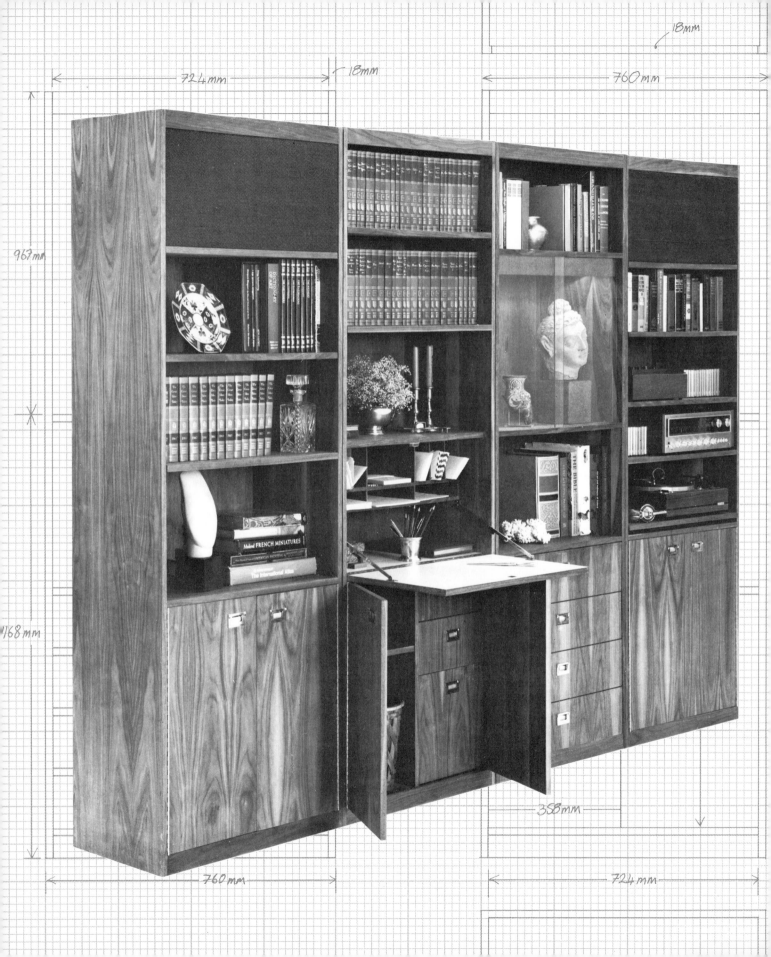

724mm

18mm

18mm

760mm

967mm

768mm

358mm

760mm

724mm

# 1 Making This Book Work for You

**Putting things within reach.** The key to using space effectively lies in storing items where you can get at them conveniently. If you approach the problem with imagination and care you can end up with a piece of furniture as handsome as the wall storage unit on the left. By studying the techniques in this volume and the construction plans that begin on page 84, you can confidently set about building these four modular units, each designed round the same basic carcass. The special features shown here—glass display case, drop-leaf desk, drawers and shelves—and their locations and numbers can be varied according to your own needs and preferences.

Even in a comfortable and pleasant home, the day inevitably comes when the clothes, books, toys, tools and kitchen utensils accumulated over the years crowd all the shelves and cupboards that seemed quite adequate when you first moved in. Fortunately, organizing the available space more efficiently and creating new storage capacity are tasks that any imaginative house owner will be able to accomplish with time-tested, straightforward do-it-yourself techniques. The skills required are quite simple; they range from using your tools in the correct way to joining together pieces of wood. The projects in this book have been carefully selected to present all the necessary working techniques in real situations and to demonstrate how one technique relates to another; thus the projects provide sufficient guidelines to enable you to undertake many enterprises besides those illustrated here.

The scope of this volume is, therefore, a great deal broader than the title alone may suggest. Absorbing its contents will, among other benefits, serve to explain thoroughly:

**Every basic woodworking tool.** As you proceed through the explanations of basic techniques found on the following pages, you will, with surprising speed, acquire an easy familiarity with all the traditional hand tools used for woodworking, as well as the most useful power tools—from chisels to routers, bradawls to electric drills, planes to power saws. A collection of tools necessary for the projects described in this book, and for others you may decide to do, is shown on pages 10–11.

**Essential woodworking skills.** For the home handyman, nothing surpasses wood as an attractive, long-lasting, easy-to-work-with and widely available building material. Furthermore, wood is a more forgiving material than metal or plastic: small errors made in cutting or joining wood can easily be corrected or concealed (page 25). By starting with simple applications of tools, you will quickly learn the correct ways to measure, mark, cut and join wood, and how to hone your new-found skills to keen efficiency. By using a sequential approach, you will advance from the basic methods for measuring, cutting and fixing to the refinements of these and other skills that are required to build cabinets, shelves, drawers and beds. It is the basic theme of this book that a simple box is the traditional building block for all types of storage projects; that if you first learn to build boxes, you can then, by adding drawer-glide assemblies, transform those boxes into drawers (pages 28–32); or, by installing hinges and adding doors, create cabinets (pages 33–37). By selecting the most suitable fixings, you can hang those cabinets securely on any wall. The various types of wall construction, with fixings for each type, are described on pages 42–43.

**What you should know about wood.** You will find a detailed discussion on the characteristics of softwoods, hardwoods and plywoods, enabling you to choose the right material for any project (pages 58–59). You will learn how to choose the right saw to cut it, the right glue to join it and the right sandpaper to smooth and finish it.

**Methods of planning your own projects.** The new skills at your command can spark the imagination. But first you must develop your ideas into workable plans, cutting diagrams for the most economical use of timber or plywood and compiling exact lists of the items you will need to buy. The chapter on job planning will help to simplify these often intimidating chores. In addition, you will learn how to incorporate ready-made items into your own plans.

**How to recognize craftsmanship.** Once you yourself have learnt how to make joints strong and true, to give surfaces a smooth finish, to install hardware properly, there are added dividends: you will be much better equipped to judge craftsmanship—or perhaps the lack of it—when you shop around for commercial pieces of furniture, and you will be more competent in talking to professional carpenters and in being able to judge their work.

**Using the book within this book.** Complete plans and instructions are provided for constructing projects in bedrooms, kitchens, attics, cupboards and under staircases. However, even if you never build these particular projects, the wide variety of skills that are spelt out in the step-by-step presentations can be applied to any project that you decide to create originally or wish to adapt from any source. The wall-storage project shown on page 6 and explained on pages 84–97, for example, includes directions for these diverse procedures: how to install drawer glides, piano hinges, movable shelves, fixed shelves, glass doors, dropleaf desk fronts, drawer pulls and laminated plastic. The more complete list on the opposite page offers a quick-reference guide to the innumerable techniques and procedures that are discussed in detail throughout this book.

If you have never tried your hand at woodworking, start simply: shop for the best buys in good basic tools and begin acquiring a home tool kit appropriate to your immediate ambitions. However, before you tackle even a simple woodworking project, get a few pieces of scrap timber and spend some time practising with them. Pick up your brand-new handsaw and use it on the scrap. Develop the skill to make eye and arm work together to saw a straight cut with minimum effort. (The trick is never to force; always let the sharp teeth of the saw do the real work.) Get the feel of your hammer; find the place near the bottom of the handle that gives you the best grip. Drive a variety of nails into the scrap boards. Discover the satisfaction of driving a nail home with a minimum of blows. Drill a number of pilot and clearance holes. Insert screws of appropriate size. Plane the scrap. Sand it.

When you feel able to use your tools with confidence, set about making the basic box; pages 12–16 tell you how to build it. Plan the job; any other approach simply means wasted effort and unnecessary expense. Buy the materials you will need. Measure and cut the wood. Glue and nail the joints together. Sand down the surfaces. And then apply the finish of your choice.

It takes only time and patience to develop the rudimentary skills. Your confidence will grow more quickly than you ever dreamt possible. And with that confidence you will be ready to tackle your own space and storage problems with creative craftsmanship.

# The Techniques of Woodworking

This is not just a book on how to use space wisely; it is a primer of many woodworking techniques. For instance, if you want to put up shelves, this book, properly utilized, will tell you how to measure, buy wood and cut it, what types of fixings and supports to use, and how to drill correctly. Or, using other techniques in this volume, you can design a chest of drawers—making the cabinet any size you like, to hold as many drawers as you need. And so forth.

The complete index that begins on page 124 includes definitions of terms that are peculiar to woodworking, as well as references to the tools, materials and different kinds of storage units described in the book. To use the index creatively in working out your own projects and designs, first list the elements you wish to incorporate in the plans; then look in the index for specific entries. For quick reference, use the list below to locate those basic techniques needed for planning and executing nearly any carpentry project in the home.

# Tool Kit for All Projects

Tools used for the projects in this volume are shown on the right. Buy the more specialized items only as you need them.

☐ To measure and mark you will need a level at least half a metre long; a steel square; a combination square; a spring-loaded steel tape measure at least 3 metres long; a bradawl, which is used for making starting holes in wood for screws; and a centre punch to make starting points in metal for drill bits.

☐ Cutting tools include the crosscut saw for across-the-grain work; a hacksaw for metal; a tenon saw for use in a mitre box; a block plane; wood chisels, and a cold chisel for harder materials, such as tiles and plaster. To keep tools well honed, an oilstone and machine oil are recommended.

☐ To hold pieces of wood tightly together while glue sets and you put in nails and screws, you will need pipe or sash cramps to span large pieces; general-purpose G-cramps; hand screws with non-marring wood jaws; and corner cramps, which will ensure that joints are square. Also necessary is a woodworking vice to hold various pieces securely while being worked upon.

☐ Tools for joining and finishing include a claw hammer; an assortment of screwdrivers, both single and cross-slotted; mole-grip pliers; and an adjustable spanner. Also useful will be a rubber or wooden mallet for striking wood chisels and tapping wood joints together; a set of Allen keys for hardware installation; nail sets, with tips 1.5 and 3 mm in diameter, to countersink fixings; and a filling knife for wood filler.

☐ Power tools require a substantial investment, but they pay off in speed, finer craftsmanship and muscle power saved. An electric drill is essential, preferably a 13 mm, variable-speed model. A circular saw makes easy work of long straight cuts. Also handy are a jigsaw, sometimes called a sabre saw, for cutting round curves and in tight spots, and an orbital sander. A router is a versatile tool that makes housing and rebate joints, and trims edges faster and straighter than a circular saw. And goggles are a necessary safety device when operating any power tool.

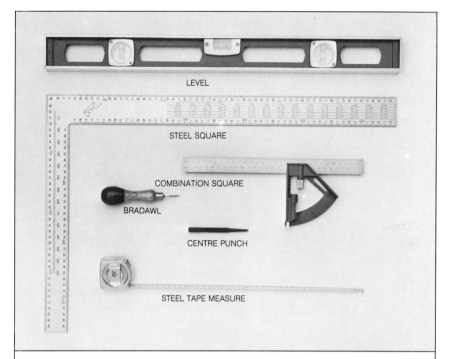

LEVEL

STEEL SQUARE

COMBINATION SQUARE

BRADAWL

CENTRE PUNCH

STEEL TAPE MEASURE

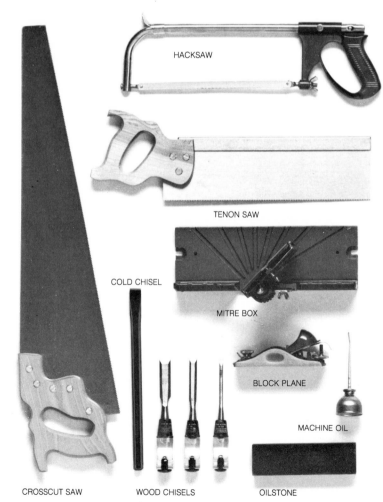

HACKSAW

TENON SAW

COLD CHISEL

MITRE BOX

BLOCK PLANE

MACHINE OIL

CROSSCUT SAW

WOOD CHISELS

OILSTONE

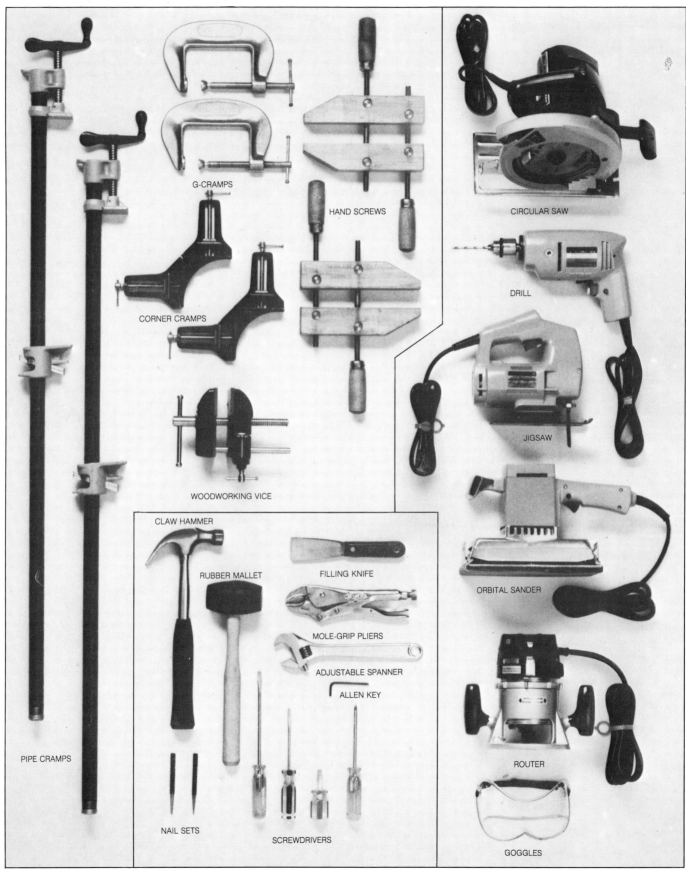

G-CRAMPS

HAND SCREWS

CIRCULAR SAW

DRILL

CORNER CRAMPS

JIGSAW

WOODWORKING VICE

ORBITAL SANDER

CLAW HAMMER

RUBBER MALLET

FILLING KNIFE

MOLE-GRIP PLIERS

ADJUSTABLE SPANNER

ALLEN KEY

ROUTER

PIPE CRAMPS

NAIL SETS

SCREWDRIVERS

GOGGLES

11

# Begin with the Box—a Basic Building Block

The basic building block for all storage units is the box. Place a box on its side and then add horizontal dividers, and it becomes a bookshelf; add a pair of doors and it becomes a cabinet; attach tracks and it becomes a drawer.

All boxes, whatever their use, share one common element of construction: the right-angled corner. The joint most commonly employed to make a right-angled corner—because it is the easiest—is the butt, which is used to illustrate the construction of a simple box on the following pages. Although it is sufficient for many purposes, the butt joint is, in fact, the weakest. Of the many choices of varying complexity and strength, five joints stand out as the most useful: the rebate, housing, mitre, corner halving and T halving; they are described on pages 17–23.

Many of the tools, techniques and procedures employed in making a butt joint are applicable to the other types of joint.

☐ MEASURING. The cardinal principle of good craftsmanship is to check and recheck the accuracy of your measurements. This rule, unfortunately, too often falls victim to impatience. Even before measuring, check the end of every piece of wood with a right-angle square; if the piece is not precisely squared, the subsequent measurements are bound to be inaccurate. Measurements should be rechecked after you have marked a piece of wood and before you start to cut. Then check yet again after cutting.

☐ MARKING. It is best to mark up wood with a hard, well-sharpened pencil, because pencil marks can be erased if you make a mistake. Always be sure, though, that the pencil is neither blunt nor soft—either of these will leave a relatively wide mark, which can lead to inaccuracies.

☐ CUTTING. As a saw cuts, its blade chews up an amount of wood equal to the thickness of the blade. The slit that results from this cut, called a kerf, must be taken into account for measuring and cutting. Always saw on the "waste" side of the mark made for cutting so that the kerf will not affect the measured area. For the same reason, when cutting several sections from one piece of wood, measure and cut the first section, and only then measure and cut the next section, and so on.

There are many kinds of cutting tool, some much more specialized than others for shaping joints. For example, for work with boxes built from pieces of wood less than 50 mm thick and no more than 100 mm wide—such as the box on the following pages—the tenon saw, with its rigid back, used in conjunction with a mitre box is ideal. For larger boxes, power cutting tools *(pages 10–11)* provide greater accuracy with considerably less effort.

☐ ASSEMBLING. The wood adhesive most often used is polyvinyl acetate (PVA), a resin glue in the form of a thick milky liquid. It is often called woodworking glue. Though only one of a wide variety of adhesives, some of which are compared on page 61, PVA is favoured because it becomes transparent as it dries. Follow the manufacturer's instructions.

When nails are combined with glue, they strengthen the box substantially. Use lost-head nails—or panel pins—whose length is three times the thickness of the wood into which they are driven first. Unless otherwise indicated, always hammer them in at a slight angle and alternate the direction to increase the holding power. Blunt the point of each nail with a hammer blow before driving it in; a blunted nail crushes the fibres of the wood instead of parting them, and is less likely to split the wood.

## Assembling the Basic Box

**1** **Measuring the wood.** To make the first side of a box with butt joints, lay a steel tape measure on a piece of wood parallel to an edge. Using a pencil, mark a point on the wood *(right)* to indicate the length you want minus the thickness of the wood to which it is to be joined. For example, if the side of the box is to be 280 mm long and the abutting piece is 20 mm thick, the wood for the side should be cut to a length of 260 mm.

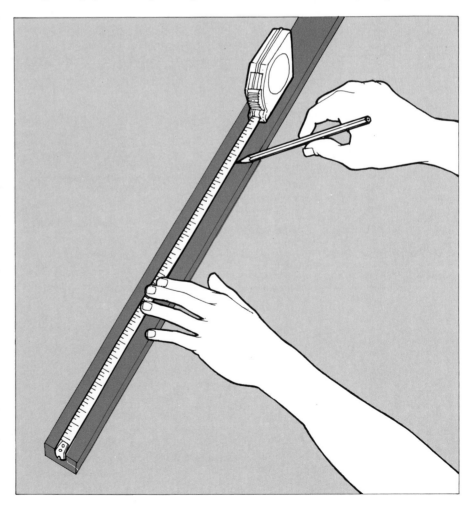

**2** **Drawing a guideline.** Place the stock of a combination square tight against the edge of the wood and position it so that the rule intersects the pencil mark made in Step 1; make another line across the board through the mark.

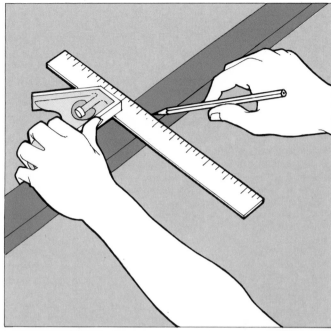

**3** **Cutting the wood.** Place the wood in a mitre box *(below)* and set the angle at 90 degrees. Align the blade to cut just barely on the waste side of the pencil line. Begin sawing on the backstroke and continue in long, smooth strokes, to ensure a clean cut. Check the cut end for squareness and smooth it down, if necessary, with a block plane. Measure, mark and cut the other three sides of the box in the same manner. Compare opposing sides with each other to make sure that the measurements are exactly the same.

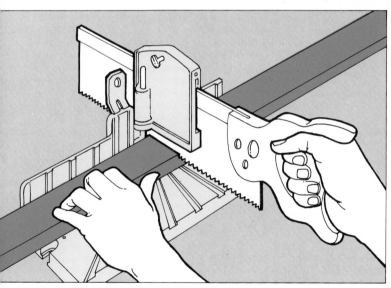

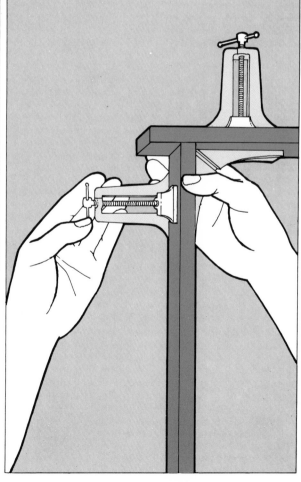

**4** **Positioning the first two sides.** Place one of the pieces of wood on its edge in a corner cramp, with the end projecting at least 50 mm beyond the corner of the cramp. Tighten the cramp screw. Place the second piece in the cramp so that it butts against the first piece and tighten the second cramp screw. (If the box is to be rectangular rather than square, join the sides in a consistent order: either butt the longer piece against the shorter piece, or the shorter against the longer, but make sure the order is the same for both joints. Butting the wrong piece will give the wrong dimensions.) Remove the first piece of wood from the cramp.

**5** **Applying glue.** Spread the glue on the end of the side that is still in the cramp, using just enough for an even coating. Return the first piece of wood to the cramp so that its end is flush with the outside edge of the piece already in the cramp; tighten the piece of wood in place.

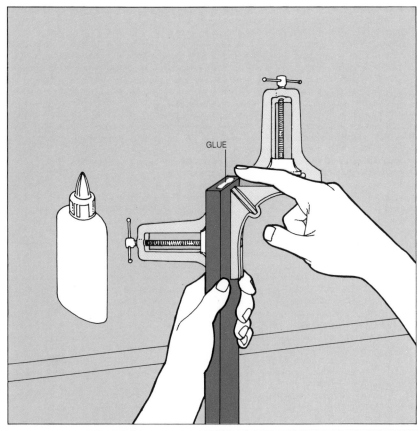

GLUE

**6** **Securing the joint.** Blunt the point of a nail and position it at a point about one-third of the way in on the top board. Holding the nail at a slight angle, drive it through the top board to secure it to the lower piece of wood (*below*): stop hammering before the nail head is flush with the surface. Measuring from the other edge, drive in a second blunted nail at a point one-third in from the end and at an angle opposing that of the first nail. If the board is wider than 150 mm, space the nails at intervals of approximately 50 mm.

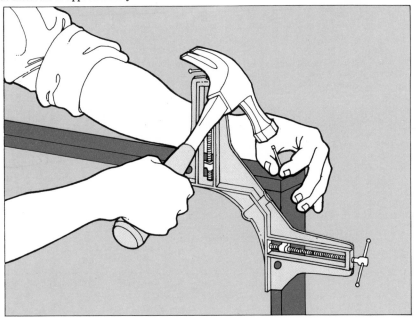

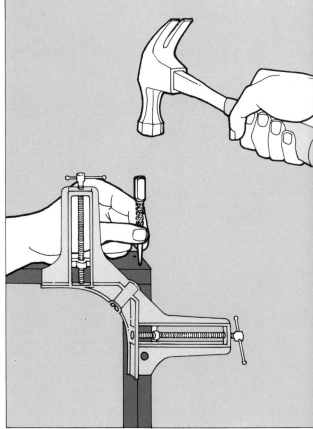

**7** **Finishing the joint.** Using a nail set no larger than the nail head, drive the nails to just below the surface of the wood. Wipe away any excess glue, and set the joint aside to dry. When the joint is dry, remove the corner cramps and repeat Steps 4 to 7 to make the second joint of the box.

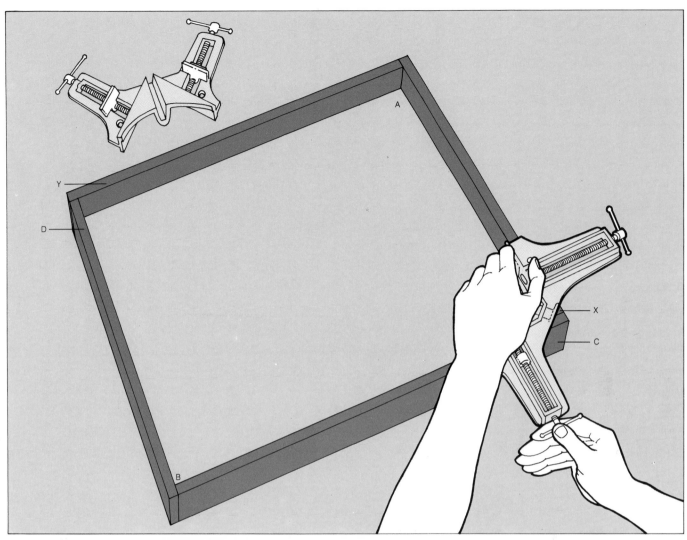

**8** **Joining the four sides.** Lay the two L-shaped sections already jointed at A and B on a flat surface so that the unjoined corners abut: X against C and D against Y. Place the cramps over the two new corners. Then loosen the matching screw on each cramp to free one of the sections and remove it. Apply an even layer of glue to ends D and X, return the free section to its place in the cramps, tighten the screws and nail the new joints in position. Set aside to dry.

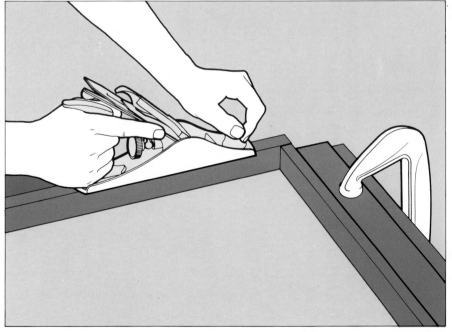

**9** **Truing the joints.** To true up any minor misalignments at the corners, remove excess wood with a plane. Brace the joint against a length of wood held tightly with a G-cramp to the top of a workbench, and begin planing at least 75 mm away from the joint. Repeat the truing process with the other three joints.

**10** **Marking off the bottom.** Lay the sides on a large board from which the bottom will be cut. After making sure that one of the corners of the board is square, align it with two of the sides, and mark off the other two with a pencil. If it matters which surface of the wood will show, be sure to mark the correct surface. Different saws splinter the wood on different surfaces: for a crosscut saw, mark the surface that will be visible; for a jigsaw or a circular saw, mark the surface that will not be seen. Cut just outside the pencil lines.

**11** **Attaching the bottom.** Spread glue along the bottom edges of the four sides and place the bottom in position, securing it with lost-head nails at one corner. Check that the box is square. Then secure the opposite corner. Secure the rest of the bottom with lost-head nails at 100 mm intervals and countersink the nails. For a neater job, you can apply wood filler to the countersunk indentations, the spaces between the bottom and sides, and any scratches. Use a filling knife for this operation *(below)*. To keep excess filler off the wood, apply just enough pressure to the knife to keep the blade slightly bent while spreading the filler towards you. Set the box aside to dry.

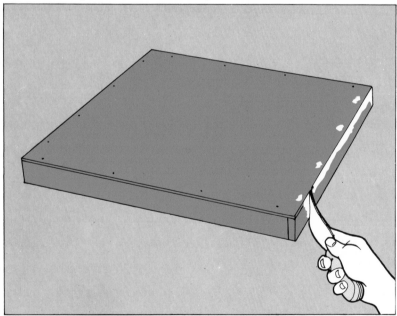
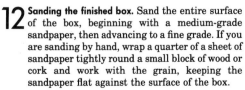

**12** **Sanding the finished box.** Sand the entire surface of the box, beginning with a medium-grade sandpaper, then advancing to a fine grade. If you are sanding by hand, wrap a quarter of a sheet of sandpaper tightly round a small block of wood or cork and work with the grain, keeping the sandpaper flat against the surface of the box.

# Strengthening the Basic Box

When storage boxes are to be pushed and pulled (as they are when used as drawers), or if they are to be hung on walls (cabinets) or loaded with heavy objects (tool chests), the corners should be strengthened. This can be done by making joints that are stronger than the butt type used for the box on the preceding pages; also, the box can be reinforced by bracing or framing.

The butt joint is relatively weak because the area of contact at the corners is limited to only one surface on each piece of wood. The stronger joints, however, may have many shared surfaces, which are formed by cutting the ends of two pieces of wood into various complementary shapes. The drawings on the right show the areas of contact for six types of joint—those most commonly used for storage units—and outline their strengths and weaknesses. Instructions for making each type begin overleaf.

Whichever type of joint you opt for, it can be made stronger by adding braces. Metal angle irons in the corners of small boxes, for instance, add rigidity and help to prevent warping. Such braces are also useful for repairing loose joints.

For larger boxes, braces of solid wood give still greater support. Such blocks can be glued inside the corners and along the full length of the joint. Wood blocks are particularly useful for making boxes from plywood, which is made of several layers of wood glued together under pressure. Joints made at the ends of most types of plywood are relatively weak; glue applied there seeps into the plies instead of adhering to the surface, and nails or screws separate the plies and do not hold securely. Wood blocks solve this reinforcing problem.

The largest—and strongest—boxes are usually constructed over a wooden frame, thereby reducing stress on the corners. Basic techniques for building frames are shown on page 24.

Before choosing a joining technique, consider the time you want to give to a project and how important the subtleties of craftsmanship are to you. In any case, practise on scraps of timber before tackling a real job with expensive wood.

## Types of Wood Joints

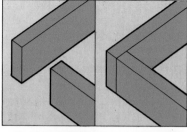

**Butt.** As indicated on the preceding pages, the area of contact for this joint is limited to the end of one side that butts against the surface of a second side. It is the weakest type of joint, but it is also the easiest to make; when reinforced with braces, the butt can hold together a large box that is not subjected to too much weight.

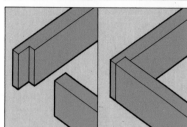

**Rebate.** The shared area of contact is increased by joining one piece of wood to a notch cut out of the end of a second piece. This type of joint construction also allows nails or screws to be used on both pieces at right angles to each other, which creates a strong, locking effect.

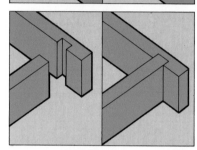

**Housing.** To make this joint, a channel is cut into one piece of wood so that a second piece of wood can butt into it. The channel should be no deeper than one-third of the thickness of the first piece of wood. Many drawers are constructed with housings, since this type of joint withstands stress from several directions.

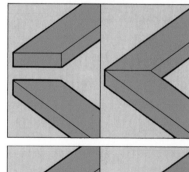

**Mitre.** For a mitre joint, the ends of two pieces of wood are cut at a 45 degree angle. The mitre, which is only marginally stronger than the butt, is used almost exclusively for appearance; the joint successfully conceals the exposed ends of each piece of wood. It is the standard type for picture frames and small decorative boxes.

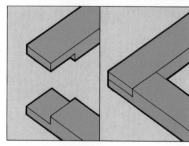

**Corner halving.** To cut this joint, half the thickness of the wood is removed from the end of each corner piece. Cutting the notches so they fit together precisely requires care and skill, but the final result is a very strong joint that is the preferred type in building frames for boxes.

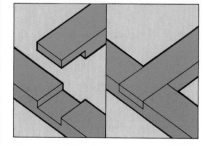

**T halving.** This type is formed by fitting the end of one piece of wood into the middle of another, with half the thickness removed from the area shared by the two pieces. It is used mostly on frames for boxes—especially large plywood boxes such as cupboards, for which the additional strength of the frame is essential.

## The Rebate Joint

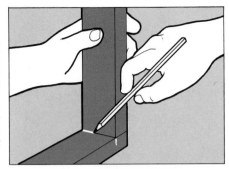

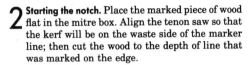

**1** **Marking the wood.** Hold the two pieces of wood together as if you were making a butt joint. With the edge of the vertical piece as a guide, use a pencil to mark a line across the surface of the horizontal piece *(right)*. Then use a rule and pencil to extend the line to approximately one-third the total depth of the wood. Too deep a cut for the notch will weaken the rebate. At right angles to the first line, mark two more pencil lines along the edges to the end of the piece of wood.

**2** **Starting the notch.** Place the marked piece of wood flat in the mitre box. Align the tenon saw so that the kerf will be on the waste side of the marker line; then cut the wood to the depth of line that was marked on the edge.

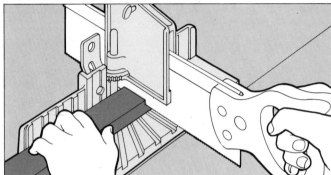

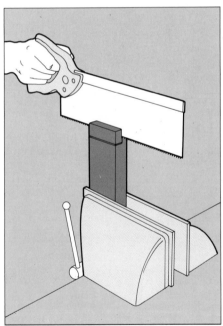

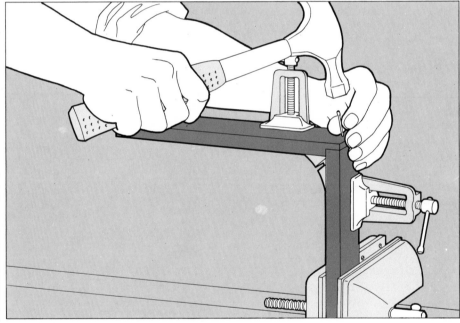

**3** **Sawing out the notch.** Set the piece of wood in a woodworking vice with cut end up. Align the tenon saw perpendicular to the saw cut made in Step 2 so that the kerf will be on the waste side of the pencil lines; then saw along the lines until the vertical and horizontal cuts meet and the block falls away. Place the two pieces of wood in a corner cramp and check for fit. Plane if necessary. Remove one piece, apply glue and replace in the cramp. The roughened surfaces created by the saw cuts are ideal for gluing.

**4** **Nailing the sides.** Secure the unnotched side in the vice. Place a nail one-third the distance from each edge of the notched piece and hammer both nails into the second piece. Loosen the cramp and countersink. To strengthen the joint further, hammer a third nail through the centre of the butt piece into the notched piece, positioning the nail at a right angle to the other nails. Retighten the cramp and allow the joint to dry.

# The Housing Joint

**1 Marking the housing channel.** Determine how far from the end of the wood you want the channel to be, and indicate the position with a small mark. To establish the outside edge of the channel, place the stock of a combination square flush against the side of the wood, aligning the blade with the small mark. Make a line with a pencil across the surface. To establish the inside edge, butt the second piece of wood against the first, align its outer edge with the pencil mark and make a line along its inside edge *(right)*. Using a rule and the pencil, extend the two lines down both edges to the desired depth of the channel.

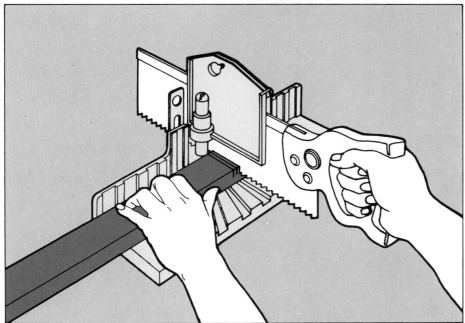

**2 Cutting the channel.** Place the marked piece of wood in a mitre box and saw along the inside of each mark to the desired depth of the channel. One or two additional cuts sawed into the wood between the first two saw cuts will make the waste fall away more easily.

**3 Chiselling out the channel.** The cut piece of wood can be set vertically *(right)* or horizontally in a woodworking vice. Pare the waste out with a chisel held perpendicular to the wood, bevelled side facing outwards. Tap the chisel gently with the mallet until the channel is flat and even.

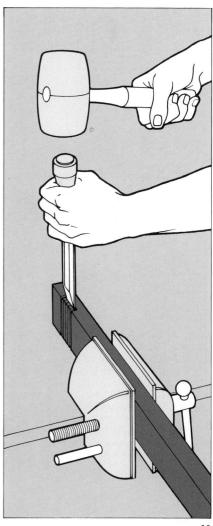

**4** **Tapering the butt piece.** If the butt piece does not fit into the channel, brace its end against a block of wood clamped to the worktable by a G-cramp. With the chisel's bevelled face down, as shown below, use it to taper the thickness of the wood slightly. An alternative method is to taper the wood with a smoothing plane until the butt piece fits tightly into the channel.

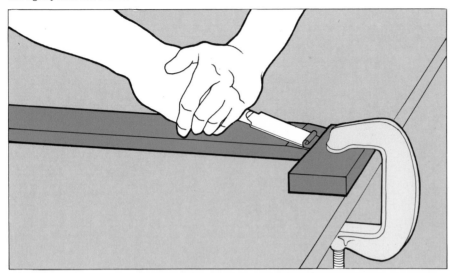

**5** **Joining the sides.** Secure the butt piece perpendicularly in a woodworking vice and apply glue to all surfaces to be joined. Place the channel over the end of the butt piece, and a corner cramp on the joint. Position two blunted lost-head nails or panel pins on the channelled piece, one-third of the way in from each edge *(left)*; drive them in flush with the surface of the wood.

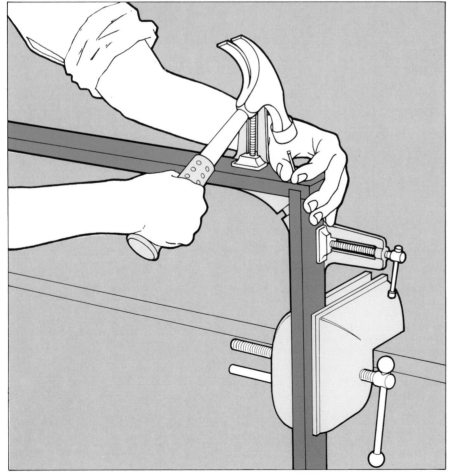

## The Mitre Joint

**1 Marking a mitre.** Place a combination square slightly in from one end of the wood, with its stock tight against the edge, and the ruled blade at a 45 degree angle across the surface. Use a pencil to mark a line *(right)*. When marking the mitre at the other end, turn the combination square over so that the angle of the second cut will be the reverse of the first.

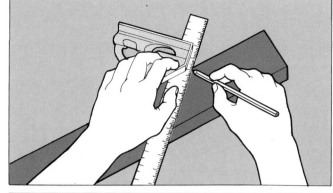

**2 Cutting the mitre.** Adjust the mitre box so that the tenon saw will cut at a 45 degree angle. Place the marked piece of wood flat in the mitre box and align it so that the tenon saw kerf will be on the waste side of the pencil mark. Cut all the way through the wood. Then mark and cut the second piece of wood in the same manner.

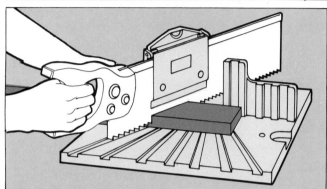

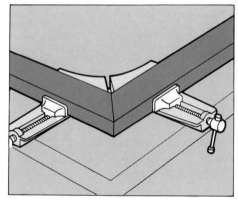

**3 Checking the mitre.** Place the two pieces of wood in a corner cramp. If the ends do not fit snugly, remove both pieces and lightly plane the rough areas. Check the fit again and repeat the procedure until the ends fit exactly. Remove a piece of wood from the cramp, apply glue to both surfaces of the joint and return the wood to the cramp.

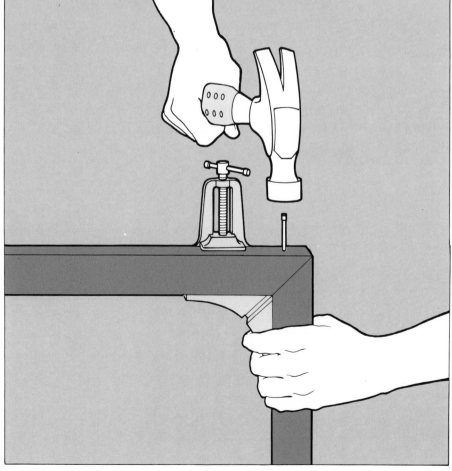

**4 Nailing the joint.** Place one piece of the mitre joint in a woodworking vice. Position at least one blunted lost-head nail in the centre of the top piece of wood, a little in from the end, and drive it into the second piece *(right)*; for the greatest holding power, hammer the nail straight in, then countersink it. Remove the joint from the vice, turn it round, and nail the other side.

## The Corner-Halving Joint

**1 Marking the notch.** Make sure the ends of both pieces of wood are squared. Lap the end of one piece over the end of the second piece so that each end is flush with the outside edge of the other. With the inside edge of the top piece as a guide, use a pencil to mark a line across the surface of the bottom piece *(right)*; using a rule, extend the line half way down the edge. Turn the two pieces over, align their edges again and mark the second piece in the same manner. Place one piece of wood in a mitre box and saw on the waste side of the pencil mark to the depth marked on the edge. Then cut the second piece of wood in the same manner.

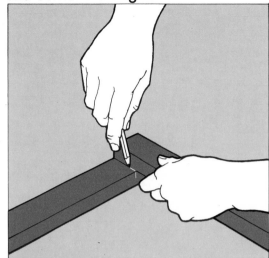

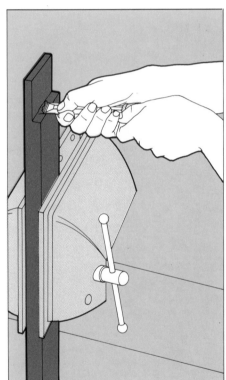

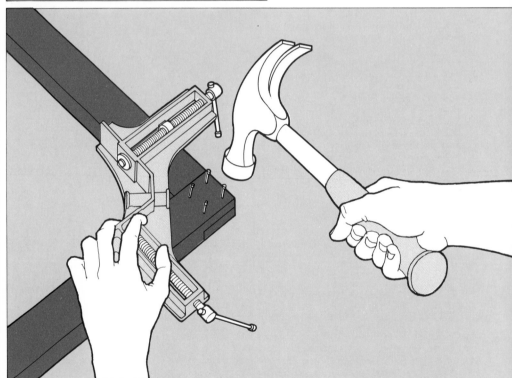

**2 Cutting out and finishing the notch.** Follow the instructions given in Step 3 on page 18 to cut out the notch on the two pieces of wood. Place both pieces in a corner cramp to check for fit.

If necessary, chisel the cut edges. Secure one piece of wood, cut side up, in a woodworking vice *(above)*. Grip the chisel with the heel of one hand against the handle and the thumb of the other on the bevel side of the blade. Make light shaving strokes, working at a slight angle to the horizontal. Repeat on all the cut edges as necessary. When both pieces fit together perfectly in the cramp, remove one piece, apply glue to the surfaces to be joined and return it to the cramp.

**3 Nailing the joint.** When the glue has set, lay the cramped pieces of wood flat. Drive four blunted lost-head nails, each slightly shorter than the total thickness of the joint, at opposing angles through the top piece and into the second piece; countersink the nails. Because of their greater holding power, you may prefer to use one or two wood screws instead of nails. If so, insert the screws from the underside of the joint.

**Another kind of halving.** This joint combines the channelling and notching techniques used in making the housing joint and the corner-halving joint. As shown on page 19 in Steps 2 and 3 for the housing joint, cut and chisel a channel the desired distance from the end of a piece of wood; make the channel as wide as the piece of wood to be joined. To mark and cut the notch in the end of the second piece of wood, follow Steps 1 and 2 on page 22 for the corner-halving joint. Then place the two pieces of wood in a corner cramp to make sure they fit together. Remove the notched piece, apply glue to both notch and channel, and replace the piece in the cramp *(right)*. Reinforce the joint with nails or wood screws.

## The T-Halving Joint

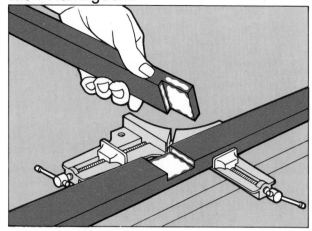

**Wood.** Rectangular wooden blocks *(top)* are frequently used to reinforce a joint along its entire length. They also make it possible to join two thin pieces of wood; attaching a wooden block to one piece of wood creates an edge to which the second piece can be joined. Triangular blocks *(middle)* occupy less space than square blocks and look neater. Attach any wooden block with glue. Because the wood is only small, nails can easily split it. Gluing on its own will, therefore, often make a more secure joint than gluing and nailing. If you do add nails, stagger them as shown. Gusset plates *(bottom)*, which are triangles of thin plywood glued and nailed to the corners, add extra strength to a bottomless box, such as an unbacked bookcase.

## Types of Joint Brace

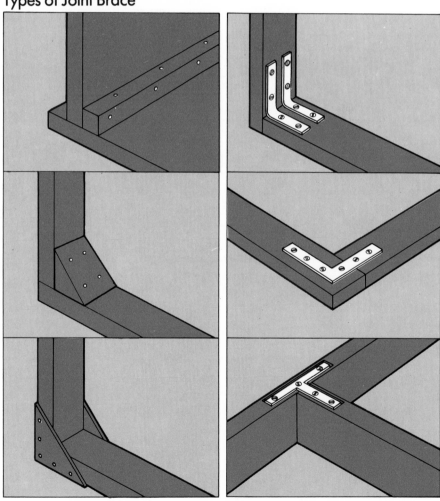

**Metal.** These devices can strengthen or repair a joint. The inside corner brace *(top)* and the flat corner brace *(middle)* reinforce a right-angled corner joint; the T brace *(bottom)* gives added support to the joints on a box frame. Braces can be screwed directly on to the surface of the wood or they can be recessed *(page 35)*.

# Framing for Greater Strength

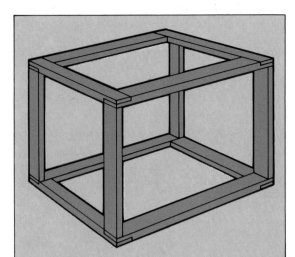

**Box frames.** If thin pieces of timber or plywood are to be used for a box, the box must be built round a frame. To build one, make two identical squares or rectangles, using the type of corner joint you prefer (corner-halving joints are shown on the left). Connect the two with butt joints at the four corners, using pieces of wood of equal length. For larger boxes *(below)*, reinforce the top and bottom of the frame with ribs (attached here by T-halving joints). To complete the box, attach the sides in the manner shown for attaching the bottom of the basic box *(page 16)*.

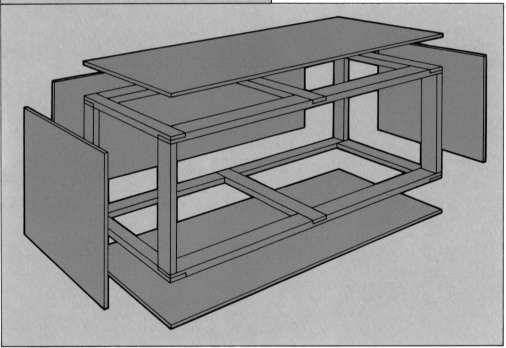

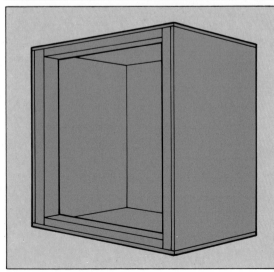

**Face frames.** If a door is to be put on a box made of thin timber or plywood, a frame secured within the opening and flush with the front edges of the box will supply all the surface area needed so that hinges can be securely mounted. Cut the four sides of the frame, making sure they fit precisely inside the box. Apply glue to the sides of the frame that will butt against the box. Reinsert the frame—sides first, then top and bottom—so that its face is flush with the face of the box. Drive and countersink nails.

# Correcting Mistakes

Cutting a housing—or any other kind of channel—in the wrong place or driving a nail where it is not wanted are common errors that anyone working with wood is bound to make sooner or later.

A housing channel that has been mislocated and then left empty not only looks unprofessional, but it also weakens the piece of wood. However, a strip of wood can be cut to the size of the channel and glued into position; it will be hardly noticeable and the piece will be as strong as ever.

A nail that has been hammered all the way in at the wrong place, or one whose head has been countersunk, can be removed only by cutting away a section of the wood with a chisel until the nail is sufficiently exposed to be grasped by a pair of pliers and carefully prized out. The area surrounding the cavity left by the nail will be marred, but the damage can be concealed with wood filler.

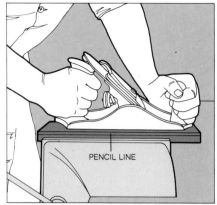

PENCIL LINE

## Mislocated Channels

**1 Cutting a housing filler.** Saw a strip of matching wood as wide and long as the housing. If the strip is thicker than the depth of the housing, mark the correct depth with a pencil line. Using a tenon saw and a mitre box (*page 18, Step 2*), remove most of the excess, leaving only a strip of wood about 2 mm deeper than the pencil line. Place the piece of wood in a woodworking vice and plane the underside (*left*) until it is smooth and the filler fits the housing perfectly.

**2 Fitting the strip.** Place the strip in the housing with the smooth surface down. The strip should fit snugly and protrude slightly above the surface. Plane the sides of the strip, if necessary, to get it into the channel. Apply glue to the housing and the strip, and clamp the strip in place. When the glue has dried, plane the strip flush with the surface. Use wood filler (*page 16*) to fill any gaps between the strip and the sides of the channels.

To fill an incorrect rebate, follow Steps 1 and 2, planing the strip flush with both surfaces.

## Misplaced or Damaged Nails and Screws

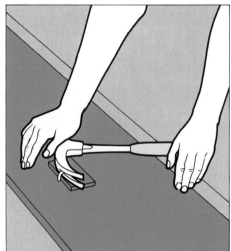

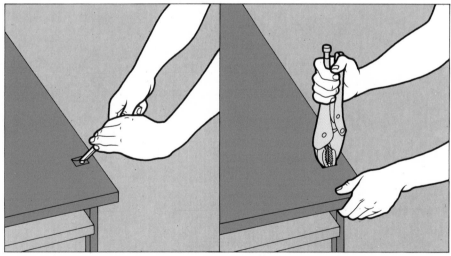

**Leverage for hard-to-pull nails.** A nail driven into the dense grain of a knot often bends or sticks fast in the wood, or the nail head breaks off when you try to remove it. First, place a piece of scrap wood under the hammer to avoid marring the wood surface. To get enough leverage, slide the claws of the hammer round the shaft of the nail and use both hands to push the hammer head down on its side (*above*) with only one claw touching the wood. Remove the hammer and repeat the process, replacing the scrap wood with a thicker piece; the nail should come out easily.

**Getting at a sunken nail or screw.** If you can reach the point of a hammered-in nail, place the concave tip of a nail set on the point and, with a hammer, tap the nail back through the board until you can grip the nail head with the hammer's claws. If, however, it is not possible to reach the point of the nail—or if you want to remove a countersunk screw whose slot has been damaged—use a marking knife to score a shallow rectangle, 20 by 10 mm round the nail or screw head. With a 6 mm tip wood chisel, chip out the rectangle to the depth scored by the knife (*above*). Repeat scoring and chiselling until you

have exposed at least 5 mm of the nail or screw. Clamp a pair of mole-grip pliers on to the head. Instead of trying to pull a nail directly up and out, rock the pliers forwards and the nail will come out more easily. To remove a screw, turn it with the pliers instead of prizing it out.

For removing both hard-to-pull and sunken nails, carpenter's pincers are another useful tool. Their jaws meet at a bevelled gripping edge, and are rounded so that the tool can be rocked back and forth. If the nail does not come out of the wood first time, move the pincers farther down the nail shaft and repeat the rocking movement.

# Two Power Tools That Make Joining Easier

With the help of power cutting tools, the work of making storage units becomes surprisingly easier and less time-consuming than when using hand tools alone. The router and circular saw, particularly, make it simple to join wood in ways that reflect true craftsmanship.

The router can be fitted with a wide variety of bits to carve almost any kind of joint on the surface or along the edge of a piece of wood. If you have not used a router before, get the feel of the tool by trying it out on scrap wood. Attach the appropriate bit for the test cut, and adjust the tool's depth indicator for the desired depth of the cut. As you should with any cutting tool, direct the router away from your body to prevent injury in case the tool slips. There

will be circumstances in which you cannot avoid working the router by pulling it towards you (particularly when dealing with large expanses of wood); in such situations, you must always stand to one side and proceed with the utmost caution. Guide the router across wood at a moderate speed: pushing it too slowly scorches the wood; pushing it too fast may burn out the motor. When the test cut is completed, use a rule to check that its depth agrees with the reading on the router's depth indicator.

The circular saw, while it is designed primarily for standard cuts on timber, can also be used to shape rebates, housings and a number of other joints. In addition, it can be tilted on its base to a 45 degree angle, providing an accurate way of cutting a

mitre—the only joint not included in the router's repertoire. The circular saw is particularly useful in cutting mitre joints too long to be made with a tenon saw and mitre box. Before making a mitre cut, try the saw on a piece of scrap wood.

Before using either a router or a circular saw, it is necessary to make sure that the tool will cut exactly where you want it to by setting up a guide—also called a fence. This is a straight-edged piece of wood clamped to the actual piece to be cut and along which you direct the tool. Directions on these pages explain how to set up a guide for both tools. Although they apply specifically to cutting a housing channel, the instructions are valid for cutting any joint that entails the use of a guide.

## The Router

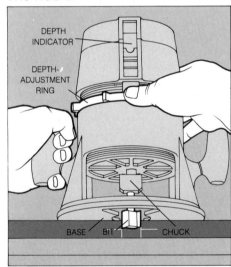

DEPTH INDICATOR

DEPTH-ADJUSTMENT RING

BASE    BIT    CHUCK

**1 Adjusting the depth to cut.** With power off, insert the bit in the router and tighten the chuck with the spanner supplied with the router. Hold the router upright above the piece of wood to be cut. Loosen the locking screw and turn the depth-adjustment ring until the tip of the bit just makes contact with the wood (*above*); turn the ring until the scale registers the desired depth, and tighten the locking screw. If your router does not have a depth scale, mark the desired depth on the edge of the wood and raise or lower the bit until its tip just reaches the mark.

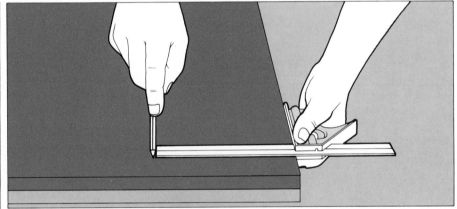

**2 Marking the housing channel.** Determine how far in from the end of the wood you want to make the housing channel. Place the stock of a combination square against the edge of the wood, with the rule extending across the surface. Mark the outside edge for one end of the channel with a pencil (*above*). For the width of the channel, measure from the first mark and indicate the position for the channel's inner edge with a second pencil mark. Extend the two marks down the edge of the wood. Indicate the position for the channel at the other end of the wood in the same way. Join each pair of marks along the surface.

**3 Marking the guide position.** Place the router on the piece of wood so that the bit lies flush with one edge of the wood and between the two marks. Make a third mark with the pencil (*left*) where the outside edge of the router base intersects the edge of the wood. Mark the far, or opposite, edge of the wood in the same manner and, using a rule and pencil, connect the two points.

**4** **Setting up the guide.** Place the straight-edged piece of wood chosen for a guide along the guideline just drawn; secure the guide in place at each end with a G-cramp. If the guide does not touch the line at all points, the edge of the guide is not absolutely straight: plane it straight.

**5** **Routing the housing channel.** Place the router on the surface of the wood so that the outside edge of its base touches the guide, and the bit nearly touches the edge of the wood. Turn on the power. Ease the router forward, bringing the bit into contact with the wood. Move the router along the guide at a constant speed. At the end of the cut, lift the router clear and turn the power off. If you must make the channel wider, move the guide and repeat the routing process.

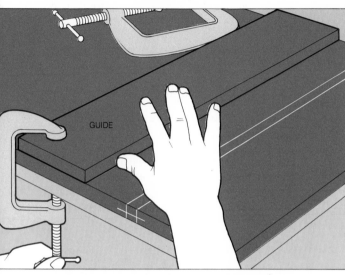

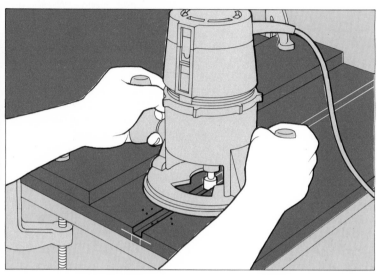

## The Circular Saw as a Router

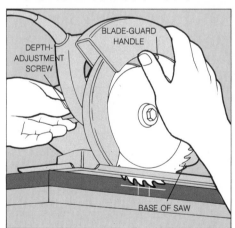

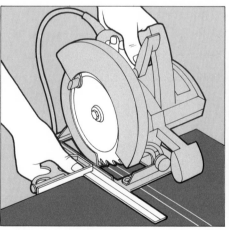

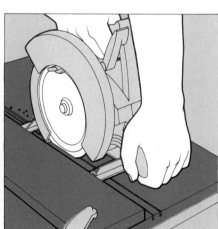

**1** **Adjusting the depth of cut.** Mark the two edges of the housing on the surface of the wood, as in Step 2 for using the router. Then mark the desired depth of the channel on the edge of the wood. After making sure the power is off, place the circular saw on the wood so that the side of the blade is flush with the edge of the wood. With your left hand *(above)*, loosen the depth adjustment screw, which is located on the front or back of the saw. With your right hand, lift or lower the blade until the point of the lowest tooth just touches the mark on the edge of the wood; at the same time lift the blade guard out of the way with your thumb. Once the blade is in place, tighten the depth-adjustment screw.

**2** **Setting up the guide.** With your left hand, hold the saw in the cutting position, just on the waste side of either line drawn across the surface of the wood; with your right hand, use a combination square to make sure the side of the saw base is at right angles to the edge of the wood *(above)*. Remove the square and mark the point where the side of the saw base intersects the edge of the wood. Measure the distance between the point and the line you want to cut along, and mark that distance at the far end of the channel to be cut. Make a line between the two marks with a pencil. Clamp a guide along the line.

**3** **Cutting the housing channel.** Hold the circular saw on the edge of the marked piece of wood so that the side of the saw base is flush with the guide, and the blade almost touches the edge of the wood. Turn the power on and move the saw forwards across the surface of the wood, keeping the side of the saw base flush with the guide. When you reach the far edge of the wood, lift the saw clear and turn the power off. Reposition the guide along the other edge of the channel, following the instructions in Step 2, and cut again. Make several cuts between the two edges of the channel until most of the wood has been removed; chisel out the rest.

# Turning Boxes into Drawers: Add Glides and Pulls

A drawer is simply a box that slides easily into and out of another larger box. To do that well, however, the box being transformed into a drawer must be built with an arrangement of joints that holds together firmly, since most drawers are heavily used and subject to a variety of stresses. The box must also be fitted with a sliding device to reduce friction and control the movement of the drawer.

A simple, sturdy drawer can be built with glue, nails and butt-jointed plywood or timber. But unlike the basic box, the front and back pieces should be inset so that they butt against the sides—otherwise the front might pull away from the sides under frequent use. Blocks of wood glued into the corners will add extra strength. Stronger drawers (below) use housings and grooves—channels cut along the wood grain—to attach the back and the bottom to the sides, and a rebate to attach the front so that it fits flush with the sides. Whichever method of construction is used, the wood should be at least 10 mm thick for the sides and 5 mm thick for the bottom; lighter wood might split.

There are many ways of equipping a drawer to slide. Hardware devices called drawer-glide assemblies are among the most commonly used because they work smoothly, are easily installed, and are available in different lengths and load capacities; the extendable type (pages 29–30) allows the drawer to be pulled all the way out without falling. But these hardware devices can be used only on cabinets constructed from wood at least 10 mm thick; thinner wood will not hold a hardware glide's mounting screws, which must be driven from the inside of the cabinet.

For such cabinets, strips of wood, attached by driving screws from the outside of the cabinet, should be used as runners (pages 30–31). The screws are then countersunk and covered. These wood runners can also be used in place of the more expensive hardware devices in cabinets made from thicker wood, in which case the runners are installed from the inside.

The type of glide will determine the width of the drawer. The metal glide used on pages 29 and 30, for instance, is 12 mm thick, so that the outside width of the drawer must be 25 mm less than the cabinet opening. When wood runners are used, the drawer should clear the cabinet by 3 mm on each side.

The finishing touch for most drawers is a false front; it can be mounted flush with the cabinet's sides (page 32), or partially overlapping the sides, or it can be fitted within the opening. A false front is essential on drawers with metal glides because the glides would otherwise be visible in the space between the drawer and the cabinet's sides. (If the false front fits within the opening, allow for its thickness when attaching the assemblies. Also, cut the false front 5 mm narrower than the width of the opening to allow a slight clearance at the sides.) A false front can be cut from finer wood than the drawer, enhancing the appearance of the project while keeping down the cost of timber.

## A Drawer with Channelled Joints

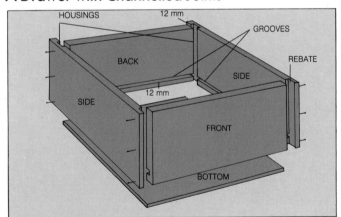

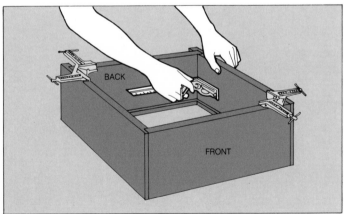

**1** **Routing the housings, grooves and rebates.** Cut the front, back, sides and bottom of the drawer. The bottom of the drawer should be cut 12 mm longer and 12 mm wider than the drawer's interior dimensions. Next, cut grooves on all four pieces to receive the bottom; locate them at least 10 mm from the lower edge of each piece. Rout the grooves 6 mm deep and as wide as the thickness of the drawer bottom—also usually 6 mm. Cut housings 12 mm from the rear edges of the side pieces 6 mm deep and as wide as the thickness of the back piece. The rebates cut at the front edges of the sides should also be cut 6 mm deep and the thickness of the front piece. Sand the bottom of the drawer smooth.

**2** **Truing the drawer.** Dry-fit the sides of the drawer by putting them in place without gluing or nailing. Place cramps on one front corner and one rear corner. Check the corners for trueness by setting a combination square into an unclamped rear corner (above). If the angle is slightly greater than 90 degrees, the front piece is too long; plane it down. If the angle is slightly less than 90 degrees, the back is too long; plane it down. Insert the bottom in the groove and recheck the corners; plane the edges of the bottom as necessary. Dismantle the drawer.

**3** **Assembling the parts.** Spread glue in the channel of both the back piece and one of the sides. Fit the back and side together and insert the bottom *(below)*. Nail the side to the back, spacing the nails 50 mm apart and nailing at a slight angle. With glue, join the other side to the back and bottom, and nail this side to the back. Finally, attach the front, using glue and nails where it meets the sides, but only glue where it meets the bottom. Put cramps on the four corners. Wipe the excess glue off with a damp cloth and set the drawer aside to dry.

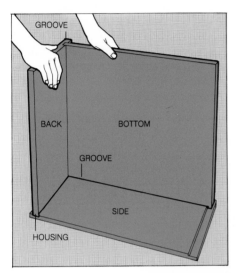

## Pilot Holes for Screws

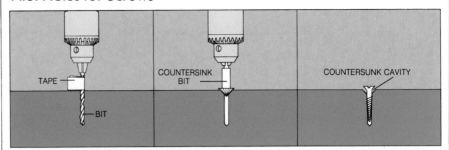

TAPE — BIT — COUNTERSINK BIT — COUNTERSUNK CAVITY

The holding power of a nail does not equal that of a screw. As well as adding strength, screws are also useful where a piece may have to be repositioned—such as a drawer-glide assembly—or where a project might be dismantled, moved and then set up again.

Holes should be drilled to receive the screws. These pilot holes prevent wood from splitting and make it easier to drive the screws. To drill a pilot hole, select a bit with a diameter slightly less than the screw's diameter at a point half way down its shank.

Hold the screw alongside the bit so that

the point of the screw is 2 mm short of the bit's tip. Wrap a piece of tape round the bit to mark a line flush with the top of the screw shank and drill until the tape touches the wood's surface *(above, left)*.

If you want the head of a screw to be recessed into the wood, use a countersink bit to widen the mouth of the hole after drilling the pilot hole *(above, centre)*. A quicker technique is to drill both the pilot hole and the countersunk cavity at the same time, with the aid of a counterbore bit. These bits are available in various sizes—choose one that matches the diameter of the screws you are using.

## Installing Hardware Glides

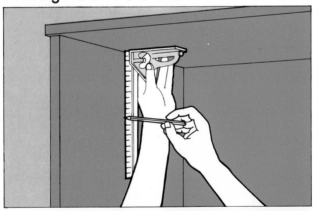

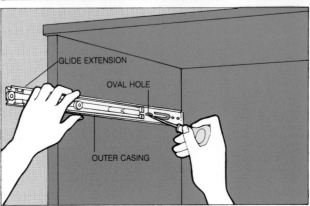

GLIDE EXTENSION — OVAL HOLE — OUTER CASING

**1** **Measuring the location.** Within the cabinet for which the drawer has been built, place a combination square so that its stock lies against the top of the cabinet and its ruled blade against one side *(left)*. Mark with a pencil a point that equals the height of the drawer plus 3 mm; for example, if the drawer is 100 mm high, put the pencil mark 103 mm below the cabinet top. Moving the square along the cabinet side towards the back, make several additional marks, each of them 103 mm from the top. With a straightedge and a pencil, make a line to connect the points. Repeat the procedure for the opposite side.

**2** **Positioning the screws.** Place the bottom of the outer casing of a glide assembly along the pencil line so that its front edge is flush with the front of the cabinet. (Note: some casings are identified for specific use on the left or right side.) Pull out the glide extension far enough to expose all the screw holes in the casing; there should be two oval holes and several round ones. Holding the casing in position, insert a bradawl through the centre of each oval hole and make a pilot hole for the screw *(left)*. Repeat for the other side of the cabinet. Attach the outer casings.

**3 Mounting the glides on the drawer.** The package containing the glide assembly will indicate the positions of the inner-glide mounting screws—usually about 15 mm from the bottom of the drawer. Place the stock of a combination square flush against the bottom edge of the drawer, with the blade running up the side. Make a pencil mark at 15 mm (or whatever the designated measurement is) and then several more marks, extending all the way from front to back. Connect the marks with a pencil line. Position the inner glide so the line appears through the centre of the screw holes and the glide is flush with the front of the drawer. Using a bradawl, make a starter hole at the centre of each oval hole and attach the glide (right). (Do not install screws in circular holes.) Repeat the procedure for the other side.

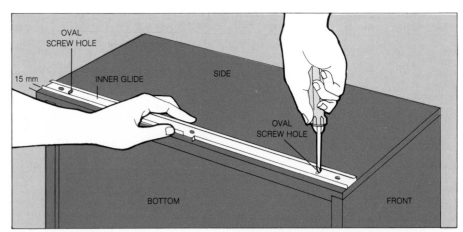
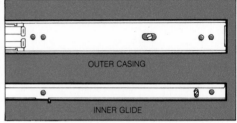

OVAL SCREW HOLE · SIDE · INNER GLIDE · 15 mm · OVAL SCREW HOLE · BOTTOM · FRONT

**4 Checking alignment.** Slide the inner glides of the drawer on to the front wheels of the outer casings. When the glides hit the stops in the casings, tilt the drawer up; this will enable the drawer to clear the stops and slide the rest of the way into position. The top of the drawer should clear the cabinet by 3 mm and the front should be level with the front of the cabinet. Check for alignment and remove the drawer.

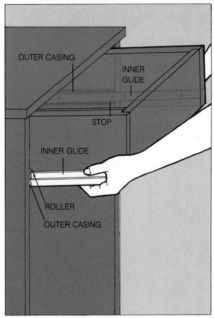

OUTER CASING · INNER GLIDE · STOP · INNER GLIDE · ROLLER · OUTER CASING · OUTER CASING · INNER GLIDE

**5 Adjusting the assemblies.** If in Step 4 the drawer was not precisely aligned with the top of the cabinet, loosen the inner-glide screws and move the glide up for more clearance or down for less clearance. Tighten the screws again and replace the drawer so that you can recheck the clearance. If the drawer does not close flush with the front of the cabinet, loosen the outer-casing screws; pull the casing forwards or backwards as necessary and retighten the screws. Recheck the fit. When the adjustments are exact, remove the drawer. Use the bradawl to make starter holes at the centres of all circular screw holes on each of the glides and casings. Install the remaining screws to fix the glides in position.

## Wood Runners

**1 Cutting and locating the runner.** For the simplest kind of drawer runner—blocks of wood on top of which the drawer rides—begin by cutting two strips of 18 mm wood, each one as long as the cabinet is deep. To position these runners, make initial pencil marks, following the same procedures used on page 29, Step 1, for installing hardware glides. Hold one runner against a side of the cabinet and align the top edge of the runner with the pencil marks. Using the runner's top edge as a guide, mark a line across the side with the pencil. Repeat for the other runner on the opposite side.

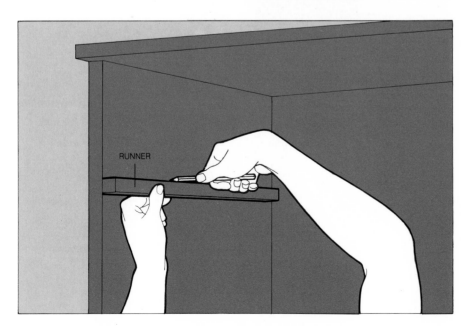

RUNNER

**2 Locating the screws.** Measure in 75 mm from the front edge of the cabinet. Place the stock of a combination square on the top of the cabinet with the blade extending downwards along the side *(right)*. Measure a distance equal to the height of the drawer, plus the thickness of the cabinet top, plus half the height of the runner, plus approximately 3 mm for clearance. If, for example, the drawer is 100 mm high, the cabinet top is 25 mm thick and the runner is 18 mm thick, the total measurement from the top of the cabinet would be 137 mm. Mark the measurement with a pencil. Make a similar mark 75 mm in from the back of the cabinet, and a third mark half way between the two. With a counterbore bit, drill clearance holes at the three marks through the cabinet wall. Repeat the procedure on the opposite side of the cabinet.

**3 Fastening the runner.** Hold the runner firmly inside the cabinet with its top edge along the pencil line. From the outside of the cabinet, push the pencil through each of the three holes in the side and make a mark on the runner. Clamp the runner to your workbench and use the bradawl to make pilot holes at the three marks. Spread glue on the runner, return it to the cabinet and align the three sets of holes. Fasten the runner in place from the outside. Repeat the procedure for the other runner, fill the countersunk cavities with wood filler. Sand off excess filler after it has dried. Finally, coat the top edges of the runner with paraffin wax. For a neater appearance, the runners can be attached from the inside of the cabinet. Saw the runners to length, and drill and countersink three holes in each runner. For positioning the runners horizontally, it is advisable to cut spacers—two strips of wood whose length is the desired distance between the underside of the cabinet top and the top edge of the runner. Hold the spacers vertically, butting against the cabinet top, and push the runners upwards against them. Insert the screws from the inside of the cabinet to attach the runners. The screws should penetrate the cabinet sides by two-thirds of their thickness.

## Channelling Drawers for Wood Runners

**1 Routing the channels.** For a steadier arrangement than platform runners, runners can be fitted into channels cut into the sides of the drawer. In that case the drawer should be built slightly smaller to allow room for the runners. Mount the runners at a point half the height of the drawer, plus the thickness of the cabinet top, plus half the height of the runner, plus 3 mm for clearance. Rout channels in the sides of the drawer 8 mm wide and half as deep as the sides are thick. The top edge of the channel should run along the midpoint of the drawer side *(right)*.

**2 Adjusting the drawers.** Slide the drawer on to the runners *(far right)*. If the fit is too tight, coat the runners and the channels with paraffin wax.

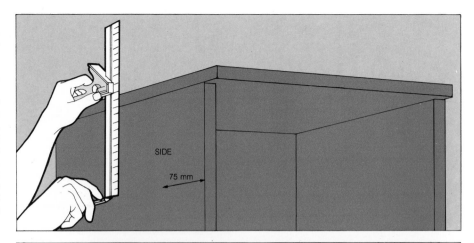

SIDE

75 mm

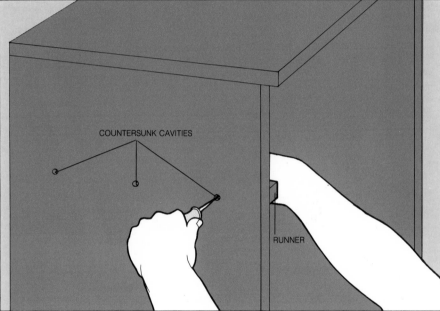

COUNTERSUNK CAVITIES

RUNNER

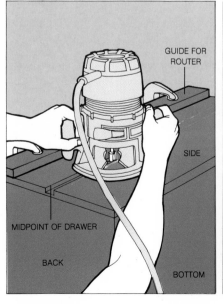

GUIDE FOR ROUTER

SIDE

MIDPOINT OF DRAWER

BACK

BOTTOM

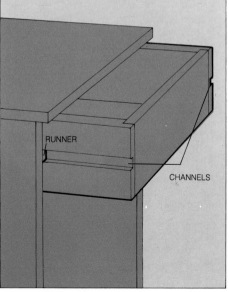

RUNNER

CHANNELS

## Adding False Fronts

**1** **Marking for a close fit.** Measure the cabinet opening from the outside edge of one side to the outside edge of the other. From a piece of wood that is at least 25 mm wider than the drawer is high, cut a length as long as the cabinet is wide. Position this false front against the front of the drawer so there is a clearance of 3 mm between it and the overhanging cabinet tops: the false front should be flush with the outside of the cabinet on both sides. Holding the false front in position, partly open the drawer and mark guidelines on the back of the false front to indicate the top and the sides of the drawer *(below)*.

**2** **Cutting and attaching the front.** Place the false front, with the drawer on top of it, on the workbench. Realign the drawer with the guidelines on the false front if necessary. Mark another line on the back of the false front, this time to indicate the bottom edge of the drawer. Remove the drawer and cut the false front on the waste side of the line indicating the bottom edge.

Clamp the drawer and the false front together, and to the workbench. Working from the inside out *(left)*, drill two pilot holes—the exact position is not critical—through the drawer front and just into the false front. Since the first is not very thick, be careful not to drill too far. Secure with screws long enough to go half way through the false front.

## Drawer Pulls

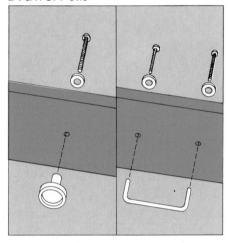

**Attaching hardware.** Use a single pull for a small drawer that will hold lightweight things; use two pulls for a larger drawer that will hold a heavy load. Knob pulls and bar pulls *(above)* serve equally well. Placement of the pulls is dictated partly by personal preference and partly by the relative size of drawer and pulls, but a good rule of thumb is to align them parallel with the unseen glides or runners; this facilitates opening and closing the drawers. A single pull should be centred. A pair is usually located 50 to 75 mm from each of the sides; for precise alignment procedure, see page 97.

Select a drill bit with a diameter of the same size as the pull's mounting bolt. Clamp the drawer to the workbench, using a piece of scrap wood as a buffer, and drill all the way through the drawer and the false front. Then insert the mounting bolts from the inside of the drawer, and screw the bolts into the pulls.

## Troubleshooting Drawers

☐ DRAWER STICKS. To find the problem area, rub chalk along the top and bottom edges of the drawer and in the channels, if any. Open and close the drawer several times. The chalk will rub off on any uneven areas where the drawer is sticking. If the uneven area follows the grain of the wood, use a plane to smooth it down. If the uneven area goes across the grain, sand the wood with a medium-grade sandpaper. Also, remove the drawer to check for protruding nail heads and countersink them with a nail set.

☐ LOOSE BOTTOM. If the bottom is flush-mounted (overlapping), insert a wedge, such as the tip of a screwdriver, at the loose area and squeeze more glue into

the crevice. Tap extra nails into the glued area. For channelled bottoms, follow the procedure explained below for tightening loose joints.

☐ LOOSE JOINTS. Use a toothpick to work glue into a joint that is loose but only slightly separated. Attach a corner cramp and nail the joint. Use wood blocks or metal brackets in the corner for greater strength *(page 23)*.

☐ LOOSE PULLS. If the pull is attached from the front, remove its mounting screws. Fill the screw holes with wood filler, or with broken matchsticks or toothpicks. Replace the screws immediately and allow the filler to dry before using the drawer. For better results, use the bolt-mounted type *(above, right)*.

# Turning Boxes into Cabinets: Install Doors

The two principal ways of enclosing boxes that will be used as cabinets are with hinged doors *(below)* and with sliding doors *(pages 38–39)*. While both methods have their advantages, hinged doors are considerably more versatile because there are several different ways in which they can be attached to boxes.

The main types of hinged doors are:

☐ LAY-ON. This type fits over the entire cabinet front, rather than into the opening. It is the easiest door to cut and install since precise measurements are not necessary. The door also covers slight irregularities in the cabinet itself.

☐ PARTIALLY OVERLAPPING. A variation for cabinets that have face frames *(page 24)*, this door requires special hinges such as the semi-concealed hinge that is demonstrated on page 36.

☐ INSET. Since it fits inside the cabinet opening, the inset door must be cut and hinged carefully if it is to open and close without any hindrance.

☐ LIPPED. This type fits both into and over the cabinet opening, creating a tight seal. The overlapping lip is usually made by cutting a rebate *(page 18)* round the edges. But the door can also be made by gluing two panels together. Since it requires hinges shaped to accommodate the lip, it is necessary to buy the hinges first, then cut the door to fit them.

☐ CONTIGUOUS DOUBLE. Double doors meet at the centre of a single large opening in this arrangement; they should always be used when an opening is wider than it is high, in order to avoid straining the hinges. The doors can be lay-on, inset or lipped. The centre edges can be rebated so that they fit into each other, as shown here, or they can simply be cut so that they just clear each other.

☐ SEPARATED DOUBLE. This type is divided by a centre partition, or stile, which gives the cabinet greater rigidity.

Most hinges for these doors can be mounted on any edge—top, bottom, left or right—depending on your preference or particular needs. Most hinges are sidemounted, but whether they are placed on the left or on the right side will be dictated for you by the location of the unit and the use to which you are putting it.

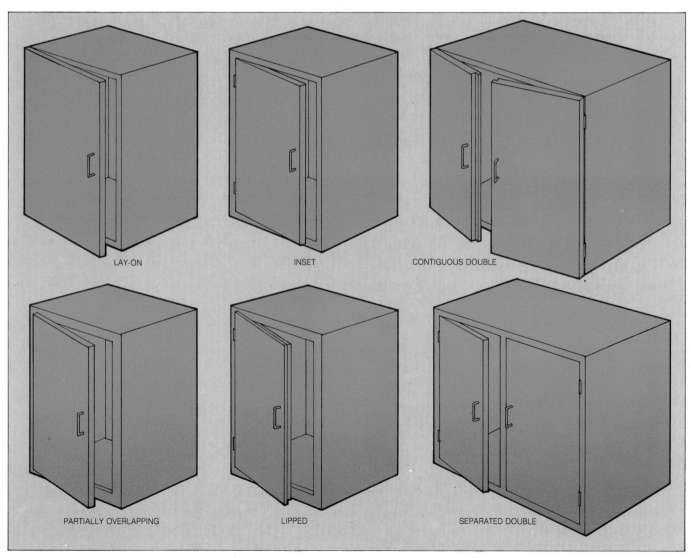

LAY-ON

INSET

CONTIGUOUS DOUBLE

PARTIALLY OVERLAPPING

LIPPED

SEPARATED DOUBLE

# Hinges: Types and Techniques

The most widely used hinge is the simple butt type, which consists of two rectangular leaves rotating on a central pin. The butt can be installed in two ways: it can be attached to the outside of a cabinet so that it is exposed—a technique known as surface-mounting—or it can be attached so that the hinge leaves are concealed between the door and the cabinet, with only the knuckle visible when the door is closed. In the latter case, the leaves fit into shallow carved-out areas, called recesses. Once you have learnt to install the butt hinge by both methods, you can use the same techniques for virtually any other type.

Butt hinges can be used only on inset doors and on lay-on or overlapping doors that cover the entire cabinet front. For lipped doors and partially overlapping doors, special hinges are required. The most popular types of special hinge, and the doors they are compatible with, are described together with auxiliary hardware on pages 36 and 37.

In addition to the plain butt hinge and the special hinges, there are many types of decorative hinge; nearly all of these are functionally the same as butt hinges, designed to be surface-mounted.

For installation of all types except the piano hinge (page 91), there are two rules of thumb: on any door that is longer than 600 mm, install three hinges; and the total length of the hinges should be equal to one-sixth the length of the hinged edge. For example, if the door is 600 mm long, use two 50 mm hinges; or if the door is 1800 mm long, use three 100 mm hinges. When only two hinges are required, they are usually placed a quarter of the way from the top and bottom of the door; when three hinges are installed, one hinge is centred and the other two are placed 100 to 125 mm from the top and bottom.

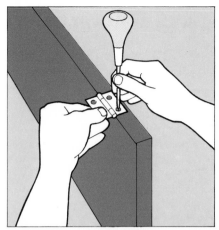

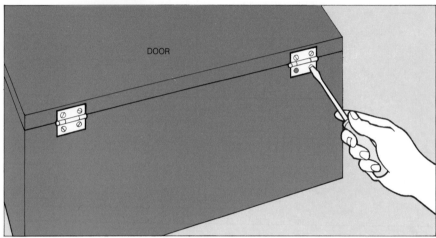

## Surface-Mounting Butt Hinges—Lay-On Door

**1** **Installing hinges on the door.** Align the leaf of one hinge on the side edge of the door so that the knuckle is centred on the back edge. Using a bradawl, make starter holes and then attach the hinge leaf. Repeat the procedure for the other hinge or hinges.

**2** **Attaching the door to the cabinet.** Lay the cabinet on its back and fit the door over the opening. On the side of the cabinet, use a bradawl to make starter holes for the screws and attach the hinges to the cabinet.

## Surface-Mounting Butt Hinges—Inset Door

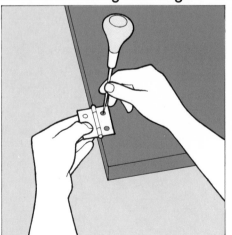

**1** **Installing hinges on the door.** Align the leaf of one hinge on the front of the door so that the knuckle is centred on the back edge. Use the bradawl to make starter holes. Attach the hinge leaf and repeat the procedure for the other hinge or hinges.

**2** **Attaching the door to the cabinet.** With the cabinet upright, set the door into the opening and wedge it in place with slivers of wood on all sides except the hinge side, where the door should fit flush against the cabinet. Make starter holes on the front of the cabinet and attach the hinges.

## Recessing Butt Hinges— Lay-On Door

**1 Marking the recess.** If your hinge has a removable pin, take it out; it is best to work with separated leaves. Place one leaf on the back of the door so that only the knuckle extends beyond the back edge of the door. Trace the outline of the leaf with a pencil.

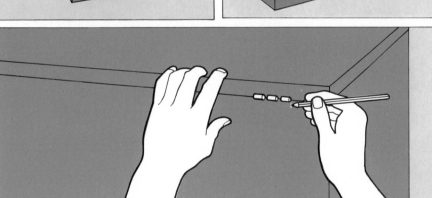

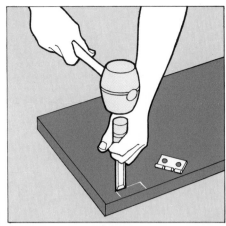

**2 Cutting the recess.** Using a woodworking chisel and a mallet, tap round the outline to make a shallow cut approximately the depth of the hinge leaf. Hold the chisel perpendicular to the door with its bevelled side towards the recess area. Then hold the chisel at a low angle to the wood—with its bevelled side down—and tap out a series of small, shallow cuts; small, even cuts make a smoother recess than longer ones. Finish by using the chisel alone to pare the recess to the exact depth that is needed to make the leaf fit flush with the surface.

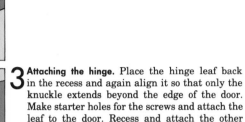

**3 Attaching the hinge.** Place the hinge leaf back in the recess and again align it so that only the knuckle extends beyond the edge of the door. Make starter holes for the screws and attach the leaf to the door. Recess and attach the other hinge or hinges in the same way.

**4 Attaching the door to the cabinet.** Lay the cabinet on its back and fit the door over the opening. Mark the ends of each attached hinge on the side of the cabinet; set the door aside. Using the marks for orientation, position the other hinge leaves on the front edge of the cabinet side and trace outlines of the leaves. Cut recesses along the outlines and screw the leaves on to the cabinet. Replace the hinge pins. (If your hinges do not come apart, follow the same procedure, but use a combination square to transfer the size of the leaves to the cabinet.)

## Recessing Butt Hinges— Inset Door

**1 Installing hinges on the door.** On the side edge of the door, recess the hinge leaves by following Steps 1 to 3 above. Be sure the knuckle extends beyond the front edge of the door.

**2 Attaching the door.** With the cabinet upright, set the door into the opening; wedge it in place with thin slivers of wood at the top and bottom. Mark the ends of the hinges on the front edge of the cabinet and remove the door. Using the marks on the front of the cabinet for orientation, position the hinge leaves just inside the cabinet with the knuckle extending beyond the front edge. Trace the outlines of the leaves, and cut the recesses. (If your hinges do not come apart, use a combination square as in Step 4.)

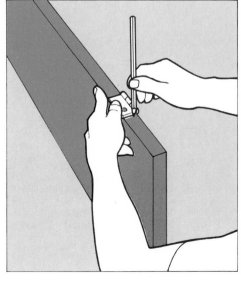

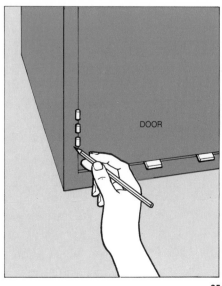

# Special Hardware

**Semi-concealed hinge.** When this type of hinge is installed, one leaf is visible, the other hidden. The semi-concealed hinge is used on lipped or partially overlapping doors. The leaf that is visible is surface-mounted on the front of the cabinet. The hidden, offset leaf is recessed into the back of the door. (For lipped doors, the hidden leaf has a double offset.)

**Piano hinge.** This hinge is, in effect, a concealed butt hinge running the entire edge of the door. Most often used on inset doors, it eliminates the need for recessing; the door is adjusted to allow the closed hinge to fit between the door and the cabinet. Its installation *(page 91)* differs from that of standard butt hinges. Sold by the centimetre, it can be cut with a hacksaw to the exact length of the door. Because of the support it gives, this hinge is well suited for attaching heavy doors.

**Cranked hinge.** This type is a useful substitute for the butt hinge on cabinets made from plywood. Since the hinge has one offset leaf, it can be screwed into the surfaces of both the door and the cabinet rather than into the edge of the plywood, which does not hold screws well. Suitable for either inset or lay-on doors, the cranked hinge must be recessed, not surface-mounted. It must be selected with care so that its offset leaf matches the plywood thickness.

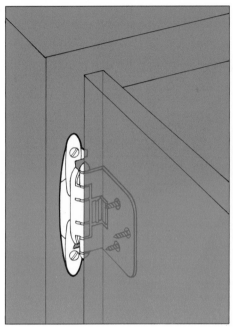

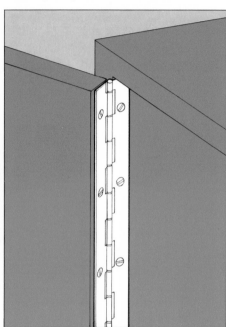

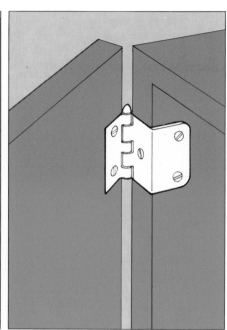

**Concealed hinge.** This type of hinge is designed for adjacent cabinets with flush doors that open alongside each other. The hinge needs no clearance since it projects the door outwards without disturbing the neighbouring doors. To attach a concealed hinge, the rounded end or boss is outlined on the inside of the door and the position of the screw is then marked on the inside of the cabinet. Careful positioning is essential. A hole for the boss is drilled to the depth specified by the manufacturer. The rectangular part of the hinge is screwed on to the inside of the cabinet. While a helper holds the door open, the boss of the hinge is slotted into the hole and screwed into place. Finally, the door is aligned by adjusting the screw and slot on the inside of the cabinet.

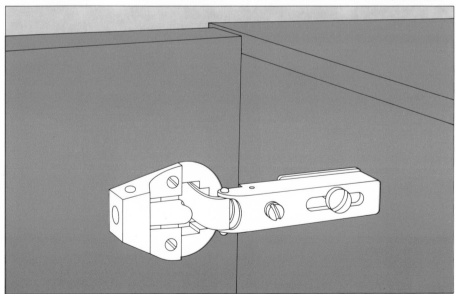

**Catches and latches.** To keep a door closed, a catch or latch is required. One popular type of catch *(below, left)* consists of an arrow-shaped "strike" mounted on the door, and a spring-loaded fastener attached to the inside of the cabinet. Precise measurement is essential to ensure that these two parts are lined up. Another type of catch, which requires less precise alignment, is magnetic *(below, centre)*. A bar latch *(below, right)*, which is decorative as well as useful, is attached to the outside of a cabinet with an inset door, and serves as both a catch and a handle.

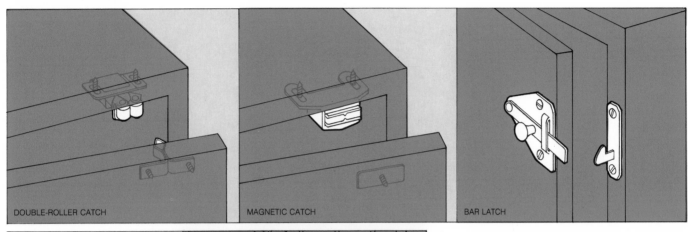

DOUBLE-ROLLER CATCH  MAGNETIC CATCH  BAR LATCH

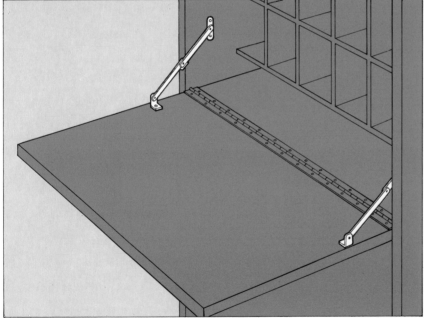

**Stay supports.** Used in addition to hinges, these collapsible retainers limit the degree to which a flap can be opened—whether the flap is the fold-down type shown here or is mounted in the usual manner. When the flap is closed, the stays fold up. Many types are available. Many are easy to attach: they simply screw to the sides of the cabinet and to the inside of the flap.

## Troubleshooting Doors

Whatever the cause, the symptoms are much the same on all malfunctioning hinged doors. They are either hard to open or will not stay closed. Here are the most common problems—together with their solutions—in the order that you should check them:

☐ WARPED DOOR. One solution, of course, is to replace the door. However, an effective alternative is to install a bar latch, if this is possible.

☐ LOOSE HINGE SCREWS. Replace all the screws with longer ones. Or, if longer screws would go completely through the wood, fill the screw holes with wood splinters (matches or toothpicks will do); replace the same screws.

☐ DOOR EDGE NOT CLEARING. To find the exact point where the door is sticking, rub chalk along the door edges. Open and close the door a couple of times. The chalk will rub off at the points where the door is sticking. Remove the door from the cabinet; plane and sand these areas.

☐ MISALIGNED CATCH. Remove the strike and reposition it on the door. It may be necessary to fill the old screw holes with wood filler and refinish.

# Tracks: an Alternative to Hinges

There are several ways, as shown on the right, to put in tracks for sliding doors: by installing hardware, by routing channels and by attaching wood strips. (An alternative to routing is to plough the channels with the specialized tool known as a plough plane.) Hardware tracks are usually best. Not only are they easy to install but they also give assured straightness and smoothness. Of the other methods, which are more traditional, routed tracks are preferable. Because the tracks are cut into the cabinet and not nailed on, they are neat and unobtrusive. However, the only way to form tracks when you do not want to use hardware or do not have a router or plough plane is by attaching wood strips.

Since they do not have to be thick enough to hold screws, sliding doors are usually made from thinner material than their hinged counterparts. In addition, a thin door slides more easily than a door made from a thick material because it weighs less and creates less friction. However, since thin material is more likely to warp, and a distorted door will not slide easily, the material used must be virtually warp proof. For most cabinets, the best-quality 9 or 12 mm plywood *(page 58)* is recommended, but less expensive 6 mm chipboard can be used for utilitarian units.

Tracks of any kind should be installed before the cabinet is assembled. However, when working with unassembled pieces, be sure to anticipate how you are going to put the cabinet together. Often, to allow space for joints, the tracks cannot run all the way to the side edges of the wood.

To ensure a perfect fit, the doors themselves, like all doors, are cut and fitted after the cabinet is assembled *(opposite)*.

As a general rule, a cabinet with sliding doors should not be much more than 600 mm high and should be at least twice as wide as it is tall. Doors running on wooden tracks are harder to push; therefore, the length of the tracks should be limited to 1200 mm. And, in order to get the doors in and out *(Step 2, opposite)*, the tracks at the top must be deeper—by at least 5 mm—than the lower ones.

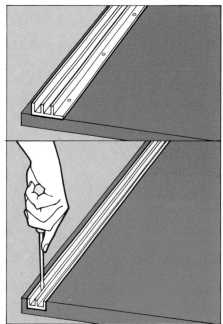

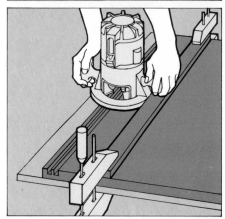

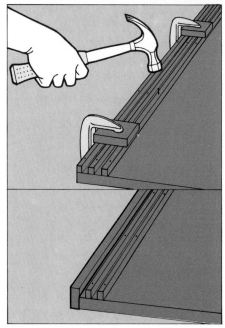

## Installing Tracks

**Hardware.** Metal or plastic tracks usually come in pairs: a shallow bottom track and a deeper top one. Available in standard lengths, they can be cut with a hacksaw to the exact measurements required. Hardware tracks may be surface-mounted *(top left)* or, for better appearance, they can be sunk into channels routed in the top and bottom of the cabinet, as shown in the lower drawing. If channels are routed, the cabinet material must be at least 10 mm thicker than the deeper track. Both top and bottom channels should be at least 10 mm inside the front edge.

**Routed.** Since these tracks are cut into the cabinet itself, the cabinet material must be 18 mm thick or more to accommodate channels at least 8 mm deep at the bottom and the same depth plus 5 to 6 mm at the top. On both top and bottom pieces of the cabinet, rout the first track 12 mm inside the front edge. Rout the second track 6 mm inside the first. Use a mortising or straight-cut bit for each track. Guide the router with a straight piece of wood clamped to the cabinet piece. Apply paraffin wax to the tracks, and round off the bottom edge of the doors.

**Wood strips.** These tracks are usually made with three pieces of hardwood *(left)*. On the bottom of the cabinet, use a length of 10 by 12 mm wood and position it to form tracks 12 mm deep. On the top, use 10 by 18 mm strips and make the tracks 18 mm deep. Space the wood strips so that each strip is separated from the others by the thickness of the door, using the actual door material as a guide. Glue and nail the strips, making sure you clamp each piece in place before nailing. Alternatively, you can replace the outer strip with a board that is nailed to the cabinet's front edge *(below)*. Whichever method is used, be sure to apply paraffin wax to the tracks.

# Making the Doors

1 **Measuring and cutting.** To determine the height of both doors *(below)*, measure from the groove of a bottom channel to the lip of the corresponding upper track; then add 6 mm so that the doors will project into the top channel when they are installed. To determine the width *(right, below)* for the first door, measure half the length of the track. For the second door, add approximately 10 mm to the measurement, so that the two doors will overlap in the centre. Cut the doors, using the dimensions thus established.

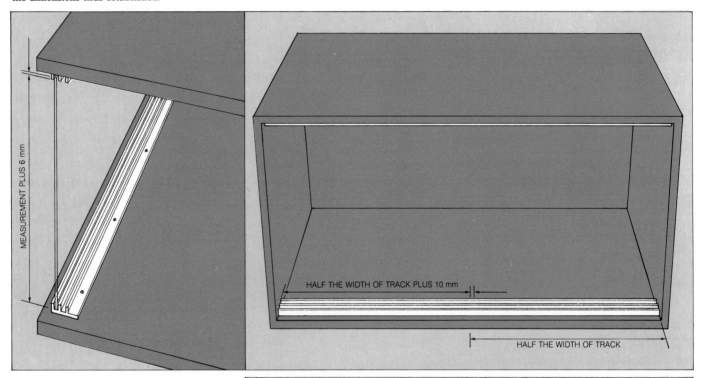

MEASUREMENT PLUS 6 mm

HALF THE WIDTH OF TRACK PLUS 10 mm

HALF THE WIDTH OF TRACK

2 **Finishing and installing.** To reduce friction, sand the door edges as smooth as possible and wax the lower ones. Add recess pulls—no deeper than the thickness of the doors—one near the left side of the left door and the other symmetrically on the right door. To do so, drill or chisel out an opening in each door to accommodate the shape of the pull. To install each door, push it all the way into the top channel; then let it drop into the bottom one. Place the wider door in the inside channel so that the two doors will appear to be the same width when they are closed.

# The Vertical Dimension: Fixing Things on Walls

Almost any object that occupies valuable floor space—from a bookcase to a bed—can be raised out of the way if it is fixed on a wall. Vertical storage is usually only one layer deep, so that items are easy to see and more accessible. And because wall units tend to range from waist height to arm's reach, stretching and bending are reduced to a minimum. To make efficient use of this vertical space, you need to find out what kind of wall you have and the most appropriate fixing to use in attaching a particular storage unit to it.

Walls appear much the same from the outside, but interior construction varies greatly. Some walls are solid: masonry block, brick or solid concrete. Others are hollow: plasterboard, hardboard or lath and plaster (these materials are usually fixed to metal or wooden support beams called studs). To identify the construction of your wall, drill a small hole in an inconspicuous spot. Note the kind of dust the drill grinds out and how much resistance it meets, then check your observations against the chart on page 42.

If the wall is solid, you will need a special carbide-tipped drill bit. If the wall is hollow, you will need to know its thickness and the amount of space inside the wall before you can select the proper fixing.

Bend the very tip of a thin wire into a right angle and poke the wire through the test hole as far as it can possibly go. The distance from the bent tip of the wire to the outside of the wall reveals the thickness of the wall plus the space behind it. Pull the wire until the bent end snags on the inside of the wall. The distance from the bent end of the wire to the outside of the wall is the thickness of the wall.

Now consider the weight the wall can bear. Some materials—for example, mortar joints between bricks or concrete blocks—cannot support loads greater than 50 kg per square metre. However, nearly everything except small ornaments runs well beyond that limit: for example, books average 100 kg per square metre; a 300 cm stack of long-playing records exerts more than double that pressure; six 5 litre cans of paint weigh 110 kg. Bathroom scales will give the weight of nearly everything you intend to hang on your wall.

If the load is to be relatively light, or if the wall is backed by wooden studs *(page 42)*, the fixings you choose can be as simple as round-wire nails or wood screws. For some situations, however, specialized fixings, like those shown below and on the right, are needed. Each type of fixing is suited to particular wall and weight combinations as outlined in the chart on page 43.

## Types of Fixing

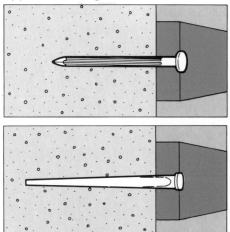

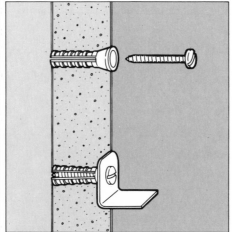

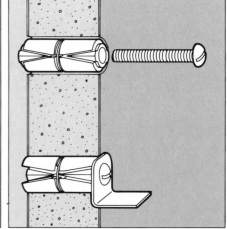

**Masonry nails and cut-clasp nails.** These fixings are used in walls made of masonry, brick or building block. Masonry nails *(top)*, which are made of hardened steel, are often finely ridged from tip to shank, and are coated with a thin layer of zinc (galvanized) to prevent rust. Cut-clasp nails *(bottom)* are stamped from sheet iron or steel. Their sharp, squared edges can sometimes split soft materials such as wood; before using a cut-clasp nail to fasten a piece of wood to any kind of masonry, drill a pilot hole in the wood slightly smaller than the thickness of the nail at its widest point. Hammer the nail through the hole in the wood and into the wall.

**Wall plugs.** Wall plugs are sheaths that expand when matching screws are driven into them. The most common types *(above)* are made of a high-strength plastic, split to allow expansion and ribbed to prevent them from pulling out of the hole. They are multi-purpose fixings for masonry, brickwork and solid concrete. To install them, drill a tight-fitting hole to match the plug. Drive in the plug, and tap a screw through the fixture into the plug. Drive in the screw until tight. A less common type is the fibre wall plug. The high density of the plug material gives it an elasticity that allows a screw to form its own thread and expand the plug without damaging its structure. Once the fixing is made, a screw can be withdrawn or replaced at will.

**Expansion shields.** Used in masonry walls to support exceptionally heavy weights, these devices vary in appearance but work on the same basic principle: when a bolt in the metal shield is tightened, the shield expands in the wall. In the shield above, wedges at each end are drawn towards the centre as the bolt turns, forcing apart a sheath bound by wire. To use an expansion shield, bore a hole the size of the shield. Tap in the shield, thread the bolt through the fixture, and tighten. Be sure to select a bolt that is long enough to pass through both the object you are fixing and the length of the expansion shield.

**Dowels with wood screws.** These home-made fixings attach fairly heavy loads to masonry and are most useful in old or crumbling walls. To make one, cut a 50 to 75 mm strip of wooden dowelling 20 to 25 mm in diameter. Using a carbide-tipped bit in your drill, bore a hole in the wall the same length as the dowel and slightly smaller in diameter. Tap the dowel in with a hammer. Drill a pilot hole in the centre of the dowel, pass a wood screw through the fixture and drive the screw into the pilot hole; once inside the wall, the dowel will expand for a firm grip.

**Collapsible anchors, or intersets.** These fixings are bolts encased in retracting sheaths. The length of the sheath shank—the smooth area near the head—must match the thickness of the wall. To install, drill a hole the diameter of the sheath. Tap the anchor into the hole *(top)*. Hold the sheath in place by setting a screwdriver in one of the open wedges in the flange and, with another screwdriver, tighten the bolt *(centre)*. The sheath will retract to grip the wall. Do not overtighten. Remove the bolt, slip it through the object to be fixed, and screw it back into the sheath.

**Toggle bolts.** Like collapsible anchors, toggles fasten things to hollow walls, but they take greater weights. One type is the spring wing—a nut split into two wings joined by a spring. To attach it, drill a hole the diameter of the closed fixing. Probe with a wire to make sure there is room for the toggle to open inside the wall. Before inserting the fixing, unscrew the bolt and pass it through the object to be fixed. Replace the toggle and force it and the bolt through the hole; the toggle will open to grip the inner surface of the wall. Tighten the bolt until the fixing is firm.

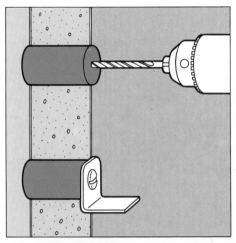

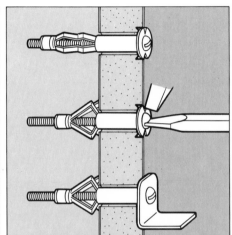

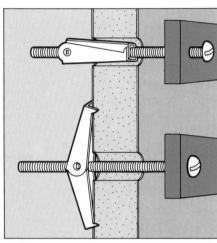

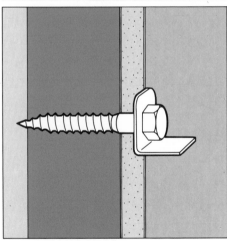

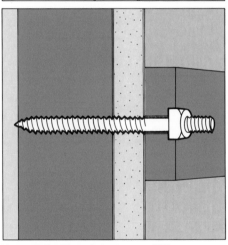

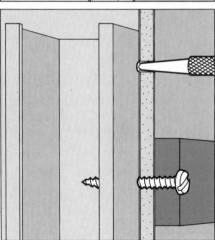

**Coach screws and bolts.** These devices are used for such extra-heavy jobs as hanging cabinets or bookcases on walls with wood studs, or in combination with wall plugs *(opposite, centre)* in masonry. They are sold in various diameters and lengths up to 400 mm, and their square or hexagonal heads are tightened with a spanner rather than a screwdriver. To insert one of these fixings in a wood stud, drill a pilot hole slightly smaller than the diameter of the screw through the wall into the stud. Thread the screw through the object that you are fixing—usually a heavy-duty bracket or metal cleat—and drive the screw into the pilot hole.

**Hanger bolts.** Threaded at one end like a coarse wood screw and at the other more finely, like a machine bolt, these fixings are also used to attach very heavy objects to wood studs. To drive one, drill a pilot hole slightly smaller than the diameter of the bolt through the wall and into the stud. Insert the wood-screw end into the hole and tighten the bolt by grasping its smooth centre section with mole-grip pliers. The smooth portion and the machine-threaded end should remain outside the wall. Drill a hole through the object that you are fixing. Then mount the object on the projecting bolt and fix it with a nut.

**Self-tapping sheet-metal screws.** Used in walls that are constructed with hollow metal studs instead of wooden ones, these screws have full-length threads and slotted or crossed heads. To drive one, drill a small hole through the wall to expose the metal stud. Make a starter point for the drill on the exposed stud by making a small dent in the metal with a centre punch *(top)*. In the stud, using a high-speed steel bit, drill a hole half the diameter of the screw. Then drill a hole in the object to be fixed. Drive the screw through the object and into the stud; the screw threads will cut their own channels in the metal.

# Matching Walls and Fixings

The chart on the right shows how to identify various types of wall construction, and the chart opposite lists the recommended fixing for a particular kind of wall. To use the chart on the right, drill a hole in your wall, then read down the left-hand column until you find a pattern that matches the kind of dust and the amount of resistance you encountered. The other column identifies the wall construction. After finding the wall type, estimate the weight of the object to be hung. Then use the chart opposite for the most suitable type of fixing.

Fixings in the light-load category are mostly suited to rough or basic work, such as securing panels to a wall, attaching skirting boards or picture-hanging.

Typical items for light-to-medium load fixings are small display cases and shelves for portable radios, decorative plates, and kitchen pots and pans. However, many of the fixings recommended for the light-to-medium range can bear heavier loads if your wall is built of solid concrete or brick.

The heavy-load fixings will bear such items as record and china cabinets. They will also support a shelf designed to carry books, a television or a large stereo system.

The best support for any heavy object is a solid wooden stud (below). However, if studs are not available or not suitably located, a heavy-duty fixing will do the job even in lighter walls.

**Locating wall studs.** Most wall studs are spaced 350 to 450 mm apart, centre to centre. Once you find one, quick measurements on the surface of the wall will locate the rest. In very old houses, studs may be randomly spaced, but a little probing will locate them. It is sometimes possible to find a stud simply by tapping the wall, but a surer method is to make a small, inconspicuous hole at an acute angle along the wall's surface. Feed a piece of stiff wire at least 500 mm long into the hole (right) until it meets resistance—a stud. Grasp the wire where it enters the wall and draw it from the hole. Hold the wire just outside the hole and at the same angle it entered the wall. The edge of the stud lies behind the point where the tip of the wire meets the wall.

## Determining Wall Construction

| If your drill in the test hole produces ... | the wall is made of ... |
|---|---|
| White dust, then grey dust; moderate, then heavy resistance to the drill bit. | Plaster over concrete block |
| Dark or brownish grey dust; continuous heavy resistance. | Concrete block |
| Brownish grey dust; continuous very heavy resistance (drill has difficulty biting into wall surface). | Solid concrete |
| White dust, then red dust; moderate resistance followed by heavy resistance as red dust appears. | Plaster over solid or hollow brick |
| White dust; lengthy moderate resistance (drill bit under 75 mm long will not break through). | Thick plaster |
| White dust; little resistance, drill bit breaks through quickly. | Plasterboard |
| White dust, then brown dust; moderate resistance, drill bit breaks through quickly. | Plaster over lath |
| White dust, then brown dust, wood shavings; continuous moderate resistance. | Lath and plaster over wood stud |
| White dust, then brown dust, metal shavings; moderate resistance followed by heavy resistance as metal shavings appear. | Lath and plaster over metal stud |
| White dust, wood shavings; little resistance then moderate resistance as wood shavings appear. | Plasterboard over wood stud |
| White dust, metal shavings; little resistance, then heavy resistance as metal shavings appear. | Plasterboard over metal stud |

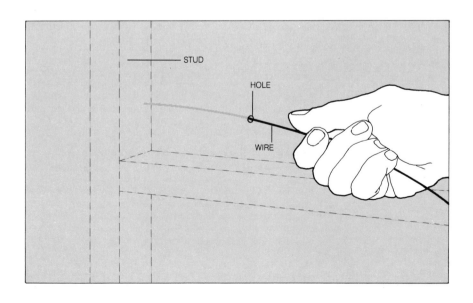

## Selecting the Correct Fixing

| Wall type | Light loads and rough work | Light-to-medium load | Heavy load |
|---|---|---|---|
| Concrete block (solid portions) | Cut-clasp nail, up to 75 mm. Masonry nail, up to 75 mm. Wooden or plastic plug with appropriately sized screw. | Plastic or fibre wall plug with 3.5–4 mm screw diameter. | Plastic or fibre wall plug with 6–8 mm screw diameter. Expansion shield 6 mm diameter or larger. |
| Brick | Cut-clasp nail, up to 75 mm. Masonry nail, up to 75 mm. | Plastic or fibre wall plug with 3.5–4 mm screw diameter. Wooden plug with 3.5–4 mm screw diameter. | Plastic or fibre wall plug with 5–8 mm screw diameter. Expansion shield 6 mm diameter or larger. Wooden plug with 6 mm or larger coach screw. |
| Mortar joints (between concrete blocks or bricks) | Cut-clasp nail, up to 75 mm. Masonry nail, up to 75 mm. Wooden wedge for nails or screws. | Plastic or fibre wall plug with 4–5 mm screws. | Not recommended. |
| Hollow brick | Metal toggle with bolt long enough to pass through object being fixed plus wall thickness. | Plastic toggle with appropriately sized wood screw. Metal toggle with bolt long enough to pass through object being hung plus wall thickness. | Metal toggle with 6 mm bolt or larger. |
| Thick plaster | 35–50 mm masonry nail. | Plastic or fibre wall plug with 4–5 mm screw diameter. | Not recommended. |
| Concrete block (hollow sections) | 50 mm cut-clasp nail. 50 mm masonry nail. | Plastic or fibre wall plug with 3.5–4 mm screw diameter. Plastic toggle with appropriately sized wood screw. Metal toggle with bolt long enough to pass through object being hung plus wall thickness. | Expansion shield 6 mm diameter or larger. |
| Plasterboard, lath and plaster | 50 mm cut-clasp nail. Collapsible anchor appropriate to wall thickness. | Collapsible anchor appropriate to wall thickness. Plastic toggle with 3.5–4 mm screw diameter. Metal toggle with bolt long enough to pass through object being hung plus wall thickness. | Collapsible anchor appropriate to wall thickness. Metal toggle with bolt long enough to pass through object being hung plus wall thickness. (Caution: plasterboard or lath and plaster may collapse under heavy load.) |
| Wooden stud behind plasterboard | Cut-clasp nail or round-wire nail long enough to be driven into stud plus twice thickness of object being fixed. | Round-wire nail long enough to be driven into stud about twice thickness of object being hung. 3.5–4 mm screw long enough to be driven into stud about two-thirds its length. | 5 mm diameter or larger screw long enough to be driven into stud about two-thirds its length. 6 mm diameter or larger coach screw, length as above. |
| Metal stud behind plasterboard | 3 mm self-tapped sheet-metal screw. | 3.5 mm self-tapping sheet-metal screw. | 4 mm self-tapping sheet-metal screw. |

# Hanging Shelves and Cabinets

Once you have determined the wall type and selected the appropriate fixing for hanging a shelf or cabinet securely *(charts, pages 42–43)*, make sure it will be perfectly level. Supports should usually be spaced from 500 to 800 mm apart, depending on the load. If supports are more than 800 mm apart, most wood shelving will sag under its own weight. Nor should the ends of a shelf extend more than 200 mm beyond the outside supports; the ends might bow and the shelf would lose stability.

If your wall is hollow, it is probably backed by wood or metal studs. Locate the studs according to the instructions on page 42; and, if possible, attach the supports to them. Since most studs are between 400 and 500 mm apart, a support attached to every other stud will work for most loads.

In levelling a shelf or cabinet, do not rely on visual judgment; use a level *(Step 4)*. Wall, ceiling and floor lines are seldom straight, even in new houses.

The most common methods for hanging shelves use brackets that are either attached directly to the wall or made to fit into upright standards installed on the wall. Brackets are usually used to support a single, stationary shelf. Heavy angle irons, like the one shown on the right, or brackets made from cast metal, can be used to support heavy weights. But whether brackets are decorative or simply utilitarian, they are all attached to walls in much the same way.

Standards, or uprights, are most often used to support several shelves on removable brackets. Most standards are attached as described in the instructions on page 46. Brackets for attaching to standards can differ, however; the most widely used, with instructions for installing them, are given on page 47.

Shelves are also installed in cupboards and corners, across windows or in hallways, where they can be supported at the sides instead of—or in addition to—the back. For this kind of installation, use the specialized mountings shown on page 48.

Heavy objects can be supported firmly—and later removed easily, if desired—with the aid of mitred cleats: wood strips cut lengthwise from 25 by 100 mm timber at a 45 degree angle, and fastened to the wall and to the back of the cabinet being attached to the wall. Directions for making these mitred cleats are on pages 48 and 49.

Wall storage devices are not, of course, limited to shelves and cabinets. One way to put vertical space to work is to use perforated hardboard, or pegboard. This composition board comes in thicknesses of 3 mm for light loads, and 5 or 6 mm for heavier jobs. Holes punched at approximately 25 mm intervals over its surface vary from under 6 mm in the 3 mm thick board to about 5 mm in the 6 mm board. Pegboard can be attached to a wall by inserting fixings through the holes. To maintain space behind the board for insertion of pegboard hooks, frame the back of the pegboard with wood strips or insert a cylindrical rubber spacer between the pegboard and the wall. Hardware shops and D.I.Y. centres carry hooks, cramps and other support devices in sizes appropriate to the thickness of the board (3, 5 or 6 mm).

With imagination, you can use pegboard in many ways, to create your own storage device from objects you have at home. Big, bulky equipment can be lifted on to brackets installed to be used as hooks. Dowels will support equipment in a garage, or plants on a patio. And wooden fruit boxes or wine cases make excellent ready-made storage compartments.

## Putting up a Shelf

1 **Levelling the first bracket.** Place the first bracket against the wall. Hold a level vertically against the bracket and the wall. Adjust the bracket until the air bubbles in the end vials of the level are centred. With a bradawl, start holes through each screw hole on the bracket. If your wall is solid, remove the brackets and use a masonry drill to make pilot holes. Centre the drill bit precisely; even a small error can throw off the alignment. Attach the bracket with the appropriate fixing *(chart, page 43)*.

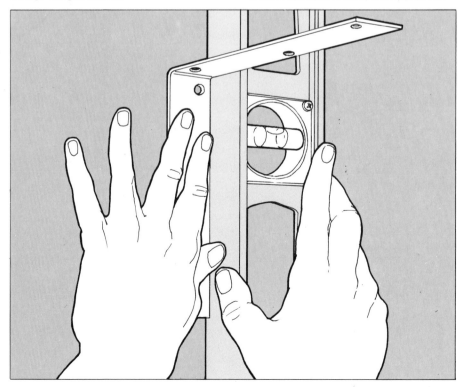

**2** **Positioning the other brackets.** If the shelf is short enough to require only two brackets, decide on the amount of overhang you want at each end. Measure in that amount from each end and mark the shelf lightly on its underside. If the shelf will need more than two brackets, mark the positions of the brackets at each end in the same manner. Then measure the distance between the position of these brackets and divide this measurement by the number of additional brackets you intend to use plus one. This figure will provide an equal distance from bracket to bracket.

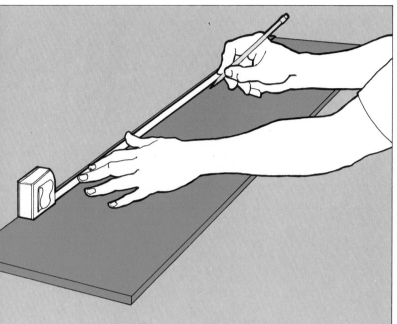

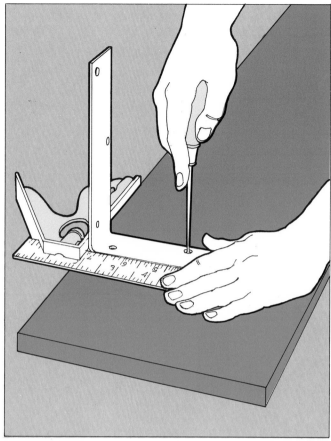

**3** **Setting the second bracket.** Set the second bracket at one of the marked positions on the shelf (except where the bracket already attached to the wall is to align). Square the bracket against the back edge of the shelf by fitting it against a combination square as shown. Make pilot holes through each screw hole with a bradawl, and attach the bracket to the shelf with wood screws. Attach all other brackets (if any) in the same way, centring them carefully on the positions marked on the underside of the shelf.

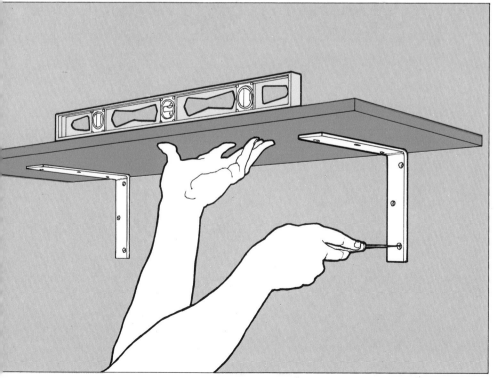

**4** **Levelling the shelf.** Rest the shelf, with its brackets attached, on the bracket already fastened to the wall. Make sure the bracket is already centred on the mark made for it on the shelf. Put a level on the shelf and adjust the shelf position until the appropriate bubble in the level is centred. With a bradawl, mark the screw positions through the screw holes in the brackets. If stronger support is required, remove the shelf and drill pilot holes or anchor holes in the wall. Replace the shelf and fix the brackets to the wall. Make pilot holes with the bradawl in the shelf through the holes in the bracket that was first fastened to the wall. Drive in wood screws.

# Hanging a Shelf Using Standards

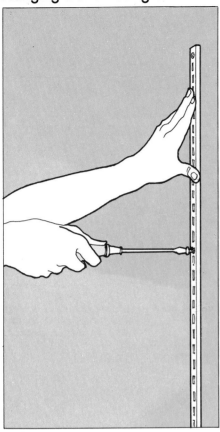

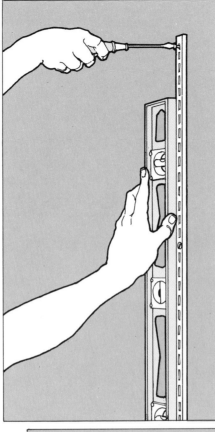

**2** **Attaching the standard.** Align the standard vertically with a level. Mark the positions of the other fixing holes and, if necessary, swing the standard aside when you drill the pilot or anchor hole. Make sure that the drill bit is centred precisely. Attach the remaining fixings.

**3** **Hanging the shelf.** Insert one shelf bracket in the first standard. Fit a bracket into the corresponding holes of a second standard. Place the second standard against the wall, centring it on the mark made for it, and set the shelf, with a level on it, on top of the brackets. Adjust the shelf until the bubble in the level is centred. Mark the top and bottom of the second standard on the wall; remove the shelf and attach the second standard as described in Steps 1 and 2. If the shelf is to be supported by more than two standards, repeat Steps 1 to 3 for each.

**1** **Positioning the first standard.** Mark the location of the shelves lightly on the wall. Determine the location of the end standards, then of the middle ones, if any, as described on page 45 in Step 2, but mark the positions on the wall, not on the shelves. Place a standard against the wall on the spot marked for an end standard. (Check to make sure the standard is top end up; some standards are made to be orientated in one way only.) Mark one fixing hole—the centre one if there are more than two—and drive in an appropriate fixing. Do not tighten, so you can swing aside the standard to insert the remaining fixings.

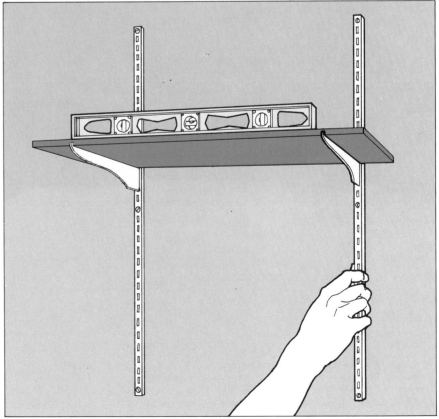

# Types of Standard and Bracket

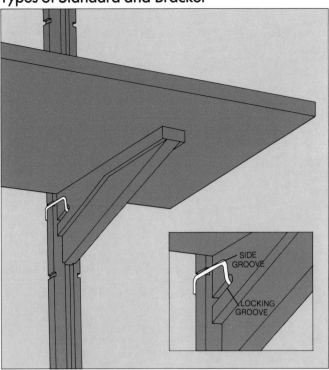

**Clip on.** These wooden brackets are attached to wooden standards by metal clips that slot into prepared grooves. Lock one leg of each clip in the side groove of the standard and gently ease the second leg across until it springs into the second side groove. Slot the protusion on the bracket into the channel in the standard and slide it downwards until it meets the clip. Ease the clip upwards until it locks into position in the up-turned end of the locking groove on the under-side of the bracket. To hold shelves securely in place, affix self-adhesive pads to the upper sur-faces of the brackets.

SIDE GROOVE

LOCKING GROOVE

**Slide and lock.** This system consists of brackets with hinged plastic wedges that slide down slotted metal standards; the brackets can be locked into place at any height you wish. To attach a bracket, slot the wedge into the channel in the standard *(inset)* and slide it downwards to the position required, maintaining an acute angle between the bracket and the standard. Then pull the tip of the bracket firmly down-wards until the wedge locks into position, fixing the bracket securely. To remove or reposition a bracket, unlock it by pushing the tip upwards.

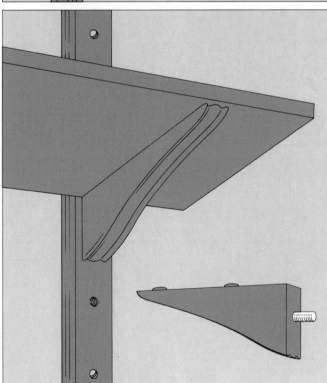

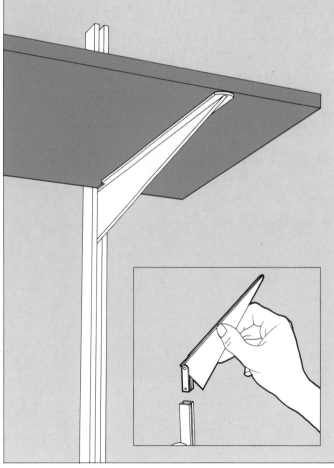

**Carved wood.** This decorative system includes pre-fixed screws on the brackets and pre-drilled threaded holes in the standards. To fix a bracket, simply position the screw into the correct hole and turn the whole bracket until it is firm and level. The shelves rest on rubber grip pads on the upper surface of the brackets.

# Supporting Shelves from the Side

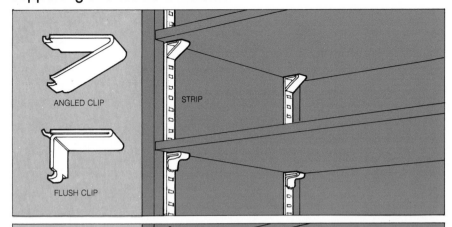

ANGLED CLIP

STRIP

FLUSH CLIP

**Strips and clips.** Slotted metal tracks, or strips, can be screwed or nailed to the side of a bookcase or wall, or housed in for a neat, flush fit. Squeeze the clips into the slots of the metal tracks with a pair of pliers. The angled clip *(top)* is able to support more weight than the flush clip *(bottom)* because it has a triangular shape.

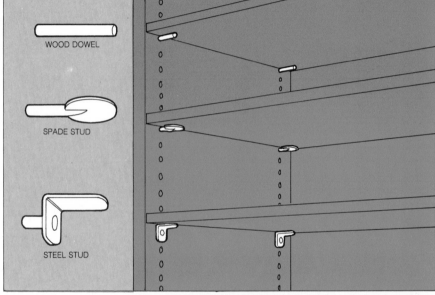

WOOD DOWEL

SPADE STUD

STEEL STUD

**Studs.** These supports fit into holes drilled to match their diameter. Wood dowels *(top)* can be fashioned as described on page 41. The load to be carried by the shelf will determine the diameter and length of the dowel. Metal spade studs *(centre)* and steel studs *(bottom)* offer a flat surface for greater stability. When marking hole positions before drilling, use a level and straight-edge to ensure evenness. You need not drill a row of holes on the side pieces if you do not plan to make frequent shelf adjustments.

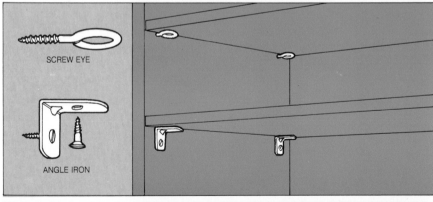

SCREW EYE

ANGLE IRON

**Screw eyes and angle irons.** A light load can be supported by screw eyes *(top)*, which are easily driven into wood. They can also be used in masonry with the help of a wall plug *(page 40)*. A small angle iron *(bottom)* can be installed in most walls fairly unobtrusively and will take 2 to 5 kg loads. Neither support is elegant, but both may serve well in a garage or attic.

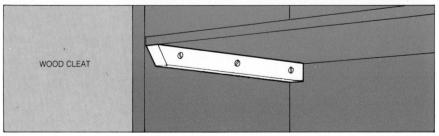

WOOD CLEAT

**Wood cleats.** For the strongest side support, cut strips of 15 to 20 mm wood about 10 mm shorter than the depth of the shelf. Saw off the front ends at a 45 degree angle before you attach the cleats to the sides of the wall or storage unit. If great strength is required, attach a third cleat beneath the back of the shelf and set the shelf on the cleats. For extra stability for a permanent instal-lation, drive small lost-head nails at an angle through the shelf into the cleats.

## Hanging a Large Unit on Mitred Cleats

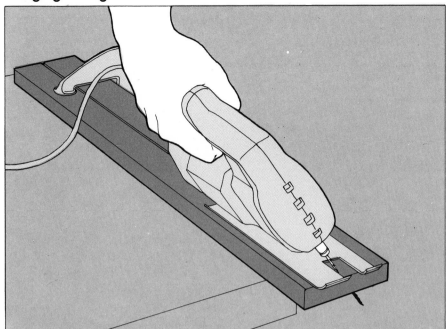

**1** **Cutting the cleats.** Using G-cramps, fix a piece of 25 by 100 mm wood or batten, slightly shorter than the width of the back of the unit, to your worktable. With a crosscut saw, or a circular or jigsaw set to cut at a 45 degree angle, cut the wood lengthwise into two cleats, as shown. A perfect cut is not necessary, since the cleats will fit together precisely along their sawn faces. But make sure to angle the saw blade away from the table while you work and reposition the G-cramps as you cut down the length of the board.

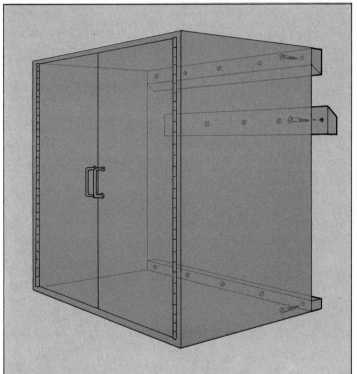

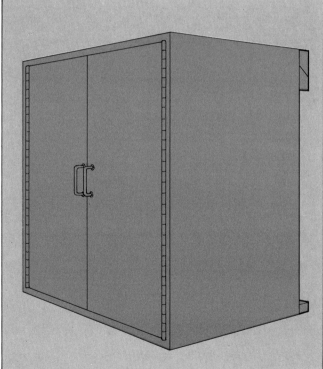

**2** **Attaching the cleats.** Fasten one of the cleats to the wall with its sawn edge up, as shown here. Then attach the other cleat, with its cut edge down, to the upper edge of the back of the unit by driving wood screws from the inside of the unit at least 10 mm into the cleat. In order to prevent the unit from wobbling or tilting after you have hung it on the wall, attach a strip of 25 mm wood to the bottom of the unit.

**3** **Hanging the cabinet.** Ease the unit on to the wall cleat, so that the two matching faces of the 25 by 100 mm board meet. When you construct a cabinet or other storage item to be hung in this way, you can hide the cleats by ensuring that the top and sides extend 20 mm beyond the back.

600 mm

600mm

600mm

133mm

564mm

18mm

900mm

747mm

20mm

600

556mm

600mm

115mm

75mm

600 mm

600mm

# 2 Planning a Project Step by Step

From start to finish. **From start to finish.** The set of working drawings *(background, opposite page)* provides the take-off point for construction of this general-purpose storage cabinet. Sturdily built, it can be used in a kitchen, living room or workshop—depending on the finishing materials chosen. As designed, it has a drawer and an adjustable shelf, but the cabinet can be easily modified to include additional shelves or drawers, by substituting hardware for the wooden pull or by adding decorative veneer strips to the exposed plywood edges.

Before actually starting to build any project, you must first ask yourself these three basic questions: What are the exact dimensions of the project you have in mind? What methods will be used to join together its various parts? What materials can be used in its construction? The answers to all these questions, taken one at a time and in their logical sequence—as they are in the chapter that follows—are indispensable to accomplishing your goal with maximum efficiency and economy.

One of the simplest projects in this book, building the general-purpose cabinet shown on the opposite page, is used to demonstrate this basic planning process. The cabinet is an example of a project conceived from scratch—one that starts as only an idea and is carried through to full realization—but the same process can be employed when you decide to modify any plans that already exist, including the instructions provided for the particular projects in this book.

Whether you are altering designs that exist already or you are working out your own, step-by-step planning demands, first of all, a complete set of working drawings, such as those shown on pages 54–57. These flat, two-dimensional representations of the project—from the side, front, top, bottom and back—show the size of each component part. The drawings are, indeed, similar to an architect's blueprints in their function; but you should not be daunted by the prospect of making them. They really are not that difficult to do and one does not have to be a professional draughtsman to produce effective results.

The sole purpose of the working plans is to provide yourself with all the essential information you will need before you go to the workbench. If you are a beginner at working with wood, it is best to start with graph paper, which is inexpensive, readily available and provides you with a built-in scale. Once you have worked on a few projects, even small ones, you may then find that you are competent enough to draw plans freehand on plain paper—as long as you are careful to record all of the measurements precisely, all of the parts and all of the joints; in short, all of the interrelationships of the various pieces, remembering to take into account the amount of space available, the location of adjacent walls and items of furniture.

Obviously, once you have completed the working drawings, you will have already answered two of the three essential questions: What dimensions? How do the pieces fit together? And the third question—What materials?—will have begun to answer itself. From the working drawings you can now compile an efficient shopping list, itemizing all the materials you will need. Furthermore, you can do so from a more informed point of view; one that will enable you to ask for materials using the often technical language of the timber merchants and D.I.Y. centres *(pages 58-61)*. This will ensure that you get everything in the sizes, types and qualities you require.

# The First Step: Using Design Norms to Determine Dimensions

When you start planning a project, you will already have a general idea of the size you want the structure to be and how it will fit into the room. However, before you can make actual construction plans, you will have to determine the exact dimensions of the unit: height, width, and depth.

Fortunately, you do not have to work out these dimensions in the abstract: there are established norms for the critical dimensions of most pieces of home furniture. The norms are based on average measurements for adult men and women; the ones to keep foremost in mind when planning storage projects are shown on the right. In the case of storage units, these dimensions should also take into account the maximum size of things that are typically stored in them. Bear in mind, however, that children's proportions vary greatly according to age; if you are building something for a child, use the same points of reference that you would use for adults, but scale to size and remember to allow for growth, since the average child grows 50 mm every year between the ages of five and 16.

The cabinet shown on page 50, which is planned through every stage on the following pages, was designed using two standard dimensions for counter cabinets. The cabinet's height, 900 mm, places the work area at a level that most individuals will find convenient to use while they are standing; it is a little lower than the average measurements from the floor to the elbow of both men and women (right). The

cabinet's depth, 600 mm, keeps everything in or on it within reach; the measurement is a good 100 mm less than that of the average outstretched arm. At the same time, because the dimensions of the cabinet are standardized, the unit will fit uniformly side by side with most kitchen cabinets and built-in appliances, which have been designed by the manufacturers with the same norms in mind.

Other factors, of course, will help you to determine the final size: available space, appearance and desired storage capacity.

Even the economical use of wood (page 60) should be taken into consideration.

Finally, to avoid the classic dilemma of the man who builds a boat in the basement only to discover he will have to tear down the house to get it out, make sure your storage unit is not too large to be moved from your work area to its eventual location. Check not only doorways but also the amount of room you will need for turning in hallways. For large projects, plan to make the final assembly in the room where the unit will be used.

**Using human norms.** The dimensions in millimetres, illustrated on the right, are averages derived from research by health education councils, standards institutes and private research associations in England, France and Germany. If you are building something for which some or all of the dimensions are optional, use the data in the drawings as a starting point, but measure yourself and your family to be sure that the project will be conveniently proportioned for those who will be using it most frequently.

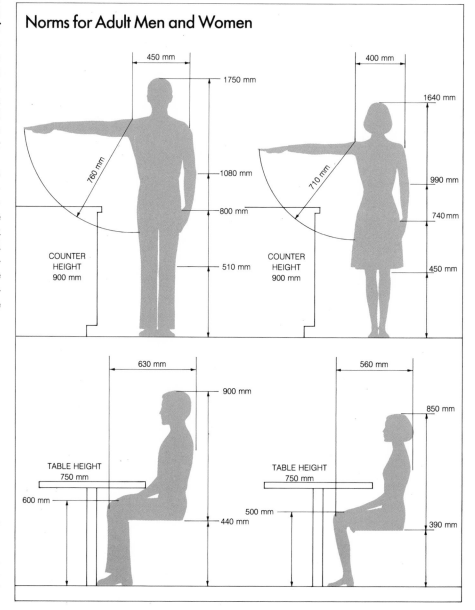

## Norms for Adult Men and Women

## Sizes of Common Household Items (in millimetres)

**Using norms for stored items.** Many of the common household items listed on the right are, of course, available in a wide range of sizes. However, for initial planning purposes, the chart will provide a good approximation of the amount of space required to store these representative items. You should list the specific items to be stored and take their relevant measurements before determining the exact inside dimensions. The abbreviations used in the chart—H, W, D, L—stand for height, width, depth and length.

### Kitchen
Frying pan, 250–500 L (with handle) × 150–300 diameter
Pressure cooker, 400 L (with handle) × 180–220 diameter
Roasting tin, 100–140 H × 320–420 L
Mixing bowls, 100–150 H × 150–300 diameter
Saucepan, 80–180 H × 200–400 L

### Cupboard
Clothes bag, 1500 H × 200–600 W × 500 D
Coat, 1100 H × 600 W
Suit (trousers folded), 1000 H × 500 W
Trousers (hung in full length), 1100 H × 400 W
Skirt, 700 H × 400 W

### Attic, basement or garage
Toolbox, 200–240 H × 400–550 L
Broom, 1250–1500 H × 200–300 W
Rake, 1250–1500 H × 400–600 W
Skis, 1200–2000 H × 80 W
Tennis racket, 650 H × 250 W
Bicycle, 1000 H × 450 W × 1500 L
Trunk, 300 H × 1000 W × 450 D
Suitcase, 450 H × 750 W × 250 D
Shoe box, 90–115 H × 180–300 W × 300 D
Boots, 450 H × 250 W × 300 L
Pram, 950–1050 H × 700 W × 1400 L
Wheelbarrow, 600 W × 1200 L
Lawn mower, 400 W × 450–850 L (with grass box)

## Standard Dimensions of Common Home Furniture (in millimetres)

**Using norms for furniture.** Norms are useful guidelines in establishing the proportions of any piece of home furniture you build. Height measurement is the most critical dimension for all the pieces listed, except for drawers and beds. The height of all the other pieces listed should not vary from the norms more than a few centimetres so that the furniture will be comfortable for most people to use. Dimensions for depth and width are less critical and can be changed according to the amount of space available for the piece and the storage room needed inside it.

| Item | Height (above floor) | Width (side to side) | Depth (front to back or head to foot) |
| --- | --- | --- | --- |
| Bed, double | 500 | 1500–1800 | 1900–2000 |
| Bed, single | 500 | 900–1000 | 1900–2000 |
| Bed, king-size | 500 | 2000 | 2000 |
| Bedside table | 400–500 | 400 | 400–500 |
| Bookcase | 2000 | optional | 250–450 |
| Cabinet, counter | 850–900 | 400–1200 | 600 |
| Cabinet, wall | 2400 (maximum) | optional | 350–550 |
| Chest of drawers | 850–1400 | 750–1050 | 450–500 |
| Cooker | 850–900 | 500–600 | 500–600 |
| Desk | 700–750 | 1500–1550 | 750–800 |
| Dining table | 750 | optional | optional |
| Drawer | – | optional | 350–600 |
| Dressing table | 600–700 | 900–1000 | 360–500 |
| Sewing table | 650–750 | optional | 400–500 |
| Sideboard | 730–850 | 1000–2050 | 450–550 |
| Straight chair | 400–450 (seat), 750 (back) | 450–500 | 450–500 |
| Typing table | 650–710 | optional | 600–650 |
| Wardrobe | 2000–2400 | optional | 550–600 |
| Workbench | 700–800 | optional | 600–650 |

# Step Two: Preparing the Working Drawings for Your Project

Like a good road map, a set of working drawings enables you to arrive at your destination by the best and quickest route. Preparing the plans is easy; with them, you can make all the main decisions for the project in advance, such as the types of joint that will hold a cabinet together, the positions of the shelves, the exact sizes of the drawers and doors, and the way the doors will open and close.

The number of drawings needed depends on the complexity of the structure you are building. For most units, the basic set of plans consist of flat, two-dimensional views of the outside from every vantage point: front, back, top, bottom and sides. In addition, any box within the basic box—such as a drawer or bin—requires its own external plans; for them, views of the object from the top, front and side will suffice.

The easiest way to make a basic set of drawings is to start with graph paper, letting each square on the grid represent 10 mm. Draw the outside dimensions of each view of the cabinet (grey lines, opposite). Within those lines, add all appropriate measurements (black lines). Any dimensions under 10 mm can be approximated, so long as the dimensions written on the plan are precise. Another set of drawings—cutaways like the ones shown on pages 56 and 57—are needed for interior parts or for those parts that are too small to be drawn accurately on the external views. These drawings, called sections, focus on such details as the way pieces go together at the joints and the way drawers, doors and other moving parts fit into the structure. The sections should be drawn larger—a scale of five graph squares to every 10 mm is recommended.

To work out the measurements on both the exterior and sectional drawings, you need to decide which of the two general types of wood—timber or plywood—you will be using for each part of the cabinet. Choosing the exact type and quality of the wood can be left for later (pages 58–59), but the width and thickness must be shown on your drawings (chart, right).

Since commonly available timber is not wide enough to be used for the large pieces of a storage unit, these parts are nearly always made from plywood. This material is usually sold in 1220 by 2440 mm sheets in thicknesses measuring 6, 9, 12, 15, 18 and 19 mm. For the large pieces that bear the greatest structural stress—the top, the bottom, sides and shelves—you will most often need an 18 or 19 mm thickness. For less critical large members—the back and the drawer bottoms—thinner plywood, usually 6 mm, can be used.

Plywood measurements are easy to calculate, because the listed thickness is the actual thickness of the wood. But the problem is more complex when timber is used, since its actual size and its nominal size can sometimes differ. Timber is most commonly used for smaller interior parts. On the cabinet shown opposite, for example, the drawer sides, base sections, runners and pull, and the blocks reinforcing the joints are all made of timber.

To adapt ready-made plans, including the ones that are shown later in this book, to your own particular requirements simply revise the measurements in the working drawings. But remember, if you change the scale of a project drastically, you may also have to change the size of wood, or even add a frame (page 24).

## Timber: Nominal Versus Actual Size

For the parts of a project that require timber rather than manufactured board, you will almost certainly be using one of the softwoods (fir, pine, cedar), since they are more readily available and less expensive than hardwoods (ash, birch, oak). By long-standing custom, the dimensions cited for the thickness and width of a length of softwood refer to the size of the rough-cut timber before it is dried and planed to make it smooth and square. As a result, the real size of the length you buy is smaller than the nominal size as shown in the chart on the right.

For example, the softwood used for the four sides of the drawer in the cabinet opposite is designated as 25 by 75 mm timber, although the boards measure only 20 by 69 mm after planing. The difference between the nominal and actual or planed measurements is usually 5 mm, but it can vary by several millimetres, depending on the type of softwood and the cutting and planing methods that are employed. In preparing your working drawings, be sure to use only the actual size of the timber.

However, this rule does not always apply to timber less than the nominal 25 by 50 mm, which is often sold according to actual size, so when buying timber with small thicknesses, check whether they are nominal or actual. The widths vary from board to board, but the thicknesses are standardized, the most common being 19, 22, 25, 32, 38, 50, 75 and 100 mm. For projects that require smaller than standard thicknesses of hardwood or softwood, ask your timber merchant to machine cut the wood to the appropriate size.

| Nominal timber sizes | Actual sizes (in millimetres) |
|---|---|
| 25 × 50 | 20 × 45 |
| 25 × 75 | 20 × 69 |
| 25 × 100 | 20 × 94 |
| 25 × 150 | 20 × 141 |
| 25 × 200 | 20 × 191 |
| 25 × 250 | 20 × 241 |
| 25 × 300 | 20 × 291 |
| 50 × 50 | 45 × 45 |
| 50 × 75 | 45 × 69 |
| 50 × 100 | 45 × 94 |
| 50 × 150 | 45 × 141 |
| 50 × 200 | 45 × 191 |
| 50 × 250 | 45 × 241 |
| 50 × 300 | 45 × 291 |

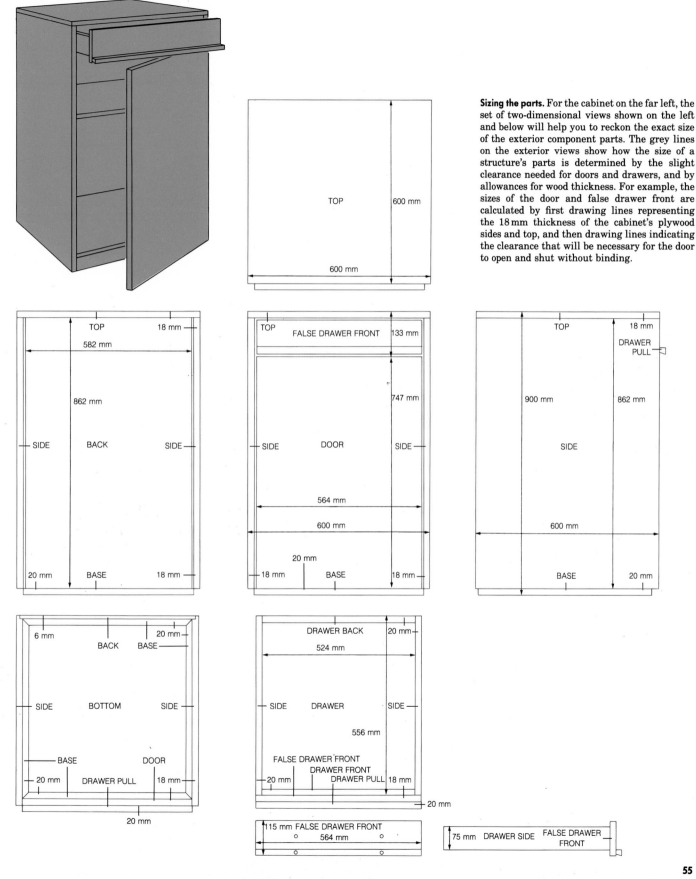

**Sizing the parts.** For the cabinet on the far left, the set of two-dimensional views shown on the left and below will help you to reckon the exact size of the exterior component parts. The grey lines on the exterior views show how the size of a structure's parts is determined by the slight clearance needed for doors and drawers, and by allowances for wood thickness. For example, the sizes of the door and false drawer front are calculated by first drawing lines representing the 18 mm thickness of the cabinet's plywood sides and top, and then drawing lines indicating the clearance that will be necessary for the door to open and shut without binding.

TOP

600 mm

600 mm

TOP — 18 mm
582 mm
862 mm
SIDE — BACK — SIDE
20 mm — BASE — 18 mm

TOP — FALSE DRAWER FRONT — 133 mm
747 mm
SIDE — DOOR — SIDE
564 mm
600 mm
18 mm — 20 mm — BASE — 18 mm

TOP — 18 mm
DRAWER PULL
900 mm — 862 mm
SIDE
600 mm
BASE — 20 mm

6 mm — 20 mm
BACK — BASE
SIDE — BOTTOM — SIDE
BASE — DOOR
20 mm — DRAWER PULL — 18 mm
20 mm

DRAWER BACK — 20 mm
524 mm
SIDE — DRAWER — SIDE
556 mm
FALSE DRAWER FRONT
DRAWER FRONT
20 mm — DRAWER PULL — 18 mm
20 mm

115 mm FALSE DRAWER FRONT
564 mm

75 mm — DRAWER SIDE — FALSE DRAWER FRONT

# Diagramming the Sections

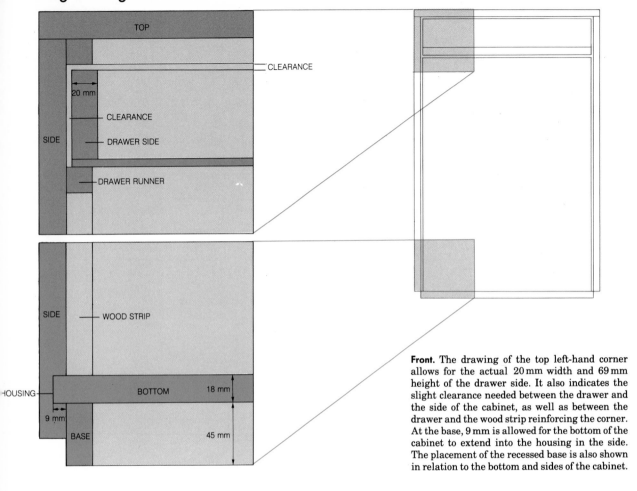

**Front.** The drawing of the top left-hand corner allows for the actual 20 mm width and 69 mm height of the drawer side. It also indicates the slight clearance needed between the drawer and the side of the cabinet, as well as between the drawer and the wood strip reinforcing the corner. At the base, 9 mm is allowed for the bottom of the cabinet to extend into the housing in the side. The placement of the recessed base is also shown in relation to the bottom and sides of the cabinet.

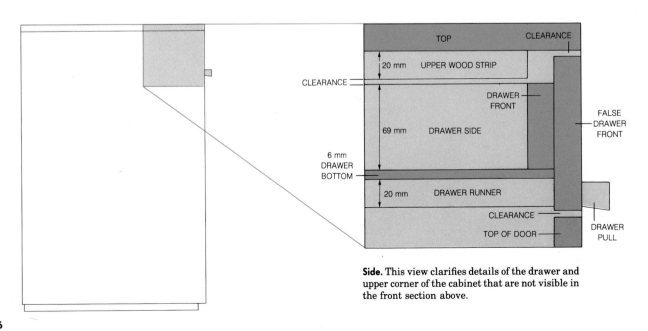

**Side.** This view clarifies details of the drawer and upper corner of the cabinet that are not visible in the front section above.

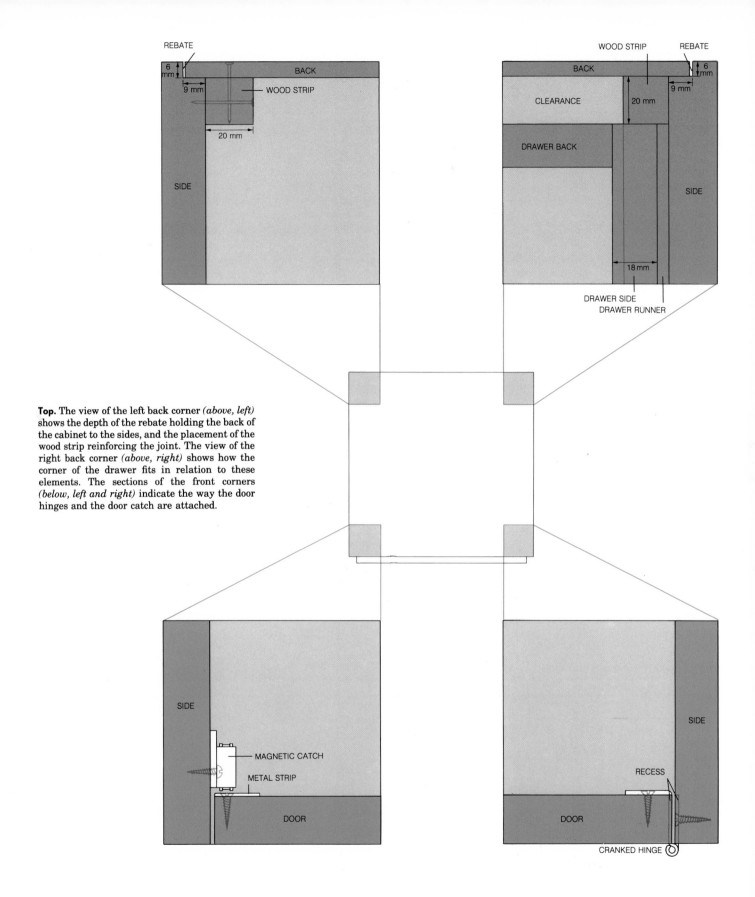

**Top.** The view of the left back corner *(above, left)* shows the depth of the rebate holding the back of the cabinet to the sides, and the placement of the wood strip reinforcing the joint. The view of the right back corner *(above, right)* shows how the corner of the drawer fits in relation to these elements. The sections of the front corners *(below, left and right)* indicate the way the door hinges and the door catch are attached.

# Step Three: Buying the Materials You Need

Once the working drawings for a project are complete, prepare a shopping list of materials. The simple list on page 60 has been compiled for the utility cabinet shown in the drawings on the preceding pages and gives specifications for the sizes and quantity of plywood and timber. Information about the working properties and characteristics of these materials can be found in the charts here and on the opposite page.

The chart below refers to three of the more commonly used types of manufactured board, and the two charts opposite categorize various types of softwood and hardwood timbers. (Not all the woods listed here are readily available, so it is best to check with your timber merchant before finalizing plans for a project.)

Plywood is the most versatile of the three manufactured boards. Obtainable from your suppliers in sheet sizes of up to 1525 by 3660 mm, it can be used to make a wide variety of projects—from shelves and wardrobes to sheds and ceilings.

Plywood consists of thin layers of wood, called plies or veneers, which are bonded together under heat and pressure. There is always an odd number of layers, each placed with its grain at right angles to the previous one. Alternating the plies in this way improves strength and stability and keeps warping to a minimum. The boards range from 3 ply to 11 ply, and each ply comes in a variety of thicknesses.

Plywood, which can be either softwood (cut from evergreen trees) or hardwood (cut from deciduous trees such as beech, birch and oak), is graded according to the quality of the surface veneers. However, this is not always easy to determine, since plywood is imported from many countries and the system of coding and grading varies from one country to another.

Plywood is also classified as interior or exterior grade, depending on the moisture resistance of the glue used to bond together the plies. Interior grades resist only normal indoor dampness. The more expensive exterior grades are needed for outdoor projects or in high-moisture areas such as bathrooms and kitchens.

Blockboard is another useful material. Composed of a hard core of wood strips sandwiched between single or double veneers of hardwood, it is stronger and more rigid than plywood and is generally used for projects which will bear heavy loads. Blockboard is easily obtainable and comes in a range of thicknesses and sheet sizes similar to those of plywood.

Chipboard—also known as particle board—is made of compressed wood particles. Although not as strong as plywood, it can serve as a cheap substitute. There are three basic types: graded density, three layer and single layer. Graded density is widely used as a furniture building material. This has a gradation from coarse to fine particles towards the surface, giving a close, smooth textured finish that can be faced with quality veneers.

Three-layer chipboard—often referred to as sandwich board—is similar, but has a layer of coarse particles sandwiched between two outer layers of fine particles. Single-layer chipboard has coarse particles throughout, producing rough, absorbent surfaces. It is suitable for projects where appearance is not important.

Like plywood, timber is imported from many countries, each with its own grading system. Because of its higher cost, hardwood is usually reserved for finer quality woodworking, whereas softwood is used mainly for general-purpose storage projects. The prime consideration to be taken into account is always suitability—and this means selecting timbers individually, according to their own particular qualities and characteristics.

## Working with Manufactured Boards

| | Plywood | Blockboard | Chipboard |
|---|---|---|---|
| Sawing | Use a tenon saw for less than 6 mm thickness, and a panel or power saw for more than 6 mm. Use a marking knife to score the surface when cutting across the grain. | Use a panel or power saw. Ensure that the core strips run parallel to the longest dimension. | Can be cut with a tenon, panel or power saw. Score veneered outer layers with a marking knife before sawing. |
| Jointing | Can often be jointed like timber when 9 mm or more thick. | All sizes can be jointed like timber. | Most sizes can be jointed like timber, but a liberal coating of adhesive is essential. |
| Nailing | Nail into the face of the sheets. Avoid edges. | Nail into the face of the sheets. Avoid the end grain of the core. | Nail through the face of the sheets into the supporting or supported member. Avoid edges. |
| Screwing | Drill pilot holes first, and use screw cups. Screw into the face of the sheets. Avoid edges. | Screw along edges and surfaces. Avoid the end grain of the core. | Double-threaded screws are recommended, but they should not be inserted too tightly. Screw into the face of the sheets. |
| Gluing | Roughen the surface with coarse sandpaper or a toothing plane. Spread glue evenly and apply even pressure. | Any woodworking adhesive is suitable. Does not glue securely on the end grain of the core. | PVA is recommended, though any woodworking adhesive can be used. |

## Softwood Timbers

| Wood | Characteristics | Nailing qualities | Screwing qualities | Gluing qualities | Finishing qualities | Uses |
|---|---|---|---|---|---|---|
| Douglas fir | A strong and durable timber. Straight-grained and highly water resistant. | Satisfactory | Satisfactory | Satisfactory | Satisfactory for staining and polishing. Poor for painting. | Plywood, flooring, windows, doors, stairs. |
| Western hemlock | One of the stiffest and strongest of softwoods. Fine, straight-grained wood. | Good | Good | Good | Good for all types of finishing. | Cabinet-making, furniture, flooring, doors. |
| Pine | Straight-grained, with a fine texture. Can be obtained almost free from knots. | Satisfactory, with care. | Good | Good | Good for staining, polishing and painting. | Plywood, panelling, flooring. |
| Western red cedar | Very soft timber, easy to work. Straight and close-grained, with conspicuous growth rings. | Poor | Satisfactory | Satisfactory | Good for staining and painting, with care. | Doors, skirting, panelling, shakes and roof shingles. |
| Redwood (Scots pine) | Strong, moderately hard timber, which is coarse and knotty. A widely available softwood. | Good | Good | Satisfactory | Satisfactory | Furniture, carcasses, flooring, kitchen furniture, doors. |
| Spruce | Straight-grained, with a fine texture. Small knots usually present. | Poor | Satisfactory | Satisfactory | Good for staining and painting, with care. | Kitchen furniture, boxes, veneer. |

## Hardwood Timbers

| Wood | Characteristics | Nailing qualities | Screwing qualities | Gluing qualities | Finishing qualities | Uses |
|---|---|---|---|---|---|---|
| Ash | One of the strongest and most flexible hardwoods. Good bending qualities. Straight-grained. | Fair | Fair | Good | Excellent for polishing. | Doors, cupboards, sports equipment, frames, shelves, drawers, tool handles. |
| Beech | A hard, strong timber. Straight-grained with a fine texture. Resistant to splitting. | Fair | Fair | Good | Excellent for all types of finishing, except painting. | Chairs, cabinets, tool handles, flooring, benches. |
| Birch | Moderately soft wood, close and fairly straight-grained. Some tendency to warp, but strong and hard-wearing. | Satisfactory, with care. | Satisfactory, with care. | Poor | Good for all types of finishing. | Plywood, chairs, general woodwork. |
| Elm | Very strong and difficult to split. Has a twisting grain that tends to warp without care. | Fair | Fair | Fair | Satisfactory for staining and polishing. | Panelling, cupboards, shelves, drawers, flooring. |
| Idigbo | Fairly coarse, uneven texture. Moderate strength, with fairly straight grain. | Good | Good | Fair | Good for staining and polishing. | Fine carpentry, door and window frames, veneer. |
| Lime | Straight-grained with a fine, even texture. Fairly soft and strong. Resistant to splitting. | Good | Good | Good | Very good for staining and polishing. | Cabinet-making, kitchen utensils, carving, musical instruments. |
| African mahogany | Medium texture and strength. Sometimes an irregular grain, but highly resistant to splitting. | Good | Good | Good | Good for staining and polishing. | Furniture, panelling, flooring, turning. |
| Oak | Hard and extremely durable. One of the most useful hardwoods. Coarse, straight-grained and free from knots. | Good, with care. | Good | Poor | Excellent for all types of finishing, with care. | High-quality furniture, flooring, doors, windows, cupboards. |
| Teak | Usually straight-grained, with a coarse, oily texture. Considered to be the strongest timber available. Highly prized. | Good | Good | Fair | Excellent for all types of finishing, except painting. | Furniture, flooring, kitchen utensils, veneer. |
| African walnut | Related to African mahogany, but with fairly coarse texture. Interlocked grain, and marked with black streaks. Tends to warp. | Satisfactory, with care. | Good | Good with care. | Very good for all types of finishing. Excellent for polishing, when filled. | Veneer, flooring, panelling, furniture. |

## Shopping List for the Cabinet

| | |
|---|---|
| 1 sheet plywood, 18 × 1220 × 2440 mm | 4 shelf bracket clips |
| 1 sheet plywood, 6 × 1220 × 2440 mm | 600 g lost-head nails, 25 mm |
| 2 lengths softwood, 25 × 25 × 2440 mm | 125 g lost-head nails, 30 mm |
| 1 length softwood, 25 × 50 × 2440 mm | 250 g lost-head nails, 40 mm |
| 1 length softwood, 25 × 75 × 2440 mm | 125 g round wire nails, 25 mm |
| 2 cranked hinges | 24,4 mm countersunk screws, 30 mm |
| 1 magnetic catch | 12,4 mm countersunk screws, 25 mm |
| 1 door pull | PVA glue |

## A Plan for Cutting Wood Efficiently

To determine how much timber or manu-factured board is required for a project, you will need to make a "cutting diagram", like the example on the right for the utility cabinet. In this diagram, every piece of the structure to be made from plywood is drawn on a piece of paper that is scaled to the dimensions of a plywood sheet, which is usually 1220 by 2440 mm.

To make a cutting plan, start with a piece of graph paper trimmed to a scale of 1220 by 2440 mm *(page 54)*. Then, using the same scale, cut pieces from another sheet of graph paper to represent each piece of plywood needed for your project. Arrange the pieces on the 1220 by 2440 mm graph paper so that the pieces fit into the most efficient pattern—that is, with the least possible waste. At the same time, arrange the pieces so that when you actually saw the wood, the first cuts can be made in straight lines along the entire length of the sheet. Indicate the cuts as Cut No. 1, Cut No. 2, and so forth as shown on the diagram. A further consideration is grain: arrange the pieces so that when the plywood is cut, the grain will create the effect you want.

When all the pieces have been carefully arranged, trace their shapes on to the sheet of paper, allowing an extra 3 mm along each cut for the saw kerf. To be doubly sure of allowing for kerfs, re-measure each cut before sawing the next one.

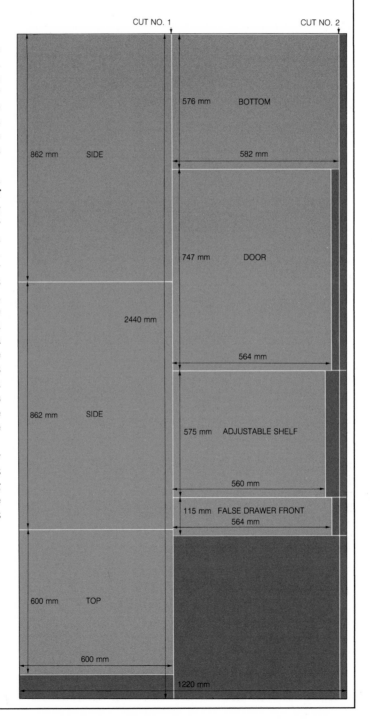

## Materials for Fixing and Finishing

The shopping list for a project is not complete unless it includes the appropriate kinds of nails, screws and glues for fastening the pieces together, as well as the wood filler and abrasive paper needed to give a neat, finished appearance.

Screws have more holding power than nails and are necessary where strength is important. They are also used to attach parts of a structure that you may later want to dismantle. Nails, when used with glue, are usually quite sufficient for parts that will be permanently attached.

There is a simple formula for selecting the right length: a nail or screw should be long enough for two-thirds of its shank to penetrate into the second of the two pieces of wood you wish to join. Screws also come in various diameters, indicated in millimetres from 1 to 10 (or in gauge numbers from 1 to 20). The screws most frequently used in woodworking range from 3 to 6 mm in diameter or gauges 5 to 14; they usually have countersunk heads that enable them to be inserted flush with the surface and concealed *(page 29)*.

Of the many types of nails sold, only three are needed for most storage construction: round wire nails, lost-head nails and panel pins. Round wire nails have large heads for greater holding power and are used only where they will not be seen. Both lost-head nails and panel pins have small heads which can be punched unobtrusively below the wood surface *(page 14, Step 7)*; they should be used on exterior parts where a relatively unblemished surface is desired.

Glue strengthens stress-bearing joints and, used in conjunction with nails or screws, can form a joint so strong that the pieces of wood will break before the joint itself will separate. Whenever you use glue, wipe off any excess immediately; otherwise the glue will clog the wood's pores when it dries, and the wood will not take a stain. Four types of adhesive are commonly used for woodworking:

☐ POLYVINYL ACETATE, known as PVA, is a ready-to-use white liquid and the most useful all-purpose adhesive for light construction. It is not suitable, however, for projects that will be exposed to moisture or high temperatures. PVA should be applied to both bonding surfaces, and the pieces clamped together until the glue dries—about 30 minutes.

☐ PLASTIC RESIN GLUE, sometimes called urea-formaldehyde, is the strongest of the common wood adhesives. It is highly moisture resistant—though not completely waterproof. Sold as a powder that must be mixed with water, plastic resin glue is slow setting, and the joint should be clamped for four to six hours.

☐ ANIMAL GLUE has been used since early Egyptian times, but is now reserved mainly for gluing veneers to plywood and chipboard, and for re-securing old joints. In the latter case, it is essential, since the new glues do not bond well over joints originally secured with animal glue.

Available in the form of small cakes or as a powder, animal glue should be soaked overnight in a pot of cold water and then heated until it reaches a soup-like consistency. It is then ready for use. The joints do not need to be clamped, but the glue takes up to 12 hours to set.

☐ CONTACT ADHESIVE is a strong glue that bonds so quickly it must be used with care. It is ideal for covering large wood surfaces with laminated plastic *(page 94)*. It is also useful for attaching strips of veneer to manufactured boards. Since contact adhesive produces an immediate bond, clamping is not necessary, but the parts must be carefully aligned before being placed together. Check the manufacturer's directions before you work with this adhesive. Most brands are quite inflammable and the fumes can be harmful if inhaled. For safety's sake, work in the open air or in a well-ventilated area, away from flames or heat.

After the project has been constructed, a wood filler is needed before the finish is applied. Fillers can be divided into two broad categories: those for filling cracks and abrasions, as well as depressions left by countersunk nails and screws, and those for filling the grain and sealing porous woods, such as mahogany or ash.

Both types of filler are sold in powder form for mixing with water. Those in the first category are also available ready-mixed, with the manufacturer's suggestion for a finish—oil, polish or varnish.

Before you apply a finish, prepare all surfaces by sanding. The abrasive papers suitable for preparing the projects in this book are listed below. They are available with three kinds of grit: glass, garnet and aluminium oxide. Glass paper and garnet paper are inexpensive, and used primarily for hand-smoothing wood to a fine finish. Aluminium oxide paper is more costly, but it tends to last much longer. It is used chiefly for power sanding. Most abrasives are rated by grit numbers, ranging from coarse to very fine.

## Types of Abrasive Paper

| | Grit no. | Typical use |
|---|---|---|
| Coarse | 40<br>60 | Removing scratches and rough spots on wood. Cleaning up old wood ingrained with dirt or paint. |
| Medium coarse | 80<br>100 | First sanding of timber and plywood before painting. |
| Medium | 120<br>150 | Final sanding of timber and plywood before painting. |
| Fine | 180<br>220 | Sanding of timber and plywood before applying varnish or other finish. |
| Very fine | 240<br>280 | Final sanding before varnishing. Sanding between varnish coats. |

# The Last Step: Cutting and Assembling

Once you have planned a project and bought the materials for it, you are ready to begin the job of actually building it: cutting the parts and putting them together. The procedures on this and the following pages explain how to cut and assemble the utility cabinet that is used as an example throughout this chapter.

For this project, the sheet of 18 mm plywood should be cut first, according to the plan on page 60. This one sheet will provide the top, bottom, sides, shelf, door and false drawer front. After making these initial cuts, use masking tape as labels for the parts. You will then need to make cuts for the joints, as shown on the right, on the sides, bottom and shelf.

Only cut the other cabinet parts from the timber you have purchased as you need them, measuring the exact space each one will occupy—thus ensuring that the dimensions originally provided in your drawings correspond to your actual cabinet. Even fractional variations in wood thickness and in cutting can change the size of the piece you need for a proper fit.

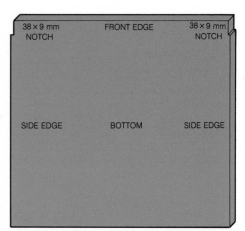

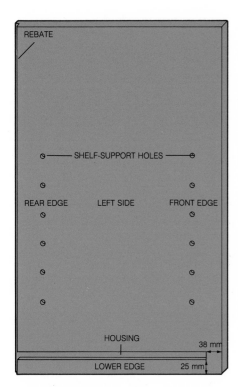

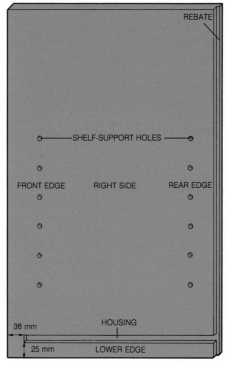

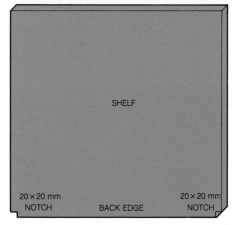

**Preparing the sides.** Along the rear edge of each cabinet side, cut rebates into which the back of the cabinet will fit. Each rebate should measure 9 mm deep and 6 mm wide. Next, cut housings on both sides to hold the cabinet bottom; locate each housing 25 mm above the lower edge. Each housing should run from the rebate to 38 mm from the front edge and be 18 mm wide and 9 mm deep. Then drill two rows of holes on each side for shelf supports. Locate one row 80 mm from the front edge, the other 60 mm from the rebate in the rear edge. Drill the first hole in each row 175 mm above the housing; drill five more at 75 mm intervals above the first holes.

**Notching the bottom and shelf.** The front corners of the bottom of the cabinet must be notched in order to fit beyond the ends of the housings on the sides. Cut each notch so that it measures 9 mm in from each side edge and 38 mm in from each front edge. The back corners of the shelf must also be notched so that the shelf will fit round the wood strips at the rear of the cabinet. Cut each notch 20 mm square.

# Putting the Pieces Together

**1** **Attaching the wood strips.** Cut two pieces of 25 mm square softwood, each piece 819 mm long, which will be used as wood strips to join the sides of the cabinet to the back. At 100 mm intervals along each strip, hammer 30 mm nails through the wood until their tips just protrude. Spread PVA glue along the side of the strips from which the nails protrude. Align each strip along each rebate between the housing and the top edge of the cabinet. Hammer the nails in. Then cut, glue and nail 556 mm long wood strips along the top edge of each side, butting them against the wood strips previously attached.

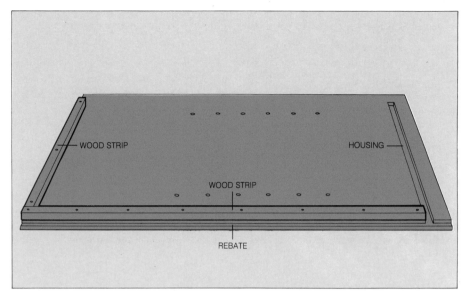

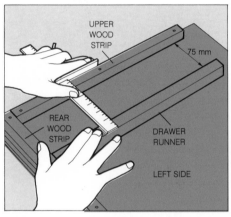

**2** **Installing drawer runners.** Cut two 556 mm pieces of 25 mm square softwood for the drawer runners. Using a combination square *(above)*, position a runner on one of the cabinet sides 75 mm below the upper wood strip and parallel to it. Hold the runner firmly in place and use it as a rule. Mark a line the full length of the runner 75 mm from the upper wood strip. Repeat on the second cabinet side. Glue and nail each runner along the line, making sure that its rear edge is butted against the rear wood strip.

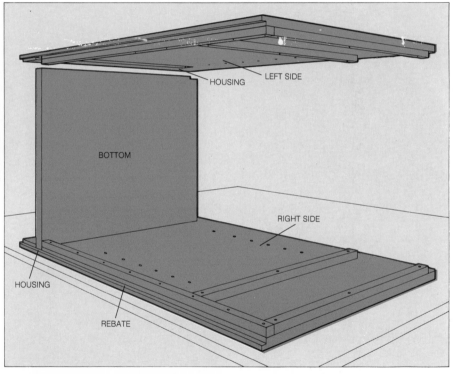

**3** **Gluing the bottom to the sides.** Place one cabinet side on a flat surface and spread PVA glue inside the housing. Also spread glue along the surfaces of the bottom edge that will fit inside the housing. Tap the bottom edge of the housing, making sure that the rebate is left clear. Apply glue to the other bottom edge and to its matching side. Tap the two pieces together. Turn the construction upright and proceed to the next step without waiting for the glue to dry.

**4** **Installing the top.** Use corner cramps to hold the top to the sides. The top will be attached by screwing it to the upper wood strips that are nailed to the sides. To locate the centres of the wood strips on the top of the cabinet, make a line 28 mm in from each side edge, using a combination square as a guide *(right)*. To indicate the positions for the screws, make cross marks on each line at points 50 mm in from the front and back edges and at 100 mm intervals in between. Then drill clearance holes for 30 mm long by 4 mm diameter wood screws at each cross mark. Countersink the screws.

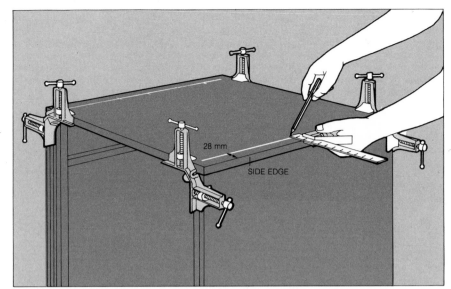

28 mm

SIDE EDGE

**5** **Attaching the top wood strip.** To join the back of the cabinet to the top, cut a 524 mm length of 25 mm square softwood. With the cabinet turned upside down, glue and nail the strip to the cabinet top, positioning it 6 mm in from the rear edge of the top so that it squares with the wood strips on the cabinet sides, as shown below.

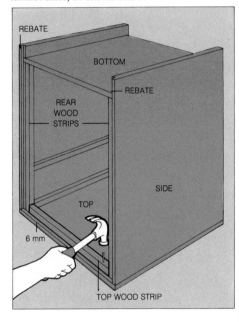

REBATE

BOTTOM

REBATE

REAR WOOD STRIPS

SIDE

TOP

6 mm

TOP WOOD STRIP

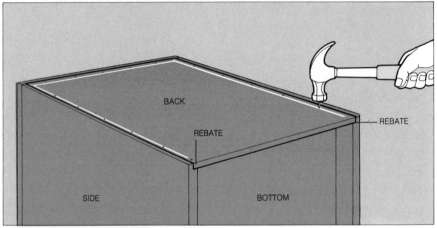

BACK

REBATE

REBATE

SIDE

BOTTOM

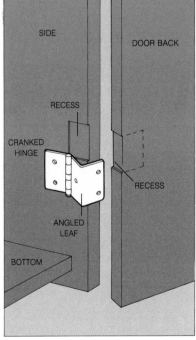

SIDE

DOOR BACK

RECESS

CRANKED HINGE

RECESS

ANGLED LEAF

BOTTOM

**6** **Attaching the back.** For the back of the cabinet, cut a piece of 6 mm plywood measuring 862 by 582 mm. Place the cabinet face down and position the back so that it fits into the rebates on the sides and butts against the top of the cabinet. Using a combination square in the same way as in Step 4, mark lines on the back of the cabinet 28 mm in from the top and side edges, locating the centres of both the top and the side wood strips. Nail the back to the strips, using 25 mm round wire nails spaced at 100 mm intervals.

**7** **Hanging the door.** Using cranked hinges *(page 36)*, attach the door according to the instructions for recessing hinges on an inset door *(page 35)*. Decide whether the cabinet's final location will make a left or right-hand opening more efficient, and then locate the hinges. The hinges should be 190 mm from the top and bottom edges of the door. Attach the angled leaf of each hinge to the door as shown; it is not necessary to cut a recess for the leaf part that will be attached to the back of the door. After hanging the door; install a catch *(page 37)* and a door pull.

**8** **Building the drawer.** Cut two 556 mm lengths of 25 by 75 mm wood for the sides of the drawer and two 524 mm lengths for its front and back. Cut a piece of 6 mm plywood measuring 564 by 556 mm for the drawer bottom. Assemble the drawer by the method described on page 28, but do not attach the false front yet. Use 40 mm lost-head nails to join the sides together and 25 mm lost-head nails to attach the bottom to the sides.

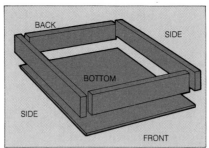

**9** **Attaching the drawer pull.** To install the wood pull shown for this project, cut a 564 mm piece of 25 mm square softwood. Using a wood cramp, align the pull on the outer face of the false drawer front 6 mm from the bottom edge. Turn the false front upside down and clamp the entire assembly in a woodworking vice *(right)*. Measure down 16 mm on the back surface of the false front to locate the centre line of the drawer pull. Make cross marks for the screws along the centre line, locating them 50 mm in from the side edges and at 100 mm intervals in between. Carefully drill clearance holes at the marks and attach the pull with 30 mm wood screws.

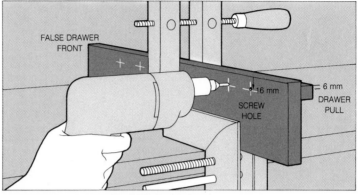

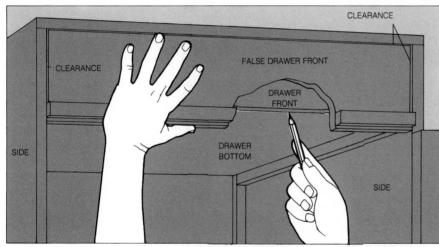

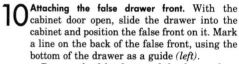

**10** **Attaching the false drawer front.** With the cabinet door open, slide the drawer into the cabinet and position the false front on it. Mark a line on the back of a false front, using the bottom of the drawer as a guide *(left)*.

Remove the false front and the drawer from the cabinet. Align the bottom of the drawer along the marker line and clamp the false front to the drawer. With a bradawl, mark positions for the two screws on the inside surface of the drawer front; locate each screw 38 mm below the top edge of the drawer front and 50 mm in from the sides. Drill clearance holes for 30 mm wood screws and screw the pieces together.

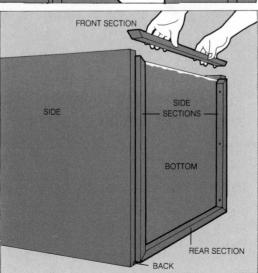

**11** **Assembling the base.** Cut two 564 mm lengths of 25 by 50 mm wood for the front and back sections of the recessed base and two 576 mm lengths for the side sections. Mitre the ends of each section, following the instructions on page 21. Place the cabinet on its back. Fit the back section into the recess at the bottom of the cabinet, and glue it in place; nails are not necessary for this section. Glue and nail the side sections to the sides of the cabinet in the same manner used for installing the wood strips in Step 1 *(page 63)*; use 25 mm round wire nails. Finally, glue and nail the front section to the bottom of the cabinet, nailing from the inside of the cabinet, using 40 mm lost-head nails.

To prepare the cabinet for a stain, varnish, paint or other finish, cover nail and screw holes with filler, and sand all surfaces *(page 16)*.

420mm

9mm

400mm

420mm

1320mm

75mm

1040mm

1040mm

**Multi-purpose divider.** The bunk bed/room divider on the left is designed to bring order—and privacy—to the confusion that often arises when two children and their possessions occupy the same room. To ease such a situation, this project takes full advantage of floor-to-ceiling space. With a bunk and storage and work facilities on each side, the unit not only partitions the room to create a separate living area for each child, but also provides more room to play in. Complete instructions for building the bunk section and the section for work and storage start on page 68.

The bunk bed/room divider on the opposite page concentrates sleeping and storage units in the normally wasted vertical space in the centre of a relatively small room, thus creating additional living space without requiring a permanent and costly alteration to your house. The divider is built using the basic techniques detailed in earlier chapters—plus some special tricks of the cabinet-maker's craft. The same is true of the other space-making projects that follow in this last chapter. Look around your house with an eye to those areas where the floor space is cramped or inadequate, and where a room's vertical potential could be exploited to get things off the floor and out of the way. Many of these objects might be placed in a modular wall-storage unit like the one described on pages 84–97.

The bunk bed/room divider and the wall-storage unit combine the functions of several pieces of furniture that otherwise would be scattered about the room, thus occupying less space and reducing clutter. In addition, the units can enhance the attractiveness of a children's bedroom or a living room by providing display areas for pieces of sculpture, books, plants, or odds and ends. And because both projects are built in separate sections, the arrangements and relationships of the sections can be varied according to taste, or you can construct only those components that you need.

Another way to gain more room for living is to use existing storage areas more efficiently. A long, sliding-door cupboard, for example, can be redesigned to contain drawers and a slide-out shelf unit without sacrificing any of its clothes-hanging capacity *(page 114)*. It may even be possible to transform a spare cupboard into a study or office, complete with desk and adjustable reading lamp *(page 115)*.

Kitchen cabinets can be fitted with roll-out storage bins *(page 102)* that not only hold more, but also make the contents more accessible. Other roll-out bins, installed in the often overlooked or poorly used wedge of space under open stairs *(page 112)*, may be an efficient solution to the problem of where to store bulky seasonal items, like ice skates or fishing tackle. Alternatively, if you have an attic or loft with an unfinished floor and areas hard to reach from a trap door, simple platforms that roll back and forth on castors *(page 110)* can be constructed to provide safe and easy access.

Many rooms have alcoves or shallow recesses that can be transformed into attractive locations for storage or display by the installation of built-in open shelves *(page 98)*. In rooms without recesses, the corners can be fitted with simple units of triangular shelves *(page 100)*.

You can construct all of the projects to the shapes and dimensions specified in this chapter by following carefully the instructions provided. On the other hand, you can modify as necessary any of these project designs to meet your particular storage requirements—or perhaps even create new plans—by referring to the techniques that are outlined in the chapter about job planning *(pages 50–65)*.

# Building a Bunk Bed and Room Divider

The combination of bunk beds and storage units illustrated on page 66 (and shown here in exploded views) offers an imaginative solution to the space problem created when two youngsters have to share one bedroom. Built to reach a ceiling just lower than 2.5 metres, with the bunks opening out on opposite sides to each other, the project functions as a room partition that not only occupies less floor space than two single beds, but also gives each child his own private living and storage area. For mobility and ease in handling, each of the five components of the project is constructed separately. The sections may be arranged as shown in the photograph on page 66 or in various combinations.

When it is finally assembled, the bunk-bed section of the room divider is 2440 mm high, 986 mm wide and 1986 mm long. The bunks are designed to hold 900 by 1900 mm mattresses. Three drawers on each side are sized to accept drawer-glide assemblies 12 mm thick; be sure to buy assemblies of this thickness.

The bookshelf-cupboard section (opposite page, bottom) is one of two identical units, each 2037 mm high, 986 mm deep and 455 mm long; each contains a 611 mm deep cupboard on one side and five bookshelves plus a drop-leaf desk on the other. The bookshelves—except for the one to which

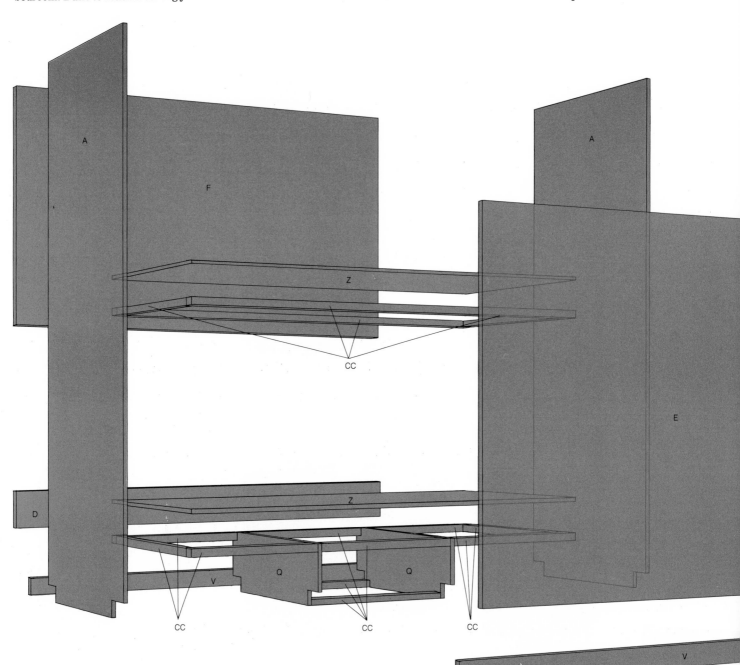

the desk is hinged—are adjustable. The cabinet *(below)*, also one of two identical units, sits on top of the bookshelf-cupboard section. Each cabinet 600 mm high, 986 mm deep and 455 mm wide; and each is divided into two compartments, one open and the other with a door.

If you build this project to full ceiling height, thus partitioning the room, be sure there is ample ventilation, heat and light on both sides. However, if you do not want it so near the ceiling or if the ceiling is lower than here, you can decrease the height by eliminating the cabinet units and then lowering the bunk-bed sections by 400 mm. You may also wish to make other modifications, such as reducing the width of the bunk beds to accommodate special-size mattresses, which would then call for corresponding alterations in the dimensions of the bookshelf-cupboard sections. Since any changes from the dimensions given on the following pages will affect your specifications, you will have to prepare a new set of cutting diagrams and working drawings by following the job-planning procedures outlined on pages 54–57 and 60.

All major parts of the bunk bed/room divider shown here are made of 18 mm birch plywood and blockboard, which can be finished with a coating of linseed oil to bring out the natural beauty of the wood.

If you paint the unit, you can economize by buying boards with a less perfect surface (see page 58 for information about manufactured boards). Do not use plywood or blockboard thinner than 18 mm; it lacks the necessary structural strength.

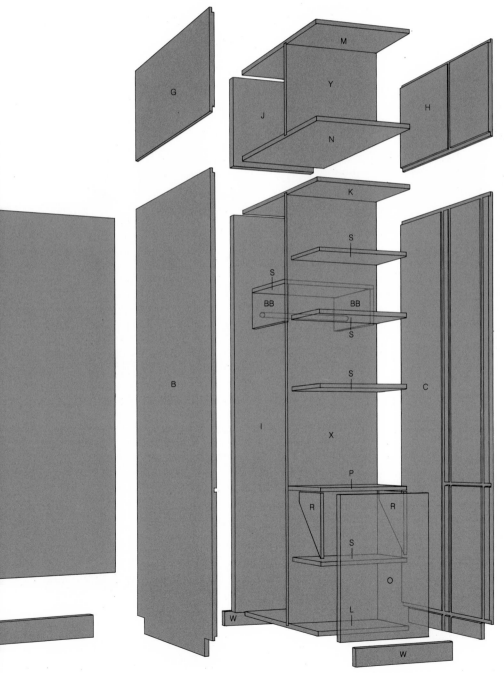

**Key to the parts.** The bunk-bed and room-divider parts shown in the exploded views on these two pages are identified in the key below. The pieces are lettered in an order that approximates to the cutting sequence *(page 70)*. Study the key and drawings carefully to familiarize yourself with the positions the parts will occupy in the finished project. Then, as you cut the parts, stick a piece of masking tape to each and write on the tape the letter-designation of the part and, where appropriate, the side that will be more visible when finished, and an arrow indicating "top".

| A | bunk-bed ends (2 pieces) |
|---|---|
| B | left bookshelf-cupboard sides (2 pieces) |
| C | right bookshelf-cupboard sides (2 pieces) |
| D | lower-bunk side |
| E | lower-bunk wall |
| F | upper-bunk wall |
| G | left cabinet sides (2 pieces) |
| H | right cabinet sides (2 pieces) |
| I | cupboard doors (2 pieces) |
| J | cabinet doors (2 pieces) |
| K | bookshelf-cupboard tops (2 pieces) |
| L | bookshelf-cupboard bottoms (2 pieces) |
| M | cabinet tops (2 pieces) |
| N | cabinet bottoms (2 pieces) |
| O | desks (2 pieces) |
| P | fixed shelves for desks (2 pieces) |
| Q | drawer support panels (2 pieces) |
| R | desk brackets (4 pieces) |
| S | adjustable shelves (10 pieces) |
| T | drawer backs and fronts (12 pieces) |
| U | drawer sides (12 pieces) |
| V | plinths for bunk-bed unit (2 pieces) |
| W | plinths for bookshelf-cupboard (4 pieces) |
| X | cupboard backs (2 pieces) |
| Y | cabinet partitions (2 pieces) |
| Z | bunk bottoms (2 pieces) |
| AA | drawer bottoms (6 pieces) |
| BB | cupboard-bar supports (4 pieces) |
| CC | bunk-bottom supports (14 pieces in 3 sizes) |

## Shopping List

2 sheets blockboard, 18 × 1220 × 2440 mm
12 sheets plywood, 18 × 1220 × 2440 mm
1 sheet plywood, 9 × 1220 × 2440 mm
1 sheet plywood, 6 × 1220 × 2440 mm
5 lengths softwood, 50 × 50
  (45 × 45 actual) × 3000 mm
2 dowels, 25 × 415 mm
1 dowel, 25 × 250 mm
18.5 metres softwood strips, 25 × 25 mm
  (20 × 20 mm actual)
60 metres 19 mm iron-on veneer
2 hardwood boards, 1520 × 125 × 18 mm
4 hardwood boards, 450 × 80 × 18 mm
6 pairs full-extension drawer-glide assemblies,
  500 mm
8 metal shelf strips, 12 × 5 × 1311 mm
8 metal shelf strips, 12 × 5 × 597 mm
250 g nails for shelf strips
32 metal strip clips
10 pivot hinges for 18 mm lay-on doors
2 magnetic catches, 32 mm
2 magnetic catches, 75 mm
2 piano hinges, 38 × 418 mm
4 piano hinges, 38 × 250 mm
72, 4 mm straight-head wood screws, 16 mm
10 drawer and cupboard pulls
200, 6 mm crosshead wood screws, 31 mm
80, 6 mm crosshead wood screws, 50 mm
60, 6 mm raised head wood screws, 38 mm
60, 6 mm screw cups
500 g lost-head nails, 38 mm
      PVA glue
¼ litre contact or synthetic resin glue
100 ml lacquer thinner
250 g wood filler
  25 sheets No. 120 grit abrasive paper
  7.5 litres linseed finishing oil

## Cutting Diagrams

**Sawing the plywood and blockboard.** Measure and saw one cut at a time; otherwise the kerf lost in cutting will affect later measurements. So that the circular saw will have the firm support of the rest of the sheet, the first cuts in the sheet should be those for the long narrow pieces extending along the sheet's 2440 mm dimension. When all the cutting is done, there should be 89 plywood and 4 blockboard pieces, identified according to the key on the preceding page. Off-cuts, indicated by a darker shade, are useful for making guides, straightedges and spacers. Handle the plywood and blockboard sheets with care so that the edges are not bruised. If an edge does become damaged, rearrange the cutting diagram to leave the scrap pieces on the edge. (Cutting of the 50 by 50 mm softwood boards to requisite lengths is done as the pieces are needed.)

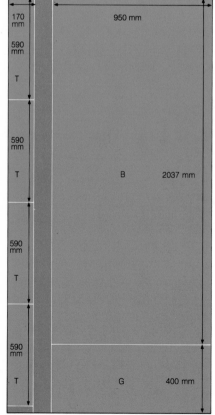

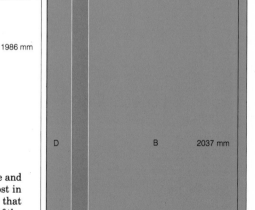

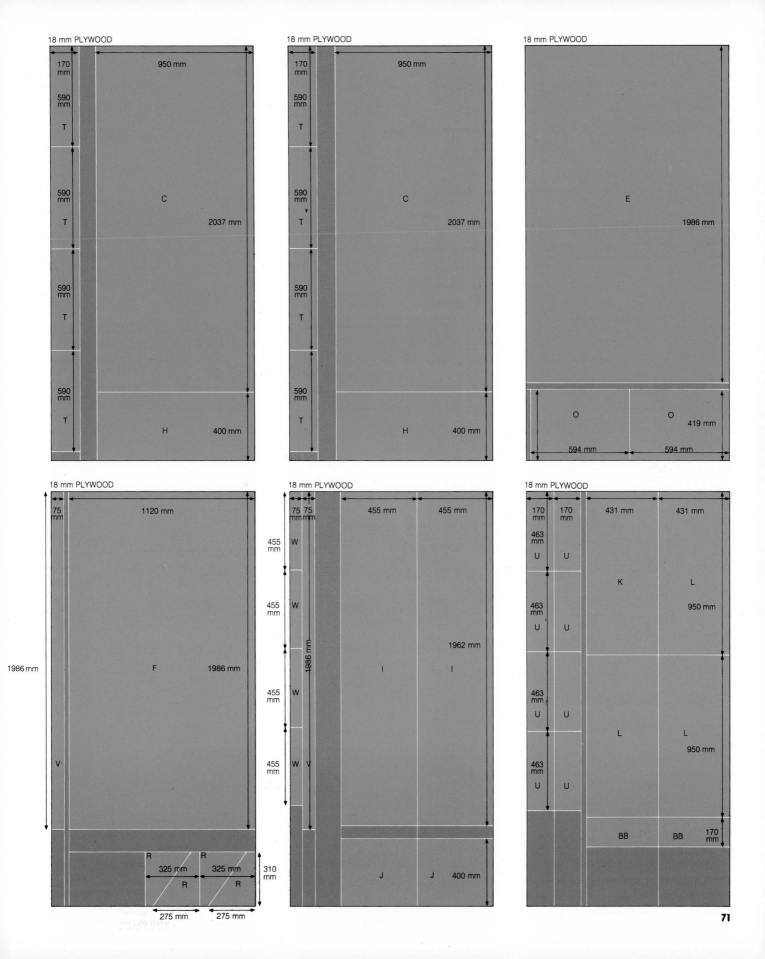

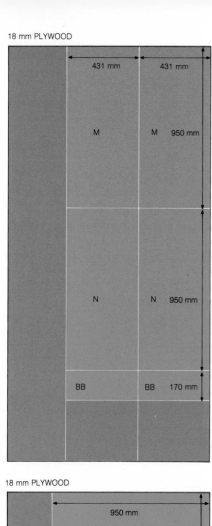

18 mm PLYWOOD

431 mm | 431 mm

M | M 950 mm

N | N 950 mm

BB | BB 170 mm

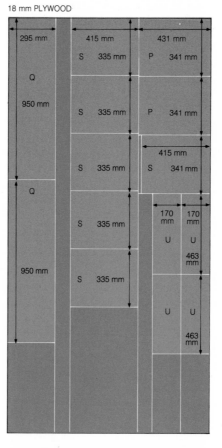

18 mm PLYWOOD

295 mm | 415 mm | 431 mm

Q | S 335 mm | P 341 mm

950 mm | S 335 mm | P 341 mm

Q | S 335 mm | 415 mm

950 mm | S 335 mm | S 341 mm

S 335 mm | 170 mm | 170 mm

U | U

463 mm

S 335 mm | U | U

463 mm

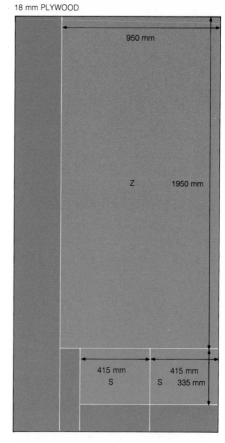

18 mm PLYWOOD

950 mm

Z 1950 mm

415 mm | 415 mm

S | S 335 mm

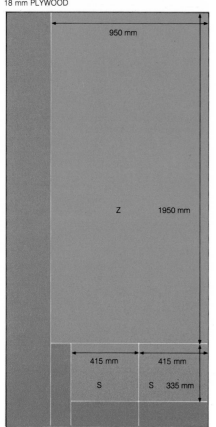

18 mm PLYWOOD

950 mm

Z 1950 mm

415 mm | 415 mm

S | S 335 mm

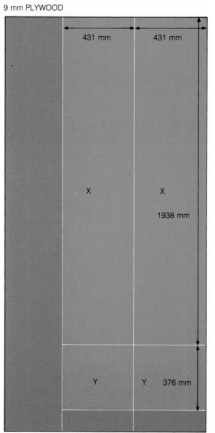

9 mm PLYWOOD

431 mm | 431 mm

X | X

1938 mm

Y | Y 376 mm

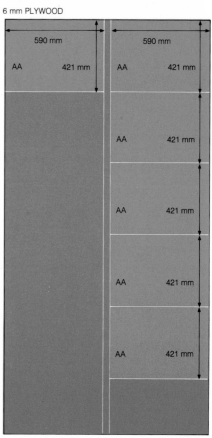

6 mm PLYWOOD

590 mm | 590 mm

AA 421 mm | AA 421 mm

AA 421 mm

AA 421 mm

AA 421 mm

AA 421 mm

# Routing the Rebates, Housings and Grooves

The chart at the bottom of this page details all the notches and channels required in the bookshelf-cupboard and the cabinet.

A router is essential for speed, precision and straightness in making the great number of channels required. If you do not own a router, hire one; with it you will be able to cut out the channels with assembly-line efficiency—including those in drawer fronts, backs and sides, and in the sides of the bunk-bed ladder (page 75). To minimize the number of times the router bit must be changed, the pieces of wood should be grouped and the channels cut in the numerical order shown in the chart and in the diagrams on the right.

Pieces that are to receive the same kind of channel should be stacked on a steady work surface at least as wide and as long as the largest pieces. If you need more room, extend the work surface by using two saw-horses adjusted to the height of the work surface. After the first piece has been routed, slide it aside and rout successive pieces, down to the last one in the stack.

Note that the bookshelf-cupboard sides (B and C) and the cabinet sides (G and H) will face each other, and that the channels routed in them must be made accordingly.

Setting up a router guide for some of the channels may be done according to the instructions on pages 26 and 27. But two home-made T squares (page 74) are needed to set up guides for making some housings and grooves; a T square also speeds the work of making identical channels on a number of pieces, and lessens the danger of error. As a further safeguard against mistakes, before routing any piece of wood make a test channel on a scrap of plywood and check its depth and width on the 1 mm scale of a combination square. Rebates, housings and grooves cut in plywood will have slightly splintered edges; sand the rough edges lightly by hand.

After the rebates, housings and grooves have all been routed, assemble the ladder and the six drawers; these parts will then be ready when you are putting together the bunk-bed section.

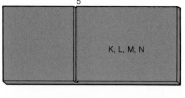

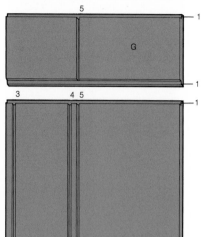

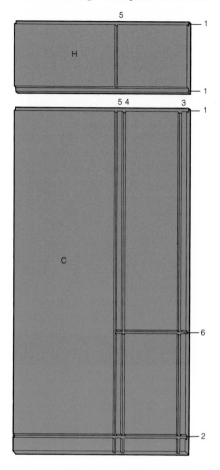

**Routing diagrams.** The numbers for the housings, grooves and rebates in the diagrams (left and below) correspond to the numbers in the chart at the bottom of the page. When calculating where to set guides for the router (pages 26–27), measure from the edge of the plywood that is closer to the edge of the planned channel.

## Data for the Routing Diagrams

| Channel | Bit (width of channel) | Depth of channel | Distance from edge of piece to near edge of channel |
|---|---|---|---|
| 1 | Rebate at top of B and C; top and bottom of G and H. | 18 mm | 6 mm | None |
| 2 | Groove at bottom of B and C. | 18 mm | 6 mm | 75 mm |
| 3 | Housing for front bookshelf support strip on B and C. | 12 mm* | 5 mm* | 35 mm |
| 4 | Housing for rear bookshelf support strip on B and C. | 12 mm* | 5 mm* | 294 mm |
| 5 | Housing for cupboard back on B, C, K and L; for cabinet partition on G, H, M and N. | 9 mm | 6 mm | 341 mm |
| 6 | Groove for fixed shelf on B and C. | 18 mm | 6 mm | 690 mm |

*Bit and depth of channel depend on width and thickness of shelf support strip used.

# Making and Using T Squares

**1 Positioning the router guides.** By following the method on pages 26 and 27, you can position the guide for groove No. 2 and housing No. 3 with a combination square. However, since the combination square does not reach far enough for housings No. 4 and 5, you will have to make two T-square fences *(right)* from straight-edged scraps of plywood.

Determine the length of the blades of the T squares by totalling the following measurements: the width of the scrap selected for the crosspieces, plus the distance from the edge of the piece of wood to be routed to the near edge of the intended channel, plus the width of the channel itself, plus the distance from the edge of the router base to the router bit. The length of the crosspieces is not critical. Be sure to square the ends of the blades. Use a combination square to check that the pieces intersect at right angles; secure the pieces with nails. For more permanent fixing, use glue and wood screws.

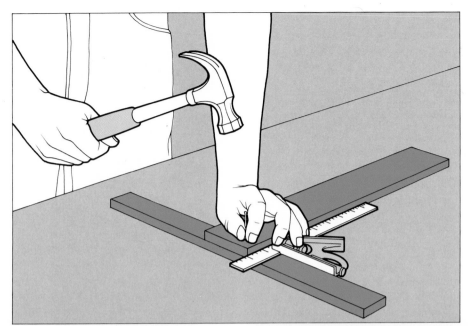

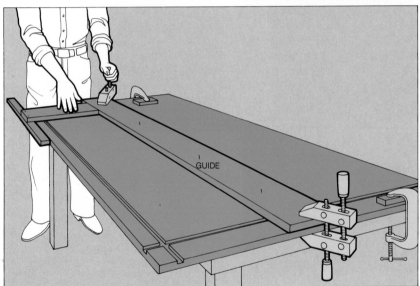

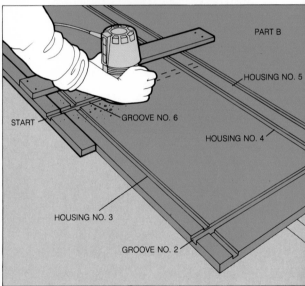

**2 Setting up a guide with a T square.** A piece of plywood about 150 mm wide and 2000 mm long, left over from cutting the large parts of the bunk bed/room divider, makes an excellent guide for the longer housings. Place the guide on the wood to be routed so that the planed edge of the plywood faces the location of the housing to be cut. At one end, hold the T against the edge of the wood to be routed and butt the guide against the T's vertical piece *(above)*. Clamp the guide to that end of the wood. Slide the T along the length of the guide, and nail down the centre of the guide temporarily with several panel pins—very small lost-head nails—to keep it from moving while you are routing. Clamp the other end of the guide to keep it steady as well.

**3 Using a T square as a guide.** To rout groove No. 6 in the bookshelf-cupboard sides (parts B and C), your longest T square can be used as a guide. Measuring each piece from the bottom edge, position the T by totalling all measurements given in Step 1 except the first. Using panel pins, tack the T square to the piece to be routed.

On parts B, start the router at the edge of the T square's crosspiece; move the bit through the crosspiece and through part B *(above)* until the bit intersects housing No. 5—but be sure not to go through the far edge of housing No. 5. On parts C, position the T square as above, but reverse the routing procedure: start at housing No. 5. Stand sideways so that you are not pulling the router directly towards your body. Continue the channel through the crosspiece of the T to avoid splintering the open end of the housing.

## Notches for the Plinths

**Cutting the notches.** To make space for the plinths, measure and, using a jigsaw or tenon saw, cut 75 by 75 mm notches at the bottom corners of the bunk-bed ends (parts A) and the bookshelf-cupboard sides (parts B and C), as well as in the drawer-support panels (parts Q). The plinths will be screwed on to the bottoms of the units on the final assembly.

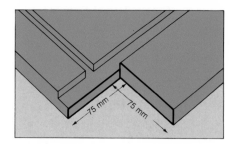

## Ladder

**1 Routing the ladder.** For the ladder uprights, use the two 1520 mm pieces of 125 by 18 mm hardwood; for the treads, use the four pieces of 450 mm long 80 by 18 mm hardwood. Place the pieces for the uprights edge to edge on the work surface and clamp them to it with hand screws. Use scrap boards, nailed across the uprights, as guides for the router in making the channels. Be careful not to nail into the work surface.

Starting 50 mm from the bottom of the ladder uprights, rout four housings 300 mm apart in each board; make the housing 6 mm deep, 18 mm wide (the actual thickness of the tread material) and 75 mm long. Saw a notch 14 by 6 mm deep at the back corners of each tread so that when the treads are assembled they will fit over the rounded ends of the housings, thus covering them. Use a jigsaw to round off the corners of the uprights at the top, and sand them smooth.

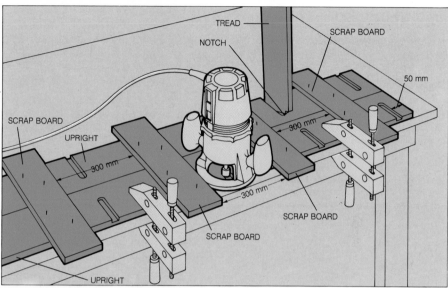

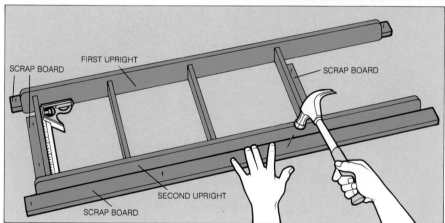

**2 Assembling the ladder.** To protect your workbench, cover it with a large off-cut board. Nail a straight scrap board as long as the uprights to the large board. The straight scrap board will hold the ladder parts in place while you glue them. Stand one of the uprights on its edge with the open ends of the housings down, and butt the upright against the nailed board. Glue the treads into the housings. Place the second upright in position and glue the other ends of the treads into its housings. With a combination square, true the top and bottom treads, and nail short pieces of scrap board to the large off-cut surface to hold the treads and uprights in position. Nail another long, straight piece of scrap board to the large off-cut so that it presses firmly against the second upright. Leave the assembled ladder in place until the glue has dried thoroughly.

## Drawers

**Making the drawers.** Rout a groove 6 mm wide and 6 mm deep 12 mm from the bottom edge of all drawer fronts and backs (parts T). Divide the drawer sides (parts U) into six left and six right sides and rout a groove in each, as above. At the front edge of each side (and on the same surface as the groove), rout a rebate 18 mm wide and 6 mm deep; at the back of each side 18 mm from the edge, rout a housing 18 mm wide and 6 mm deep. Assemble the drawers, following the procedure on pages 28 and 29. A false front will be added later when you assemble the bunk bed.

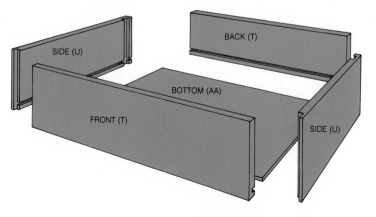

# Trimming the Plywood Edges

All plywood edges that will be visible in the completed bunk bed/room divider should be covered with wood lipping or veneer edging; besides giving your work a more professional appearance, such covering keeps the cut edges of plywood from splintering. Also, if you plan to paint the plywood, lipping provides a ready base for the paint. If you do not use a covering, the edges of the plywood should be sealed with wood filler and then sanded smooth.

Because of the large size of many of the pieces in this project, it is easier to apply edge covering after all router cuts have been made and before the pieces are assembled. Two kinds of covering can be used:

☐ LIPPING. Strips of 18 by 18 mm (actual) softwood or hardwood will protect edges that get the most wear, such as the beds and the fronts and sides of the desks.

☐ VENEER EDGING. On edges that do not require any extra protection, use veneer edging. This flexible wood trim is available in a variety of woods, such as oak, mahogany and teak, to match the most commonly used plywoods; for this project you will need 60 metres.

The most convenient edging comes with a heat-and-pressure-sensitive glue already on the back. It is sold in rolls about 2 metres in length, and is available from most D.I.Y. shops. To apply the edging, you simply press it in place with a warm iron, starting at one end of the plywood and slowly moving along its length. To ensure that bonding is effective, run a block of wood or a wooden dowel along the edging while it is still warm. When the edging has cooled, it can be shaved with a razor blade or a trimming knife to the correct width, as shown on the opposite page. Alternatively, it can be trimmed with a file.

Veneer edging also comes without ready-glued backing; such edging generally comes in thin strips 1 to 2.5 metres long and is applied with a contact adhesive (page 61). Care must be taken to position it correctly (right, below), since the adhesive bonds instantly when the two glued surfaces touch. Use inexpensive stiff-haired brushes to spread the glue. When the glue dries on the brush, it is best to discard the brush and use a new one: cleaning the glue off is difficult and time-consuming.

Before applying edging, refer to the chart below and mark the edges to be covered with coloured pencils—one colour for lipping and one for veneer edging.

## Edges to be Covered

| Piece | Edge | Type of covering |
|---|---|---|
| Lower-bunk side, part D | Top edge<br>Side and bottom edges | 18 × 18 mm lipping, 2011 mm<br>Veneer edging |
| Lower-bunk wall, part E | Top edge<br>Side and bottom edges | 18 × 18 mm lipping, 2011 mm<br>Veneer edging |
| Upper-bunk wall, part F | All four edges | Veneer edging |
| Desks, part O | Front edge<br>Sides<br>Back edge (where hinge will be mounted) | 18 × 18 mm lipping, 444 mm<br>18 × 18 mm lipping, 619 mm<br>Veneer edging |
| Desk brackets, part R | All four edges | Veneer edging |
| Fixed shelves, part P | Front (431 mm) edges | Veneer edging |
| Adjustable shelves, part S | Front (415 mm) edge | Veneer edging |
| Bookshelf/cupboard sides, parts B and C | Top of bookshelf edge to shorter groove<br>Top of shorter groove to bottom of bookshelf edge<br>Edges of cupboard end | 18 × 18 mm lipping, 1354 mm<br>Veneer edging<br>Veneer edging |
| Bookshelf/cupboard tops, part K | 431 mm edge nearest to housing<br>431 mm edge farthest from housing | 18 × 18 mm lipping, 456 mm<br>Veneer edging |
| Bookshelf/cupboard bottoms, part L | Both 431 mm edges | Veneer edging |
| Cabinet sides, parts G and H | 400 mm edge nearer housing<br>400 mm edge farthest from housing | 18 × 18 mm lipping, 425 mm<br>Veneer edging |
| Cabinet tops and bottoms, parts M and N | 431 mm edge nearest to housing<br>431 mm edge farthest from housing | 18 × 18 mm lipping, 456 mm<br>Veneer edging |
| Cupboard doors and cabinet doors, parts I and J | All edges | Veneer edging |
| Plinths, part V and W | Short ends | Veneer edging |

## Lipping Strips

**1** **Attaching lipping.** Each small piece to which lipping will be attached should be clamped in a woodworking vice with the edge to be covered facing up. Large pieces can be clamped, edge up, to one side of the worktable with hand screws. Cut the lipping about 25 mm longer than the edge it is to cover. For an especially strong bond, use PVA woodworking glue (page 61); spread it liberally along the plywood edge and one face of the lipping. Bring the surfaces together. Every 150 to 200 mm, drive in lost-head nails, 38 mm long, and countersink them with a nail set.

Wipe off excess glue with a wet rag. After the glue has dried, use a tenon saw to trim excess lipping flush with the ends of the piece, except on parts M, N and K. Fill the countersunk nail holes with wood filler and sand all surfaces.

**2** **Making cutaways for joints.** To allow enough space for the joints, the lipping on the storage-cabinet top (M) and bottom (N), and the bookshelf-cupboard tops (K) must be indented instead of being trimmed flush with the side edge of the plywood. Use a combination square and a pencil to mark a saw line across the lipping 6 mm in from the plywood edge. With a jigsaw or a tenon saw, cut along the line just until you reach the glued edge of the plywood. Gently tap the excess lipping from the rear with a hammer; it will break off cleanly at the saw cut.

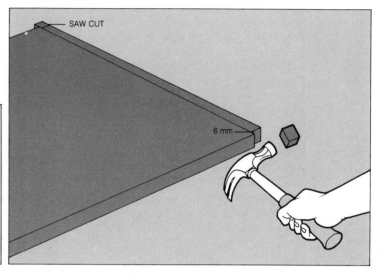

SAW CUT

6 mm

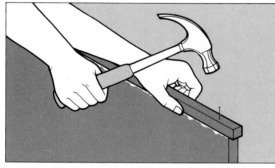

## Veneer Edging

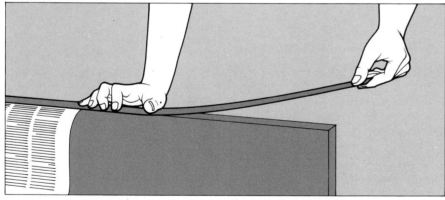

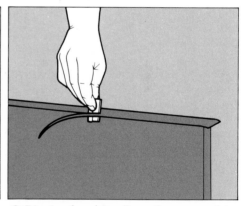

**1** **Applying veneer edging.** If you are using edging without a ready-glued backing, first cut a strip of edging at least 20 mm longer than the plywood edge to be covered. Using a small brush, apply contact adhesive on to the plywood edge and the veneer edging, moving the brush in one direction only to ensure an even coat; allow the coat of glue to dry according to the manufacturer's instructions. Add a second coat of glue to the plywood edge—the first coat will have soaked into the wood—and let it dry. On shorter edges, apply the edging to the plywood in one step, from end to end. On longer edges, it may be difficult to align the full length of edging simultaneously. However, because contact adhesive adheres only to itself when partially dry, you can use newspaper or brown wrapping paper to cover approximately half of each long edge and thus prevent the edging from making accidental contact. Place the edging about half way along the edge and work towards the uncovered corner; remove the paper and lay the edging to the other corner.

**2** **Trimming the edging.** Press the veneer edging firmly into place by rolling it several times with a wooden dowel; continue rolling past the corners of the plywood edge to make a crease in the overhanging edging. With a single-edge razor blade—or a trimming knife—slice off the overhanging edging and any excess edging along the edge. Using No. 120 grit abrasive paper, lightly sand the edges of the veneer edging to blend them into the surface of the plywood. Be careful not to sand the surface of the edging. Contact adhesive that has dried on the plywood should be removed by careful chiselling and sanding.

# Assembling the Bunk Bed and Room Divider

Putting together the parts of the three largest sections of the bunk bed/room divider calls for no extraordinary skills. Even though the bunk-bed section is 1986 mm long and 986 mm wide, it is—like the bookshelf-cupboard and the cabinet sections—essentially a box, and it is assembled with the same basic techniques used for other boxes: measuring and marking, drilling holes, gluing, and inserting screws.

Because the bunk-bed section is so large, you should assemble it in the room it is to occupy. The less bulky bookshelf-cupboard sections and the cabinet sections can be put together elsewhere and moved into the room, but first make sure that there are no impossibly tight corners to turn.

As you assemble each section, you will occasionally need a helper to change the position of the piece you are working on or to exert force against a part while you drill. A helper can also hold parts or wipe glue when you are joining a number of parts at the same time and you must work fast before the glue sets.

After the five sections are assembled and in position, they can be attached to one another with screws to ensure greater strength and stability.

Assembling the various parts can be managed faster and with less effort by following certain practices throughout:

☐ Because the numerous pieces must fit precisely, check often and carefully with a straightedge and combination square to make sure that the pieces are perfectly aligned before you secure them.

☐ Drill countersunk pilot holes for all of the countersunk screws; follow the instructions given on page 29 for the size of drill bit in relation to screw size. (Pilot holes for raised-head screws should not be countersunk; the screw cups used with them have a countersunk feature.) Do not drill pilot holes for piano-hinge screws; use a bradawl to make starter holes for them.

☐ Use a 9 mm variable-speed drill with a screwdriver bit to insert the crosshead screws speedily. (It is preferable to use crosshead screws with an electric drill: their double slots keep the bit firmly in the screwhead. Screws with single slots, driven by drill or hand, will hold the structure just as well, but they require more care and effort to insert.)

For a project this size, use PVA glue (*page 61*) because of its great bonding strength. Be sure to wipe off any excess glue immediately, or the affected area will not accept a stain or oil finish. Use wet sponges or rags for wiping (old towels are good) and rinse them out frequently.

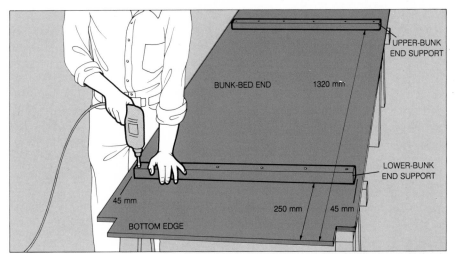

## Joining the Parts: Bunk-Bed Section

1 **Bunk-end supports.** Saw the 50 by 50 mm (45 × 45 mm actual) softwood as follows: two pieces 1950 mm long, four pieces 860 mm long, and eight pieces 638 mm long. The 860 mm lengths are horizontal supports for the ends of the bunk bottoms; set the other lengths aside for use in later steps.

Position the supports for the lower-bunk bottom 250 mm from the bottom edges of the bunk-bed ends (parts A) and 45 mm from the side edges. Position the supports for the upper-bunk bottom 1320 mm from the bottom edges of the bunk-bed ends. Glue and screw the supports in place, using six 5.5 mm wood screws 50 mm long, placed at 175 mm intervals on each support.

2 **Lower-bunk side.** Cut a piece of scrap plywood 1950 mm long and approximately 75 mm wide to use as a spacer; clamp it to the back of the lower-bunk side (part D) so that the spacer is 18 mm from each end of part D.

Set the bunk-bed ends on their long edges with the bunk-end supports facing inwards; use two saw-horses to keep the ends from falling. Position the lower-bunk side across the bunk-bed ends with its bottom edge 175 mm above the plinth notches; butt the bunk-bed ends against the clamped-on spacer. Drill pilot holes and attach the lower-bunk side to one bunk-bed end with three screw cups and raised-head screws 35 mm long. Attach the lower-bunk side to the other end in the same manner.

**3** **Upper-bunk wall.** Clamp the spacer used in Step 2 to the back of the upper-bunk wall (part F) and along its bottom edge. Position the wall across the bunk-bed ends; butt the bunk-bed ends against the spacer. The top edge of the wall should be flush with the upper corners of the ends; use corner cramps to square the corners.

Attach the upper-bunk wall to the bunk-bed ends with screw cups and raised-head screws. Drill pilot holes and insert the screws first at the four corners of the wall; then add five more screws along each side of the wall, spacing them about 175 mm apart. With a helper, carefully stand the bunk-bed section upright.

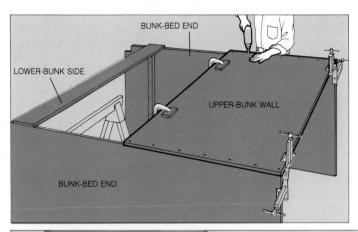

**4** **Lower-bunk wall.** Clamp the plywood spacer to the back of the lower-bunk wall (part E) and along its top edge. Clamp a pair of hand screws to the bunk-bed ends and against the undersides of the 50 by 50 mm supports for the lower-bunk bottom. Rest the lower-bunk wall on the hand screws with the clamped-on spacer butted against the bunk-bed ends. Hold the wall to the bunk-bed ends with sash cramps, and attach the wall to the ends with screw cups and raised-head screws, following the procedure in Step 3.

**5** **Upper-bunk side supports.** The two pieces of 1950 mm long 50 by 50 mm wood cut in Step 1 are side supports for the upper-bunk bottom. Hold them in position on the upper and lower-bunk walls (parts F and E) with temporary rests made of off-cut boards clamped to the undersides of the upper-bunk end supports already mounted on the bunk-bed ends *(below)*. Attach the side supports to the upper and lower-bunk walls with glue and wood screws that are 50 mm long.

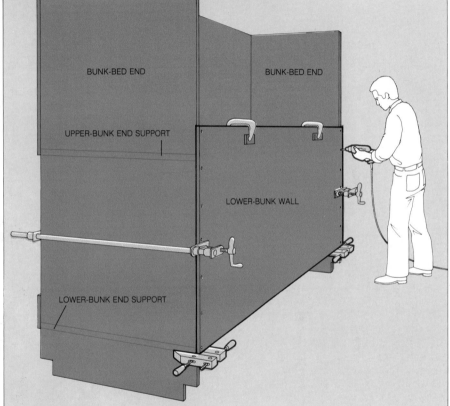

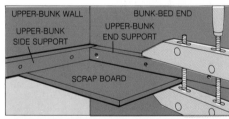

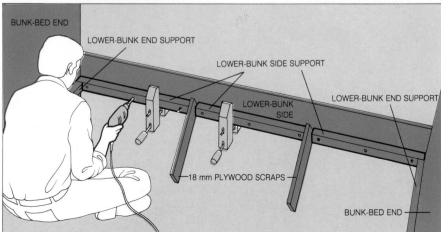

**6** **Lower-bunk side supports.** Six of the 638 mm long 50 by 50 mm wood sections that you cut in Step 1 serve as side supports for the lower-bunk bottoms. Clamp three of these side supports on the lower-bunk side (part D) at the same level as the end supports that are already attached to the bunk-bed ends. Keep them separated with 18 mm plywood scraps *(left)* to allow spaces for inserting the drawer-support panels in a later step *(page 80)*. Glue and screw the side supports in place with wood screws that are 50 mm long and remove the scrap plywood spacers. Repeat all steps of the procedure in attaching the other three supports to the lower-bunk wall (part E) opposite the place where you have been working.

**7 First drawer-glide outer casing.** To position the first outer casing, use the junction of the bottom of the lower-bunk side and the bunk-bed end as a reference point *(below)* and measure down 173 mm (the depth of the drawer plus a slight clearance). Mark that point, and from it extend a horizontal line across the bunk-bed end to indicate the position for the bottom of the outer casing. Screw the casing in place, following Steps 2 and 3, pages 29 and 30. Since slight adjustments may have to be made later, do not tighten the screws for the outer casings until you are ready to mount them permanently in Step 11.

**8 Remaining drawer outer casings.** To install the other casings, cut a plywood guide the length of the drawer casing you attached to the bunk-bed end in Step 7. The guide should be the same height as the space between the bottom of the casing and the floor. Be sure the edges of the guide are straight and the corners square. Using the guide *(below)*, position and mount three more of the remaining 11 outer casings at the other three corners of the bunk-bed ends. Use the guide to position four outer casings on each of the two drawer-support panels (parts Q), placing them in the same relationship to the 75 mm notch as are the outer casings on the bunk-bed ends. Still following the instructions in Steps 2 and 3 on pages 29 and 30, make pilot holes in the oval-shaped screw locations of the casings. Slip the panels into the spaces between the 50 by 50 mm lower-bunk side supports; position the casings over the pilot holes, and screw them loosely in place. Install a pair of inner glides on each drawer, according to the instructions in Step 4 on page 30. Check all six drawers for fit before continuing with the assembly procedure.

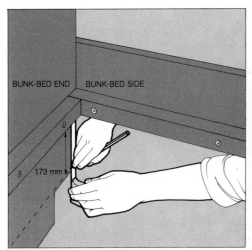

BUNK-BED END   BUNK-BED SIDE

173 mm

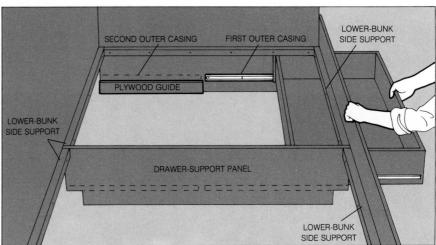

SECOND OUTER CASING   FIRST OUTER CASING   LOWER-BUNK SIDE SUPPORT

PLYWOOD GUIDE

LOWER-BUNK SIDE SUPPORT

DRAWER-SUPPORT PANEL

LOWER-BUNK SIDE SUPPORT

PLINTH

PLINTH (INSTALLED)

50 × 50 mm (INSTALLED)

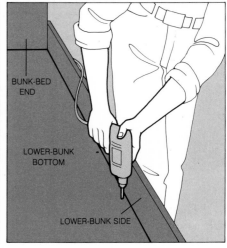

BUNK-BED END

LOWER-BUNK BOTTOM

LOWER-BUNK SIDE

**9 Plinths.** Before attaching the plinths, remove the drawers. Drill two pilot holes for raised-head screws with screw cups at each end of the two plinths (parts V); the centres of the holes should be 9 mm from the edges. Insert screws loosely to hold one plinth in position and, with a pencil, mark a line on the back of the plinth at the inner edges of the two drawer-support panels *(above)*; repeat the procedure with the other plinth. Glue and screw the two remaining 638 mm pieces of 50 by 50 mm wood between these marks so that they are flush with the bottom edges of the plinths. Screw the plinths to the bunk-bed ends.

**10 Bunk bottoms.** Both bunk bottoms (parts Z) are installed in the same way. Place each bunk bottom on its supports. Make pilot holes for 50 mm screws 150 mm to the left and right of the middle of the long edges, drilling through the bunk bottoms into the supports beneath *(above)*. While you are drilling, get a helper to push against the bunk walls to close any gap between the walls and the bottom. Screw the upper-bunk bottom in place; remove the lower-bunk bottom. If there is no one to help you, clamp sash cramps across the bunk to hold the walls in place.

**11** **Drawer-support panels.** To hold the panels in place temporarily, drive two nails at an angle through each drawer-support panel and into the lower-bunk side supports. Drill pilot holes for 50 mm screws *(below)* through the drawer-support panels and into the ends of the 50 by 50 mm lengths attached to the back of the plinths. To wield the drill, you may have to make the holes at a slight angle. Insert the screws and pull out the nails. Put the drawers in place and check that the glides move freely in the outer casings. Make any necessary adjustments. Remove the drawers and tighten the screws in all the drawer casings and glides. Insert screws in the remaining holes.

**12** **False fronts for the drawers.** With the drawers in place on both sides of the bunk-bed section, clamp to and across their fronts the 175 mm wide strips of blockboard that are left from cutting the bunk-bed ends. Insert spacing pieces approximately 2 mm thick between these strips and both the lower-bunk side (part D) and the lower-bunk wall (part E). Using a pencil, mark the blockboard strips with straight lines for cutting false-front pieces *(below)*; mark at the midpoint of each drawer-support panel and also 2 mm in from the outer edges of the bunk-bed ends so that the drawers will clear the bookshelf-cupboard section after the final assembly.

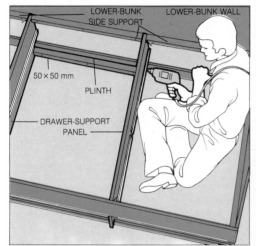

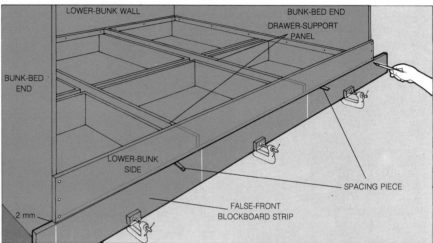

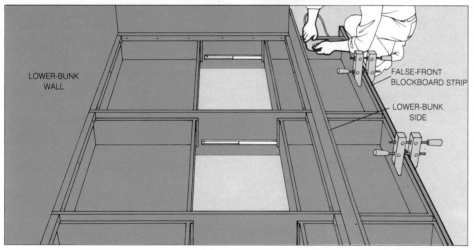

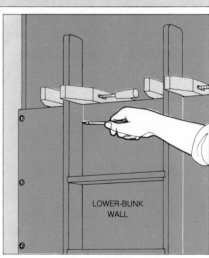

**13** **Final assembly.** Pull the three drawers open, taking care not to disturb the false-front blockboard strip still clamped across them. Leave the G-cramps in place and, for additional stability, use hand screws to hold the drawers and the blockboard strip together. From the rear of each drawer front, drill four clearance holes for 30 mm screws *(above)* through the drawer and just into the false front. The marks will serve to position the false drawer fronts after they have been cut to size. Unclamp the

strip and saw it into sections along the lines made in Step 12. Install drawer pulls on all three false-front pieces; countersink the screws flush with the blockboard surface. Line up the clearance holes in each drawer front with the pilot holes in the false-front pieces. Drive the screws all the way into the false-front pieces. Repeat this entire procedure for the drawers on the opposite side. Place the lower-bunk bottom in position and drive 50 mm screws through the pilot holes drilled in Step 9.

**14** **Ladder.** After choosing the location for the ladder, attach hand screws to its uprights to suspend it against the lower-bunk wall *(above)*. With a pencil, mark each edge of both uprights; remove the ladder and, between each pair of marked lines, drill five holes for each upright through the lower-bunk wall. Replace the ladder with the hand screws still on it. Get a helper to hold it while, from the other side of the lower-bunk wall, you insert a slightly smaller drill bit through the holes; then drill pilot holes into the ladder uprights. Use screw cups and 40 mm raised-head screws to attach the ladder to the wall.

## Joining the Parts: Bookshelf-Cupboard Sections

**1 Drop-leaf desk.** To keep the drop leaf level and hold the brackets in position when the desk is raised, mount two pieces of 18 mm square hardwood—each 75 mm long and with a notch at one end measuring 12 by 18 mm—on the underside of the drop leaf (part O), as shown below. So that the hardwood can be swivelled aside when the drop leaf is down, make the clearance holes in the hardwood (but not in the drop leaf) slightly larger than the diameter of a 6 mm screw 30 mm long. Place the drop leaf and a fixed shelf (part P) flat, undersides up and butted together (*below*). Centre a 418 mm piano hinge over the crack between the parts. With a bradawl, make starter holes and insert 16 mm screws. Repeat the procedure for the other desk.

**2 Support strips.** Place a bookshelf-cupboard side (part B or C) flat on the work surface or across two saw-horses and insert four support strips (*page 48*) in the housings previously cut for them. Two 1311 mm strips go above the fixed-shelf housing and two 597 mm strips go below. Do not allow the strips to extend into the fixed-shelf housing; whether you are screwing or nailing, be sure to align the holes in the matching strips exactly, so that the shelves will be level when installed. Secure the strips and repeat for the other bookshelf-cupboard sides.

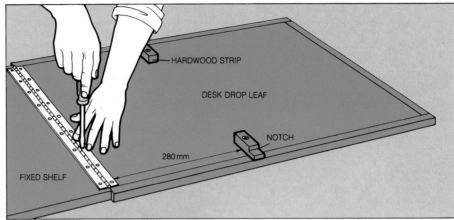

HARDWOOD STRIP
DESK DROP LEAF
NOTCH
280 mm
FIXED SHELF

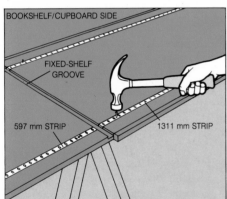

BOOKSHELF/CUPBOARD SIDE
FIXED-SHELF GROOVE
597 mm STRIP
1311 mm STRIP

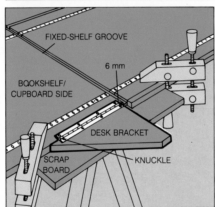

FIXED-SHELF GROOVE
6 mm
BOOKSHELF/ CUPBOARD SIDE
DESK BRACKET
SCRAP BOARD
KNUCKLE

**3 Desk brackets.** Lay a bookshelf-cupboard side on the worktable or across two saw-horses. Clamp a piece of scrap board under the side to support the desk bracket in its open position (*left*). Butt the desk bracket (part R) against the bookshelf-cupboard side and 6 mm below the fixed-shelf groove. Position a 250 mm piano hinge with its knuckle aligned on the edge of the bookshelf-cupboard side. Attach the hinge with screws according to the instructions in Step 1. Mount the hinges for the other three desk brackets in the same way. Fold the brackets back against the bookshelf-cupboard sides and use masking tape to hold them there during the next steps.

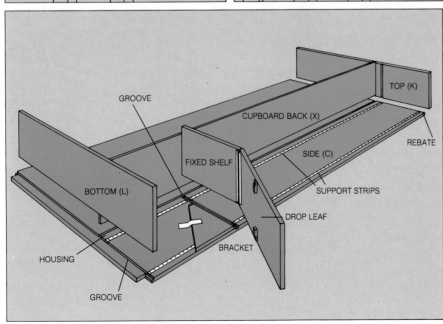

GROOVE
TOP (K)
CUPBOARD BACK (X)
REBATE
FIXED SHELF
SIDE (C)
BOTTOM (L)
SUPPORT STRIPS
DROP LEAF
HOUSING
BRACKET
GROOVE

**4 Final assembly.** From the channel side of each bookshelf-cupboard side, drill pilot holes for 40 mm screws in the grooves and rebates; start 25 mm from the ends of these channels and space the holes about 150 mm apart. Drill only deep enough to break through the wood on the outside, turn over the pieces and finish drilling; countersink the holes slightly on the outside.

Dry-fit the parts into one of the bookshelf-cupboard sides in the following order: bottom (part L), cupboard back (part X), fixed shelf with attached drop leaf, and top (part K). Dismantle, spread glue rapidly in the rebate and all the channels in the side piece and on the edges of the parts to be joined to them, and reassemble. Glue the other side on. Insert screws into all the pilot holes. Quickly wipe off any excess glue before it dries. Using raised-head screws and screw cups, attach the plinths (parts W) in the 75 mm notches cut for them. Repeat the procedure for the other bookshelf-cupboard section.

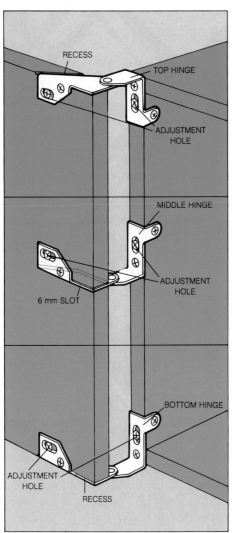

RECESS

TOP HINGE

ADJUSTMENT HOLE

MIDDLE HINGE

6 mm SLOT

ADJUSTMENT HOLE

BOTTOM HINGE

ADJUSTMENT HOLE

RECESS

**5** **Cupboard door.** Tape the drop leaf to the sides of the bookshelf-cupboard and turn the entire unit so that the cupboard opening is facing upwards. Lay the door over the opening to check for a flush fit. If necessary, plane the edges to allow for the thickness of the veneer edging. Install pivot hinges in recesses chiselled in the top and bottom edges of the door *(upper and lower details, left)*.

To attach the middle hinge, chisel a horizontal slot 6 mm wide in the edge of the door; shape the slot to fit the contour of the hinge (indicated by dash lines in the centre detail of the drawing). Position the door level with the cupboard opening and screw the hinges in place, starting at the adjustment holes. Then install a door pull and a magnetic catch, following the directions on pages 32 and 91. If you are unable to obtain a pivot hinge, use a concealed hinge *(page 36)*.

**6** **Cupboard-bar supports.** For the clothes rod in each cupboard, use the two pieces of 25 mm dowel 415 mm long. Bore holes for the rods in the four cupboard-bar supports (parts BB); make the holes 125 mm from the front edge of each support and 50 mm from the bottom edge. Insert the rods in the holes and mount the supports on the sides of each cupboard, butted against the cupboard back; the bottom edges of the supports are 1360 mm from the cupboard floor. Use two 30 mm screws in each support. Rest an adjustable shelf (part S) on each pair of cupboard-bar supports.

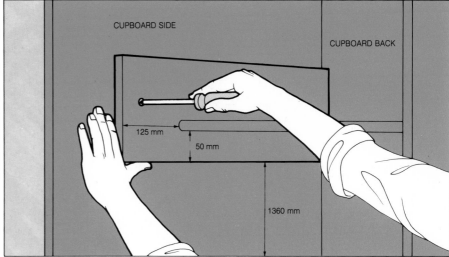

CUPBOARD SIDE

CUPBOARD BACK

125 mm

50 mm

1360 mm

## Joining the Parts: Cabinet Sections

**Assembling the cabinets.** Following the procedures described in Step 4 for assembling the bookshelf-cupboard, drill pilot holes in the rebates in the four cabinet sides (parts G and H). Place a cabinet side flat on the work surface and dry-fit the parts in the following order: cabinet partition (part Y), cabinet top (part M), cabinet bottom (part N) and the second cabinet side (part H). Dismantle the parts and apply glue to all channels and edges; then reassemble and insert 40 mm screws in all pilot holes. Mount the cabinet door (part J) with two pivot hinges as in Step 5, and attach a door pull and magnetic catch. Repeat for the other cabinet.

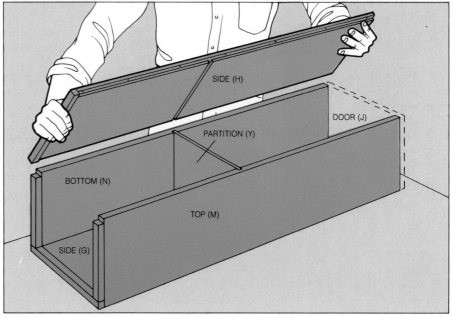

SIDE (H)

DOOR (J)

PARTITION (Y)

BOTTOM (N)

TOP (M)

SIDE (G)

83

# Organizing Space with Modular Units

The four interchangeable units on these pages demonstrate the concept of modular storage. Each unit is 2135 mm high, 760 mm wide and 403 mm deep, and all together they provide more than 2.25 cubic metres of vertical storage space. Because the units are free-standing, you can build as many as you want; and set them up in any combination—in the centre of a room as a divider, round a corner in an L configuration, back to back or, as shown in the photograph on page 6, along a wall. If you plan to use several units in combina-tion, be sure that the surface of the floor is level so that all units will be in proper alignment with each other; if the floor is uneven, place wood spacing pieces beneath the units to position them correctly.

The units share a basic design, but each has been adapted for different storage re-quirements. The first unit *(left, below)* has adjustable bookshelves, space for a stereo speaker at the top, and, at the bottom, a cabinet with an adjustable shelf. The second unit, in addition to shelves and a cabinet with drawers, has a drop-leaf desk with a laminated-plastic surface and a set of compartments inside (without the com-partments, the space could serve as a bar). The third unit has a display case behind glass doors, with optional glass shelves inside; four large drawers below provide storage space for linen, silverware, place mats or anything else. The fourth unit matches the first, with the exception of a pull-out shelf to hold a record player.

If you decide to undertake the complete four-unit project, you will need all the wood, hardware and accessories detailed in the shopping list on page 86. But you can easily alter the size of the units or add to them as you choose by following the in-structions on pages 54–57 for revising or making new plans. The number of doors, drawers and shelves can be reduced or increased at will. You may also choose materials other than those specified in the shopping list. See pages 58 and 59 for a description of types and qualities of wood.

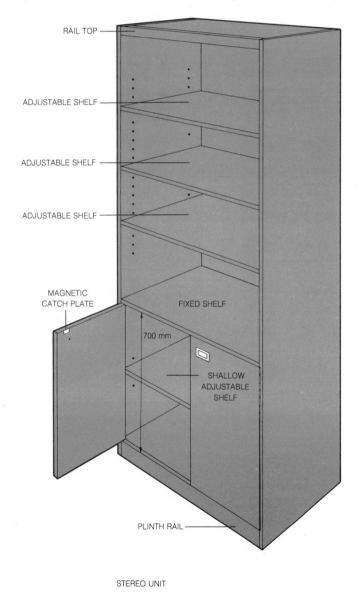

STEREO UNIT

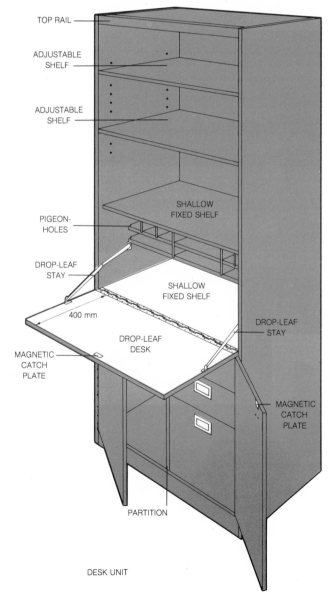

DESK UNIT

After gathering together the necessary wood and hardware called for in the cutting list, cut the sheets of plywood and the timber into the required pieces indicated in the cutting diagrams *(pages 86–87)*. The joints should then be cut according to the routing diagrams on page 88. Before starting to assemble the pieces, use medium-grade sandpaper to smooth all of the surfaces that will be visible.

Since the carcasses of the four units have the same structure—they are all, essentially, rectangular boxes—the instructions for assembling one of them serve for all *(pages 89–90)*. As soon as these carcasses are assembled and all of the fixed shelves are installed, apply veneer edging to the visible edges of the plywood *(page 77)* before installing the doors, drawers, pull-out shelf or the drop-leaf desk.

Instructions beginning on page 91 explain in detail how to install the special features of each unit. (All the drawers are dimensioned to accept drawer-glide assemblies that are 12 mm thick.)

Veneer should be applied to the edges of drawers and doors only after they have been installed. Before gluing the veneer, slip a piece of scrap veneer between closed doors and drawers and the cabinet walls to make sure that there is sufficient clearance. Plane the edges of the plywood, if necessary. When the assembling and veneering are finished, sand the unit with fine-grade sandpaper in order to prepare the surfaces for wax or oil, or another finish.

**Planning the project.** The perspective drawings that appear below will serve as a useful guide for building the wall-storage units. If you should not want to make all four units, or if you want to change dimensions or eliminate or add certain features, revise the plans accordingly and alter the cutting diagrams *(pages 86–87)* to reflect the changes. Each piece of the units is labelled for easy cross-reference to the cutting diagrams. The internal and external dimensions marked on the stereo unit on the right, below apply to all of the units. Measurements for special interior features are located within each unit.

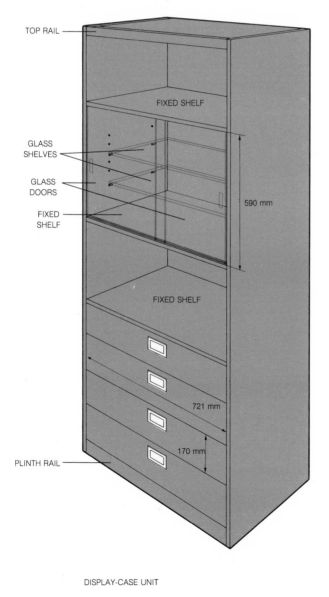

DISPLAY-CASE UNIT

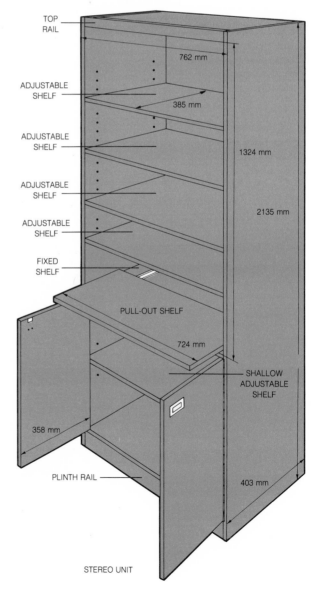

STEREO UNIT

85

## Shopping List

7 sheets plywood, 18 × 1220 × 2440 mm
4 sheets plywood, 6 × 1220 × 2440 mm
3 pieces scrap plywood, 3 × 38 × 300 mm
3 lengths hardwood, 12 × 250 × 722 mm
1 length softwood, 25 × 200 × 3800 mm
1 length softwood, 25 × 200 × 4200 mm
2 glass doors, 606 × 380 mm
2 glass shelves, 722 × 250 mm
6 piano hinges, 690 mm
1 piano hinge, 721 mm
6 door pulls
7 drawer pulls
7 magnetic door catches
4 pairs drawer-glide assemblies, 350 mm
3 pairs drawer-glide assemblies, 300 mm
1 pair shelf-glide assemblies, 375 mm
2 drop-leaf stays
60 metres 19 mm veneer edging
2 litres contact adhesive
1 litre lacquer thinner
1 litre PVA glue
1 length wood dowel, 1830 mm length × 6 mm
   diameter
450 g lost-head nails, 38 mm
200 countersunk wood screws, 20 mm
  8 shelf-support pegs
  1 laminated-plastic sheet to yield 2 pieces,
    390 × 733 mm, 347 × 724 mm

## Cutting Diagrams

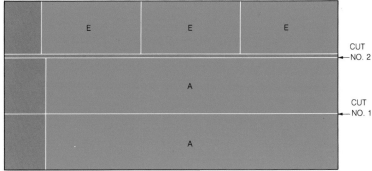

18 mm PLYWOOD, 1220 × 2440 mm

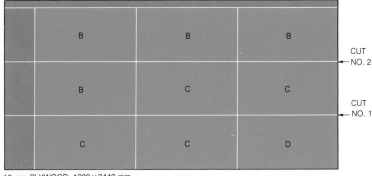

18 mm PLYWOOD, 1220 × 2440 mm

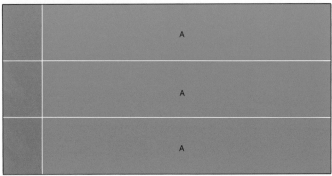

18 mm PLYWOOD, 1220 × 2440 mm

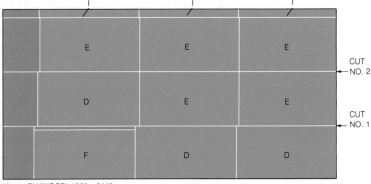

18 mm PLYWOOD, 1220 × 2440 mm

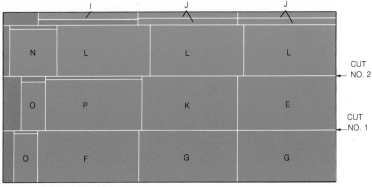

18 mm PLYWOOD, 1220 × 2440 mm

**Making the basic cuts.** To build all four units, cut the plywood sheets and lengths of timber into the pieces shown in these diagrams. Do not, however, cut the plinth rail (parts I) or the top rail (parts J) until each basic unit has been assembled *(page 90, Step 4)*. The cuts identified as Nos. 1 and 2 should be done in order, to minimize waste and avoid errors. The diagrams have been laid out so that lengthwise cuts precede crosscuts; exceptions have been indicated. Remeasure each piece before cutting to allow for the saw kerf. Dark-shaded pieces are scrap; save them for additional shelves or other features you may want to install. Make masking-tape labels for each part to indicate its name, key letter and, where appropriate, the side that will be more visible. Mark the top with an arrow. The name and dimensions of each piece, identified by letter in the diagrams, are given in the key below.

A| side, 2135 × 403 mm
B| top, 736 × 385 mm
C| bottom, 736 × 385 mm
D| fixed shelf, 736 × 385 mm
E| adjustable shelf, 721 × 385 mm
F| shallow fixed shelf, 736 × 363 mm
G| shallow adjustable shelf, 721 × 363 mm
H| narrow adjustable shelf, 363 × 356 mm
I| plinth rail, 724 × 56 mm
J| top rail, 724 × 48 mm
K| roll-out shelf, 718 × 385 mm
L| door, 690 × 358 mm
M| wide-drawer front, 721 × 170 mm
N| desk-drawer front, 341 × 341 mm
O| desk-drawer front, 341 × 172 mm
P| desk-cabinet partition, 712 × 363 mm
Q| drawer side, 351 × 335 mm
R| drawer back, 335 × 305 mm
S| desk drop leaf, 721 × 400 mm
T| cabinet back, 2079 × 736 mm
U| wide-drawer bottom, 673 × 358 mm
V| desk-drawer bottom, 336 × 299 mm
W| pigeon-hole upright, 240 × 195 mm
X| pigeon-hole dividers, 240 × 128 mm
AA| pigeon-hole shelf, 722 × 240 mm
BB| wide-drawer back, 679 × 164 mm
CC| desk-drawer back, 305 × 166 mm
DD| wide-drawer side, 373 × 164 mm
EE| desk-drawer side, 351 × 166 mm

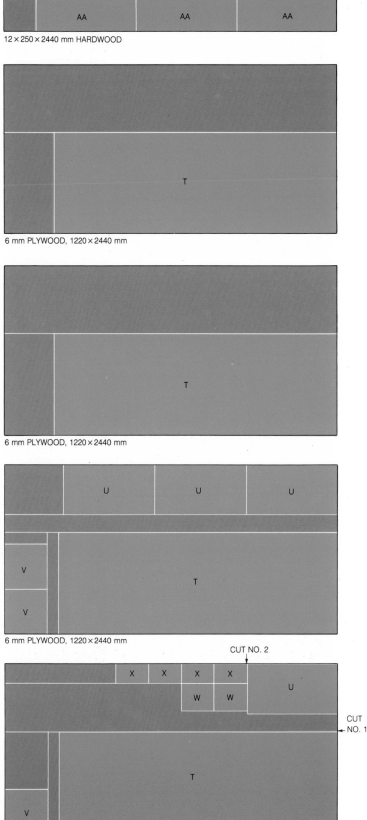

12 × 250 × 2440 mm HARDWOOD

6 mm PLYWOOD, 1220 × 2440 mm

6 mm PLYWOOD, 1220 × 2440 mm

6 mm PLYWOOD, 1220 × 2440 mm

6 mm PLYWOOD, 1220 × 2440 mm

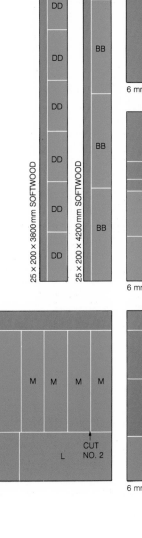

25 × 200 × 3800 mm SOFTWOOD

25 × 200 × 4200 mm SOFTWOOD

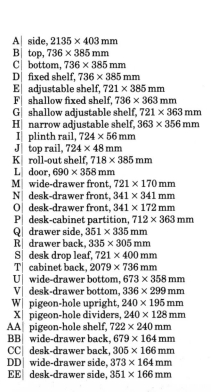

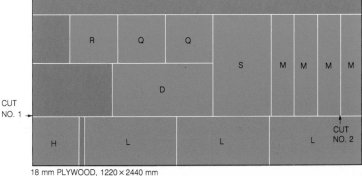

18 mm PLYWOOD, 1220 × 2440 mm

# Cutting Joints and Peg Holes

**Channels and peg holes for side pieces.** The left side pieces for all four wall-storage units are represented in the three diagrams on the right (the sides of the two stereo units are identical). The right side pieces must be cut to make mirror images of the left sides—with one exception; do not drill any peg holes near the bottom of the right side of the desk unit; instead, drill them in the desk partition *(diagram A, right, below)* to match the peg holes in the left side piece. All the peg holes are 12 mm deep and 6 mm in diameter. The number and location of the peg holes can be changed to suit your particular storage needs. Cut the 6 mm wood dowel into 25 mm lengths to make the pegs.

The housings at the bottoms and the rebates at the tops of each side piece are all 18 mm wide and 6 mm deep. Start routing these cuts from the back edge, and stop 12 mm from the front edge. The bottom line of the housings is 32 mm from the bottom edge; the round ends of the housings and rebates need not be squared off.

Exact positions of the middle housings, which are also 18 mm wide and 6 mm deep, are indicated by the figures in the diagrams. The middle housings in the desk unit must be squared off 22 mm from the front edge. All grooves along the back edges are 6 mm wide and 6 mm deep; their outside edges are 12 mm from the back edge.

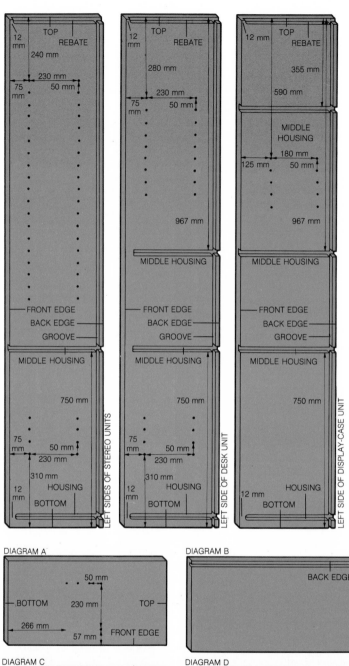

**Channels for smaller pieces.** All top and bottom pieces have a channel 6 mm wide, 6 mm deep and 12 mm from the back edge, as in diagram B. Cut them on the underside of the top pieces and on the top surface of the bottom pieces. The bottom of the desk unit *(diagram C)* has an additional channel, 18 mm wide and 6 mm deep, 353 mm from the right edge.

Cut a channel in the desk unit's shallow fixed shelf *(diagram D)* 18 mm wide and 6 mm deep, 353 mm from the right edge. On the underside of the top shelf in the display-case unit *(diagram E)*, cut two channels 6 mm wide and 12 mm deep. One channel is 6 mm from the front edge and the other is 18 mm from the same edge. On the top surface of the bottom shelf for the display case *(diagram F)*, cut two channels 6 mm wide and 6 mm deep. One channel is 6 mm and the other is 18 mm from the front edge.

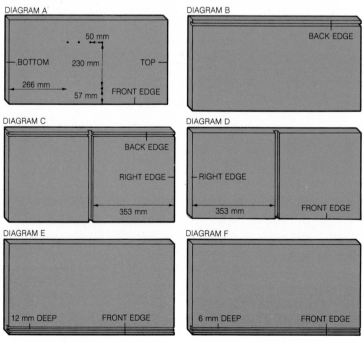

## Assembling the Basic Pieces of the Wall-Storage Units

**The basic structural components.** The three different wall-storage units appear in exploded diagrams below, with channels cut according to the diagrams opposite. Two basically similar stereo-speaker units were built for the complete four-unit installation shown on page 6. Instructions for installing doors, drawers and desk compartments begin on page 91.

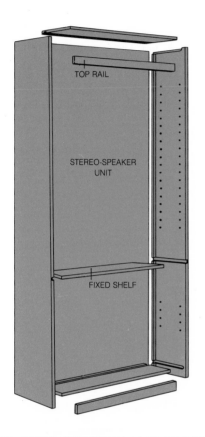

TOP RAIL

STEREO-SPEAKER UNIT

FIXED SHELF

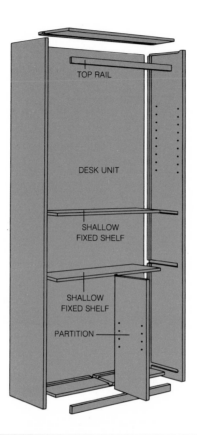

TOP RAIL

DESK UNIT

SHALLOW FIXED SHELF

SHALLOW FIXED SHELF

PARTITION

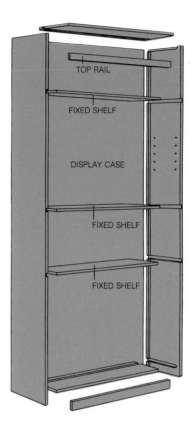

TOP RAIL

FIXED SHELF

DISPLAY CASE

FIXED SHELF

FIXED SHELF

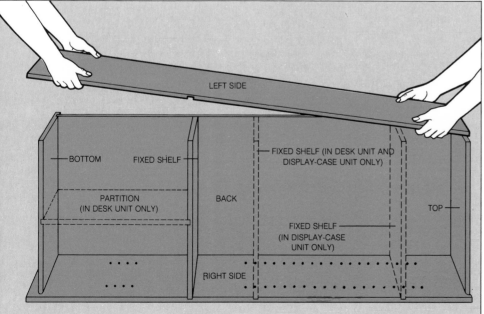

LEFT SIDE

BOTTOM    FIXED SHELF

PARTITION (IN DESK UNIT ONLY)

BACK

FIXED SHELF (IN DESK UNIT AND DISPLAY-CASE UNIT ONLY)

TOP

FIXED SHELF (IN DISPLAY-CASE UNIT ONLY)

RIGHT SIDE

**1 Gluing the units.** Sand the interior surfaces of all pieces with 150 grit sandpaper. Dry-fit all pieces and plane or sand any channels that are too tight. Lay the unit's right side on the floor. Apply glue to the groove in the rear edge of the right side and slip the back of the unit into this groove. For all units except the one with the desk, apply glue to the groove, housings and the rebate on the bottom and top. Set in place the bottom, top and all fixed shelves (including those for the display case, as indicated by broken lines on the left). To finish the framework, apply glue to the edges of the shelves, the top and the bottom, and the channels in the left side of the unit; lower the left side into place *(left)* and wipe off excess glue.

To assemble the desk unit, install the back in the right side, glue the edges of the partition (indicated by broken lines) and the housings in the middle of the bottom and in the fixed shelf; join these pieces and install them in the right side. Then assemble the top, the remaining fixed shelf and the left side in the same way.

**2** **Nailing the pieces.** Mark guidelines lightly on both of the side pieces to indicate the centre of the top, bottom and shelf pieces. Drive three 38 mm lost-head nails along each of these lines through the sides into the top, bottom, and shelves. Nails are not required in the back panel. Drive all nails below the surface.

**3** **Squaring the units.** Check the corners of all units with a steel square before the glue has had time to set. If a unit is not square, clamp a steel square tightly into one corner with hand screws *(below).* Leave the hand screws in place until the glue has dried. Squaring one corner should bring all of the other corners into alignment.

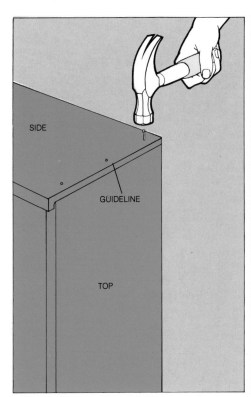

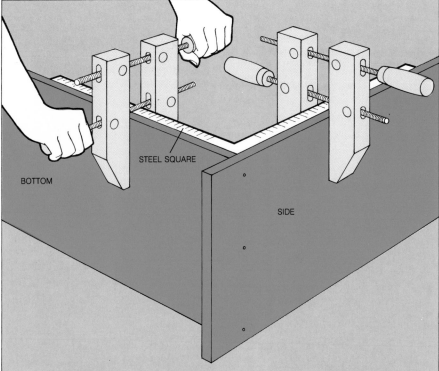

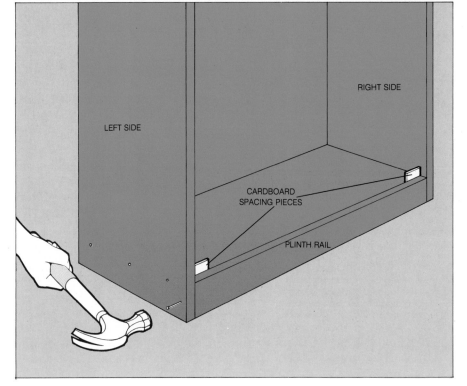

**4** **Installing plinth rail and top rail.** Measure the inside distance between the two sides of the unit at the top and at the bottom. Using these measurements for the lengths, cut the top rail 48 mm wide and the plinth rail 56 mm wide from 18 mm plywood. Apply glue to all the surfaces that touch. As you slip the rails into place, insert behind them two pieces of cardboard about 1 mm thick *(right).* These distance pieces hold the rails out far enough for their surfaces to be flush with the veneer that will be applied later. Drive two lost-head nails through each side into the rails, and three nails through the fronts of the rails into the top and bottom pieces.

## Hanging the Cabinet Doors

**1 Attaching hinges to doors.** Before hanging the doors, apply veneer edging to the front edges of the cabinet walls *(pages 76–77)*. Place the door in a woodworking vice with the edge to be hinged facing upwards. Measure the length of the edge and, with a hacksaw, cut a piece of piano hinge to the same length. Make the cuts at least 5 mm away from the screw holes. Lay the open hinge on the door edge with the flat side of the hinge downwards and the knuckle just beyond the front edge *(below)*. The unattached leaf of the hinge should extend over the front side of the door. Start the screw holes with a bradawl. Screw the hinge down, beginning with the end and middle screws, then working from each end towards the middle. Repeat the procedure to attach a hinge to the other door.

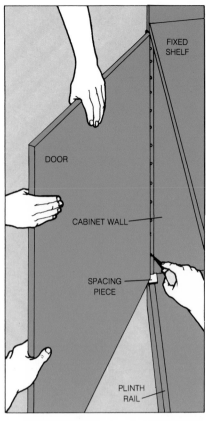

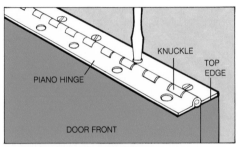

KNUCKLE

TOP EDGE

PIANO HINGE

DOOR FRONT

**2 Attaching hinges to the cabinet.** Place a clearance spacer on top of the plinth rail, and against the cabinet wall. Rest the door on the clearance spacer and put the door in place. Hold the unattached leaf of the hinge firmly against the cabinet wall, and get a helper to adjust the position of the door so that the knuckle protrudes just beyond the edge of the cabinet wall *(left)*. Properly positioned, the door should open freely and close flush with the unit's front.

Mark the centres of the top and bottom screw holes with a bradawl and drive in these two screws first. Test the swing; if the door does not open and close properly, take the screws out, readjust the position of the door and attach the door to the cabinet again—this time inserting screws in the second holes from each end. When the door is hung correctly, put in all of the screws. Repeat the procedure for the other door.

## Installing Door Catches

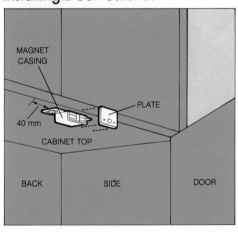

MAGNET CASING

PLATE

40 mm

CABINET TOP

BACK    SIDE    DOOR

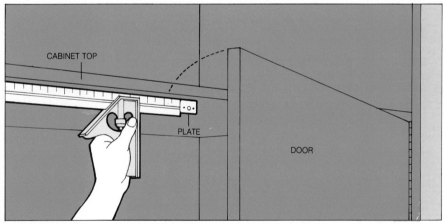

**1 Positioning the magnet.** Magnetic catches that hold cabinet doors closed consist of two parts: a magnet in a plastic or metal casing that is screwed to the cabinet, and a metal plate that is screwed to the inside of the door.

Place the magnet casing on the underside of the cabinet top about 15 mm from the front edge and about 40 mm away from the point where the side edge of the door meets the cabinet top. Attach screws in the centres of the casing slots, leaving the screws just loose enough to permit the magnet to move back and forth freely. Place the separate metal plate in position on the magnet *(above)*.

**2 Attaching the plate.** With the metal plate in position against the magnet casing, use a combination square to measure the distance from the edge of the plate to the point where the cabinet door meets the cabinet top *(above)*. Transfer the measurement to the inside of the cabinet door to mark a guideline for mounting the plate on the door. This method works even if the cabinet has a wall or partition at the edge of the door, as in the desk-unit cabinet.

For this unit, which has no such divider, simply close the door on the plate, reach inside with a pencil and mark a guideline on the door at the edge of the plate. Install the plate on the door. To set the magnet casing to its correct depth, close the door flush with the edge of the cabinet top, reach inside and slide the magnet casing forward so that it is against the plate. Holding the magnet casing in position, open the door and tighten the casing screws.

## Assembling the Pigeon-Holes

**1 Cutting the joints.** The three shelves and the two uprights required for the pigeon-holes are shown below. All of the housings are 3 mm deep and 6 mm wide. The dimensions of the halving-joint slots are given in the diagrams. The housings are best made with a router and a 6 mm straight bit. The halving-joint slots can be cut with multiple passes of a circular saw, as in Step 2. To mark the location of all cuts on the three shelves, begin by measuring at the centre of each board—that is, 361 mm from the ends. This ensures that the channels will be in correct alignment and the compartments will be square—in case you discover that the shelves must be trimmed for correct fit. To allow both drop-leaf stays to close completely, cut out pieces 9 mm wide and 12 mm deep at the front corners of the middle and bottom shelves.

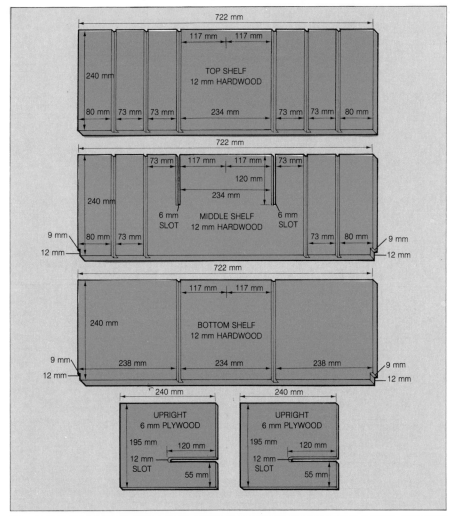

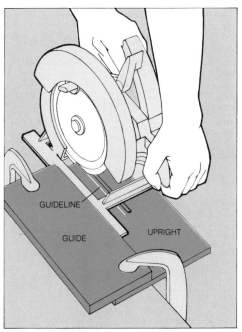

**2 Cutting the housing-joint slots.** Use a circular saw with the blade depth set at 18 mm *(above)* to cut the housing-joint slots in the uprights and in the middle shelf. Instructions for setting up a circular-saw guide, like the one shown here, are given on page 27. After marking the location of both sides of the slots with a pencil, make as many passes with the saw as necessary to cut them out, but take care to stay within the pencil lines.

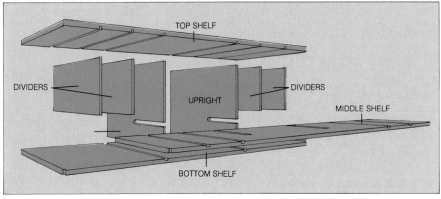

**3 Dry-fitting all the pieces.** This exploded diagram shows how the three shelves of 12 mm hardwood fit together with the two uprights and the four dividers of 6 mm plywood to form a set of compartments that will be installed above the desk. After making the cuts described in Steps 1 and 2, dry-fit each piece into its channels; sand or plane any housing or slot that is not wide enough. All the pieces will be glued together (no nails or screws are used) following the assembly procedure that begins on the opposite page.

**4 Assembling uprights and middle shelf.** Apply glue to the sides of the two slots in the middle shelf and to the slot in each upright, and slip the uprights down over the shelf as shown below. With a mallet, tap the uprights all the way down into the shelf slots until the edges are flush. Check the joints with a square. If the uprights are not at right angles to the shelf, attach corner cramps and leave them until the glue has set.

**5 Assembling dividers and top shelf.** When the joints of the uprights and the middle shelf have dried, set the assembly on a table with the housings facing upwards. Apply glue to the housings in the shelf, and slip the dividers into these channels. Apply glue to the tops of the dividers and of the uprights, and to the housings on the top shelf. Carefully lower the top shelf on to the dividers and uprights so that each vertical piece slips into the appropriate housing on the shelf.

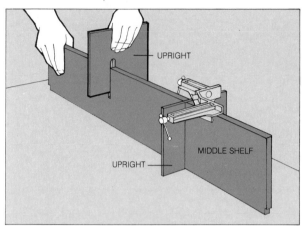

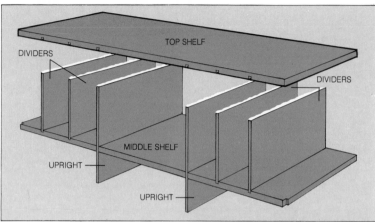

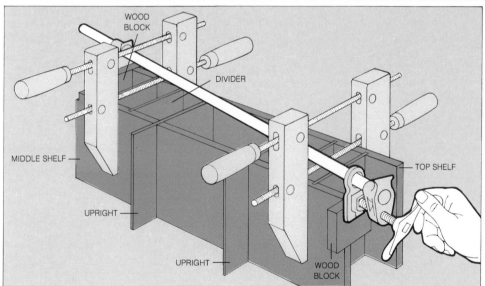

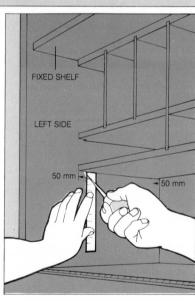

**6 Clamping dividers and shelves.** After the dividers, uprights and top shelf have been glued and assembled, but before the glue has dried, place hand screws across the shelves, outside the uprights. Check the joints with a square. It is likely that the unit will be askew and that you will have to use a pipe cramp or sash cramp to straighten it. If the top shelf twists to the left, place the screw end of the cramp on the middle shelf and the other end on the top shelf *(above)*. If the top shelf twists to the right, put the screw

end of the cramp on the top shelf. Place blocks of scrap wood between the cramp faces and the shelf ends to protect the shelves. Tighten the cramp until the joints are square. When the glue has dried, remove all the cramps. To complete the assembly of the compartments, apply glue to the bottoms of the uprights and the housings of the bottom shelf; slip the shelf on to the uprights and then place hand screws across the shelves so that they are in line with the uprights; tighten the hand screws and allow the glue to dry.

**7 Drilling peg holes.** Position the pigeon-hole assembly firmly under the fixed shelf above the desk, and against the back panel, either by means of pieces of scrap wood wedged underneath, or with the aid of a helper. With a bradawl, mark the locations for four peg holes—two underneath the compartments on the left side and two on the right side. The centres of all four holes should be 4 mm below the assembly. The centres of two of the peg holes should be located 50 mm from the front edge of the assembly and the other two holes should be centred 50 mm from the back edge. Remove the pigeon-hole assembly and bore 12 mm deep holes with a 6 mm bit. Then insert the pegs.

# Installing the Drop-Leaf Desk

**1** **Laminating the shelf.** Using a circular saw with a plywood-cutting blade, cut a piece of laminated plastic with the good side down, 347 mm deep and 724 mm wide, to cover the shelf of the drop-leaf desk. These dimensions leave 16 mm uncovered at the front of the shelf to accommodate the piano hinge. Cover the top surface of the shelf and the back of the laminate with contact adhesive. Allow approximately 20 minutes for the adhesive to become touch-dry. Place the back edge of the laminate above the back edge of the shelf, taking care to keep the glued surfaces apart until the pieces are in the correct position. Let the back edge of the laminate drop into place; lower the laminate on to the shelf, and press the whole surface firmly with the heel of your hand.

PLASTIC-LAMINATED SHEET

SHELF

**2** **Preparing edges for the hinge.** To bevel the edges of the pieces that will be joined by the piano hinge, draw guidelines 4 mm along the top back edge of the drop leaf *(below)*; draw the same guidelines along the top front edge of the shelf. If the knuckle of your hinge is wider than the standard 3.5 mm, mark the guidelines that much deeper. Clamp the drop leaf to a worktable for support. Hold a plane at a 45 degree angle to the top of the drop leaf and cut away the triangle of wood marked by the guidelines; repeat for the shelf. Use a wood chisel, bevelled side up, to finish bevelling the corner of the shelf.

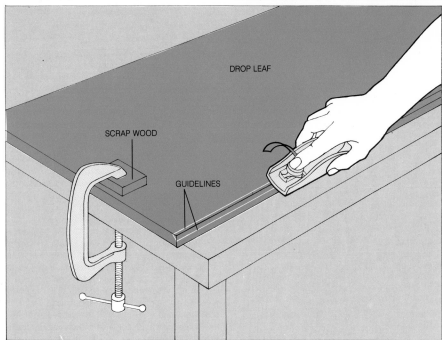

DROP LEAF

SCRAP WOOD

GUIDELINES

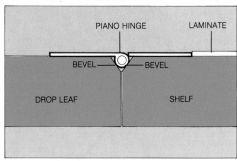

PIANO HINGE    LAMINATE

BEVEL    BEVEL

DROP LEAF    SHELF

**3** **Attaching the hinge to the drop leaf.** With a hacksaw, cut a length of piano hinge 721 mm long. Hold the drop leaf in position against the shelf and place the knuckle of the hinge into the bevelled channel between the two pieces. If the hinge does not lie perfectly flat, as shown above, chisel the bevels until it does. With the drop leaf and hinge in position, mark the end screw holes on the drop leaf with a bradawl. Clamp the drop leaf to the worktable. Screw the hinge down, starting with the end and middle screws, then working in from each end towards the middle.

**4 Laminating and attaching the drop leaf.** Cut a sheet of laminated plastic 390 by 733 mm to cover the drop leaf. Lay the drop leaf on a worktable for support, and apply contact adhesive to the top of the drop leaf and the back of the laminate. Place the back edge of the laminate against the edge of the hinge and lower the laminate on to the drop leaf so that the laminate overhangs the drop leaf about 5 mm all round. Press the laminate firmly on to the drop leaf. Trim the laminate edges with a router and flush-trimming bit *(right)*.

Apply veneer edging to the three sides of the drop leaf that will be visible (see page 77 for directions on edge lipping). While a helper holds the drop leaf and hinge in position against the shelf, mark the end screw holes on the shelf with a bradawl. Screw the hinge to the shelf, starting at the end and working towards the middle.

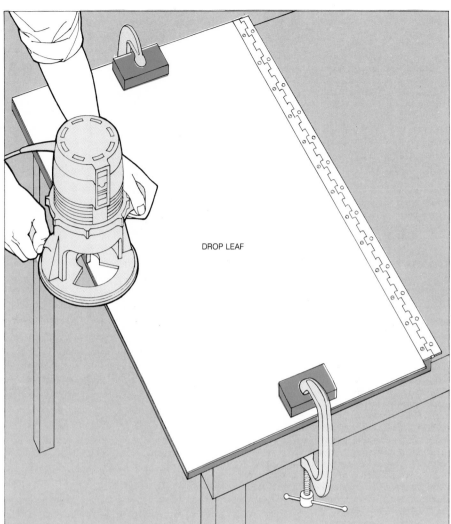

DROP LEAF

WALL END
18 mm
SHELF
DROP-LEAF END

**5 Attaching the drop-leaf stays.** Put the pigeon-hole assembly in place on its pegs. Place the drop-leaf end of a fully extended stay near the back edge of the drop leaf, and the opposite end on the side of the cabinet, above the shelf. The exact positioning will depend on the kind of stay you are using. To ensure that the joint of the stay clears the upper shelf when folded, hold the wall end of the stay in place and move the drop-leaf end so that its base is 18 mm inside the cabinet *(above)*.

Still holding the wall end of the stay in place, mark the screw holes on the cabinet wall, and install the screws. Repeat this entire procedure for the second stay. Extend both stays fully, with the bases resting on the drop leaf. Place a level half on the drop leaf and half on the shelf. Once the drop leaf is level, use a bradawl to mark the laminate with the positions of the screw holes for both stay bases. Then drive in the screws.

ROUTER BASE

CATCH PLATE OUTLINE

**6 Attaching the catch plate.** Place the catch plate in the middle of the front edge of the drop leaf, 22 mm from the edge, and trace its outline on the laminate with a pencil. Mount a 6 mm straight bit in a router and adjust the bit depth to equal the thickness of the plate. Hold the router at an angle over the plate outline on the laminate, with the router base pressed against the edge of the drop leaf to steady it *(left)*. Then lower the rotating bit gently but firmly into the laminate and rout out the area within the outline. Screw the catch plate into the routed area. Remove the pigeon-hole assembly, then apply wood finish to the unit. When the finish has dried, put the assembly back in place and attach the magnetic catch for the drop leaf under the cabinet shelf.

## Constructing the Drawers

**Cutting the joints.** Housings, grooves and rebates for the drawers *(right)* may be cut with a router or a circular saw *(pages 26–27)*. All housings on the sides of the front pieces are 18 mm wide and 9 mm deep, and end 6 mm from the top. Note, however, that on the desk-unit drawers one housing is 12 mm from the right side of the front piece, and the other is 6 mm from the left side. All grooves are 6 mm wide, 6 mm deep and 6 mm from the bottom of each piece. All the rebates are 18 mm wide and 9 mm deep.

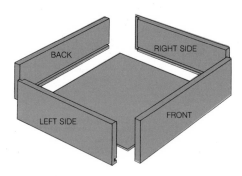

**Assembling the pieces.** Although the drawers come in three different sizes, their parts fit together in the same manner, as shown in the exploded diagram above. Before applying glue, dry-fit all the pieces to make sure the joints have been properly cut. Begin by placing the front piece on the worktable with the outside face down. Place the two sides in the housings on the front, slip the bottom into the grooves on the sides and front, and lower the back into position on the sides and bottom. Dismantle the drawer, then trim any joints that are too tight, and sand the inside surfaces smooth. Assemble the pieces again in the same order, this time applying glue to all joints. Place sash cramps along the sides and along the back. Nails are not necessary.

## Adding the Finishing Touches

**Installing glass shelves and doors.** Before you install the sliding doors, put the shelves into the display case. For support, use clear plastic pegs, which are less noticeable than wooden ones under the glass shelves.

With a cotton-tipped swab, apply paraffin wax to the channels on the bottom shelf of the display case, so that the glass doors will slide easily. Hold the rear door almost vertical, with the milled slot towards the side of the cabinet *(right)*. Slip the top of the door into the rear channel on the underside of the top shelf, then swing the bottom of the door in and lower it into the rear channel on the bottom shelf. Install the other door in the front channels in the same way.

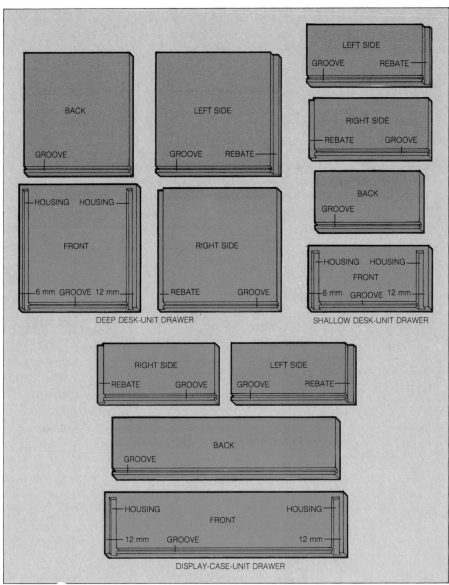

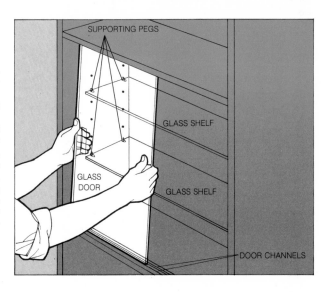

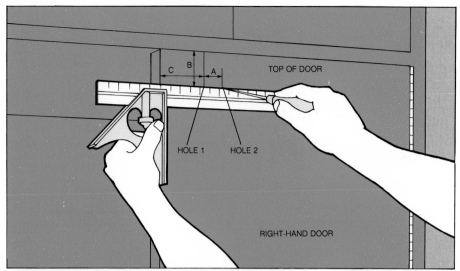

**Attaching door and drawer pulls.** Most pulls, like the ones used here, are installed by drilling holes through the door or drawer and attaching the pull with screws. The procedure varies with other types of pull, but no matter what type you use, be sure to install it parallel to the edge of the door or drawer. To position the pulls correctly on the cabinet doors, mark the position of the first screw hole about 50 mm from both edges of the door (hole 1 in the diagram, left). For hole 2, measure the distance between the centres of the screw holes on the pull and, with a combination square, transfer this measurement (A) to the door. Drill holes at these points and install the first pull. Then measure the distance from hole 1 to the top of the door (B) and to the side of the door (C), and transfer measurements A, B and C to the second door to position the screw holes.

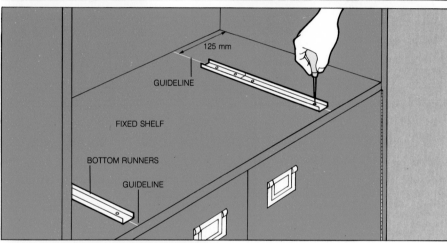

**Installing shelf glides.** To install the glides that support the roll-out shelf in the stereo unit, use a steel square to mark guidelines on the fixed shelf, perpendicular to the front edge of the shelf and 125 mm from the sides. Centre the roll-out shelf on top and transfer the guidelines to the front edge of the roll-out shelf. Remove the roll-out shelf and attach the bottom runners of the glides to the fixed shelf, with the centres of the screw holes on the guidelines, and the glides 25 mm from the front edge. Start the screw holes with a bradawl *(left)*. Begin at the guidelines on the front edge of the roll-out shelf and mark parallel guidelines on the underside. Attach the upper runners in the same way.

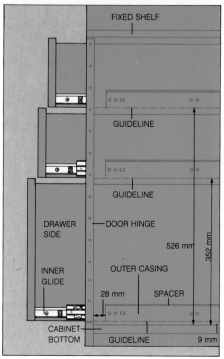

**Installing drawer-glide assemblies.** To install the three drawers of the desk-unit cabinet, attach the inner glides to both sides of each drawer, following the instructions on page 30. Locations of the outer casings on the right side of the desk-unit cabinet appear in the diagram on the left. Using a pencil and a steel square, mark three guidelines, one for each outer casing, on the inner cabinet side; mark three matching guidelines on the right side of the cabinet partition. The lines are respectively 9, 352, and 526 mm above the bottom of the cabinet.

Cut three clearance spacers of 3 mm thick wood 38 mm wide and 300 mm long. Hold each outer casing on one of the clearance spacers and place the spacer against the inner side of the cabinet with the bottom edges of both the casing and the spacer precisely on the guideline. The front edges of both the casing and the spacer should be 28 mm from the rear edge of the cabinet-door hinge. (The spacer is necessary so that the glide assembly will clear the hinge.) With a bradawl, mark the casing screw holes on the spacer; drill clearance holes through the spacer and just into the cabinet side. Screw the casing and spacer into place. Following the same procedure, mount three other casings on the partition, but without using spacers. The front edges of the casings are 28 mm from the front edge of the partition. Install glide assemblies for the four drawers in the display-case unit following the same procedures. Mark the outer-casing guidelines on the cabinet sides 10, 182.5, 355 and 527.5 mm above the cabinet bottom.

# Assemblies Built on to a Wall

An assembly of open shelves nailed to the walls piece by piece can attractively satisfy a variety of needs. Made with plain butt joints, such shelving is easier to install than a ready-made cabinet because it need not be manoeuvred on stairs or through doorways, or painstakingly shaped to the contours of the walls.

Most open shelves are rectangular, and fit into the corner of a room or a three-sided enclosure of walls—for example, between a fireplace and a corner. Some shelves are triangular to take advantage of a corner, generally for storage or display. Shelves of either type can be supported by a simple system of adjustable clips that snap into vertical metal standards.

The dimensions of shelving units depend on the room and the purpose. In height they should leave at least 300 mm of work-space between the top and the ceiling. The length of the unit can be anything you like but the length of a single shelf should not exceed 800 mm: in longer units, use partitions to support shelves of 800 mm or less. The depth of the shelves depends on what you plan to store on them: paperback books fit on shelves 200 mm deep, while stereo equipment requires 450 mm or more.

Before beginning construction, try to prise the skirting board from the walls that will contain the shelving. Starting at a corner, lever the skirting board out with a utility bar, using a wooden block as a fulcrum to protect the wall; slip a wooden wedge behind the skirting board to hold it away from the wall, then move the bar about 400 mm at a time. (You can cut and re-use the old board to trim any wall space left on each side of the shelving.) If the skirting board is pinned behind layers of flooring, leave it in place but mark and cut the base of the shelving to its shape.

If you have taken the skirting board off, you may find clues to the locations of studs behind the wall: the bottoms of plaster-board seams that lie over studs, or the nail holes where the board was secured. To confirm these locations, tap lightly on the wall until you hear the solid sound that usually comes from a stud; if necessary, drill holes and probe inside the wall with a length of wire to find the studs (page 42).

## Rectangular Shelves along a Wall

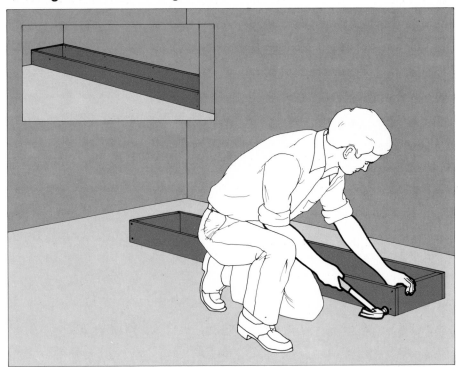

**1 Making the base.** For shelves in a corner, make the base with 25 mm (20 mm actual) timber cut to the height of the skirting board. The long pieces should be 20 mm shorter than the length of the unit, and the end pieces 115 mm shorter than the depth. Set the pieces in a rectangle and nail through each long piece into the short ones.

Nail the back and side to the walls; where you cannot nail into studs, use collapsible anchors.

To build shelves in a recess (inset), cut front and back pieces to the length of the back of the recess and nail the back piece to studs in the wall; nail the side pieces to the flanking walls, then fasten the front piece to the sides.

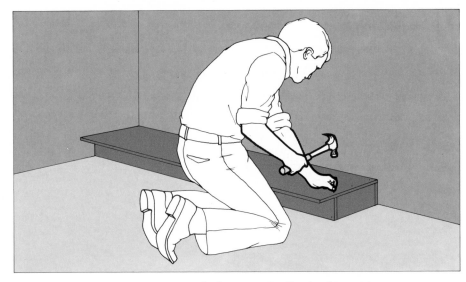

**2 The bottom shelf and sides.** For these and other parts, use 25 mm timber or, if the shelves are deeper than 291 mm, 18 mm plywood. Nail to the base a bottom shelf that is as long as the base and 75 mm wider, driving lost-head nails every 150 mm. Fasten to the corner wall a side as wide as the bottom shelf and long enough to reach from the shelf to the underside of the unit top,

using lost-head nails or anchors.

For a corner unit, cut the other side piece to reach from the floor to the underside of the unit's top and make a notch in the lower front corner 75 mm wide and the height of the base.

For a recessed unit, cut a second side piece to match the first and fasten it to the wall at the other side of the wall recess.

**3** **Nailing the top.** For a corner unit, cut a top 20 mm longer than the bottom shelf. While a helper holds the loose side piece in place, nail the top to each side with lost-head nails every 150 mm. Then nail the bottom of the exposed sidepiece to the end of the base.

For a unit built in recess, measure between the top outer edges of the side pieces, cut the top to these dimensions and nail it to the sides.

**4** **Installing partitions.** Cut partitions the same size as the corner side piece. Inside the unit, mark off equal spaces along top and bottom; then, 10 mm to one side of each mark, draw a line for the partition edge. Nail each partition through the top of the unit. Nail a scrap of wood along the line on the bottom, tap the partition against it and drive nails through the partition into the bottom; remove the scrap and repeat from the other side of the partition.

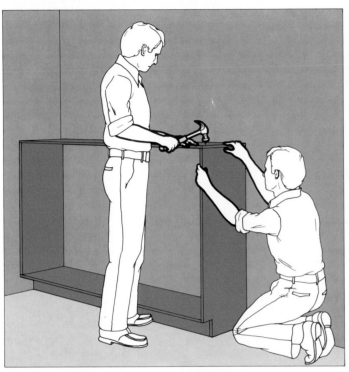

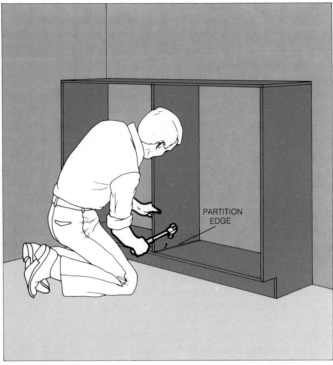

PARTITION EDGE

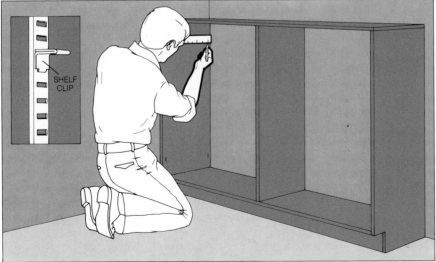

SHELF CLIP

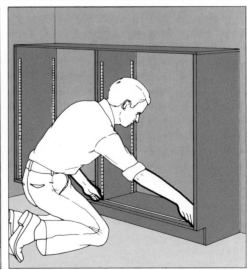

**5** **Installing the standards.** Near the top and bottom of each side, mark the wood 25 mm from the front and from the back. On each partition, mark one side 25 mm from the back and 40 mm from the front, the other side 40 mm from the back and 25 mm from the front. Set a standard just inside each top-and-bottom pair of marks, with its lower end resting on the bottom shelf; use a bradawl to make starter holes and fasten the standard with the screws provided. Snap shelf clips (*inset*) into the standards.

**6** **Cutting the shelves.** On the bottom shelf of the unit and at each set of shelf clips, measure between the standards at the front and back of the cabinet. Cut a shelf 3 mm shorter than the shortest of these measurements and set the shelf on the clips.

# Triangular Shelves for a Corner

**1** **Making a template.** Cut a square of 18 mm plywood with sides about 19 mm longer than the planned sides of the shelves. Measuring from a corner, mark the length of the shelf sides—usually about 450 mm—on two edges of the plywood square. Using a straightedge, draw a line between the marks for the front of the cabinet, and a parallel line 75 mm closer to the corner for the front of the base. To check the layout, use a combination square to draw a 45 degree line from the corner to the front line *(inset)*; this line should be exactly half as long as the front line.

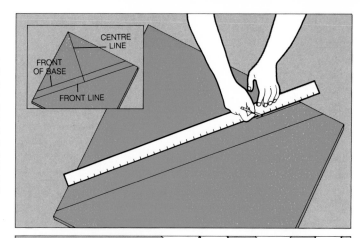

**2** **Making the base.** To mark the front of the base, select a 25 mm (20 mm actual) board as wide as the skirting board of the room and set it on edge, just behind the line for the front of the base. Trace a short line on the template along the back of the board at each edge of the template. Mark the position of each edge of the template on the front and back of the board *(right)*. At each pair of marks, cut the board at a 45 degree angle.

To mark the sides of the base, set a 25 mm board on the edge of the template with its end at the template's corner. Mark the front and back of this board where it touches the traced lines; set a second 25 mm board on the other side of the template, butted against the first *(right, below)* and mark it in the same way. Cut the sides at angles of 45 degrees at the marks and secure them to the walls; nail the front piece to the ends of the side pieces.

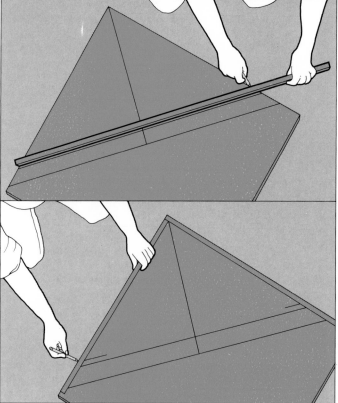

**3** **Cutting the bottom of the unit.** Cut the template along the line for the front of the unit. If you use a portable circular saw, measure the distance between the side of the blade and the left edge of the base plate, temporarily nail a straightedge this distance from the marked line and run the base plate along the straightedge to make the cut. Fasten the bottom to the base with lost-head nails every 150 mm.

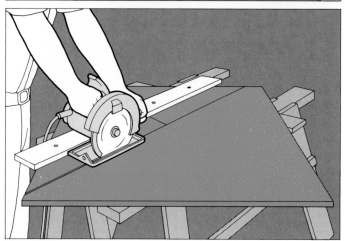

**4** **Bevelling the sides.** On the bottom shelf, measure the distance from the corner of the wall to the corner of the triangle; mark this across the face of a side piece. Using a circular saw, cut the piece lengthwise with a 45 degree bevel cut that matches the angle of the base, then cut the piece to the desired height and fasten it to the wall. Fit the second piece by butting it against the first at the corner, and cut it in the same way.

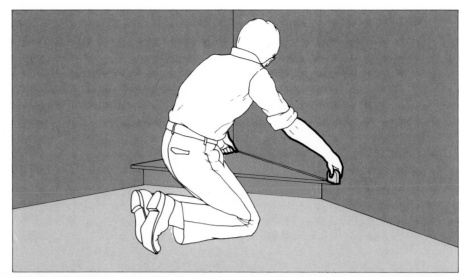

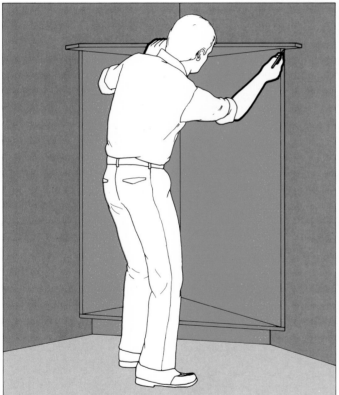

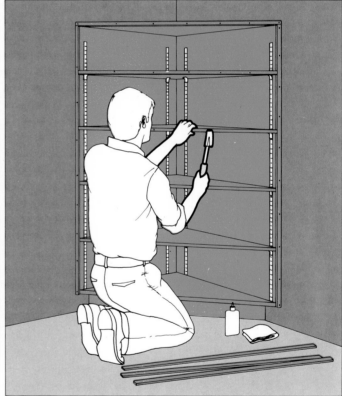

**5** **Marking the top.** Set the other half of the template on top of the side pieces, with the square corner snug against the corner of the wall, and mark the outer corners of the side pieces on the underside of the template. Cut the top as you did the bottom *(Step 3)* and nail it to the sides.

Install shelf standards on each side piece, 25 mm from the front and 50 mm from the back, and snap in the clips. To mark and cut shelves, set rectangular pieces of plywood on the clips, mark them at the corners of the side pieces and cut along a line drawn 6 mm inside the marks.

**6** **Finishing the edges.** Cover the exposed plywood edges of the unit with veneer edging *(page 77)* mitred to match the angles of the shelving. Squeeze a bead of PVA woodworking glue along each edge and smear it along the edge evenly. Press the veneer edging into the glue, flush with the edges of the plywood; wherever you squeeze wet glue out of a joint, wipe it off immediately— do not let it dry.

# Building Extra Space into Kitchen Cabinets

A ready-made kitchen cabinet that provides only one drawer and a shelf is wasteful of space and frustrating to find things in. But the cabinet can be turned into an efficient storage unit by adding purpose-built, roll-out bins like the ones shown on these two pages.

The plans and instructions for building these bins were designed to fit a wooden or hardboard counter cabinet with a depth of 585 mm and a door opening 375 mm wide and 540 mm high; if your cabinet is a different size, adapt bin dimensions accordingly. Perhaps one large bin instead of two side by side would serve you better. And by tailoring shelf locations and dimensions to the kitchen appliances and utensils you need space for, you can make bins that will solve many storage problems.

Before starting to build the bins, you may have to remove an existing shelf. If the shelf is fixed in housings, you can remove it by cutting a wide V into the shelf with a jigsaw so that the point of the V is at the back. When the V drops out, the remaining shelf pieces can be pulled easily from their housings. You may find it necessary to remove the cabinet door if it does not open wide enough to give full access to the inside.

The housed and grooved joints specified here give the bins extra rigidity and strength, both desirable qualities if the bins are to be used for storing heavy utensils or canned goods, as these are designed to do. Such joints are more time consuming to make, however, and they require the use of a router *(page 26)* or a power saw. If the bins will be used only for lightweight items, they can be built with simple butt joints that are reinforced with glued wood blocks *(page 23)*.

**Dual bins for convenient storage.** The left-hand roll-out bin in the drawing below is designed to hold long-handled frying pans in its rear compartment and saucepans in the top front shelf, with space below for lids. The right-hand bin in the drawing on the opposite page has a front compartment for tall items that never seem to fit anywhere, such as a 2 litre vacuum flask or large containers. The tray on top can hold large cutlery, spatulas, wooden spoons and flat items while the shelves that are towards the back are for baking tins and mixing bowls.

## Shopping List

2 lengths pine, 12 × 250 × 2440 mm
1 length pine, 12 × 200 × 2440 mm
1 piece hardboard or plywood,
  6 × 573 × 534 mm
4 pieces wood for glide mounts (for instructions on
  size, see page 106, Step 6)
  PVA glue
100 lost-head nails, 25 mm
  6 lost-head nails for ledge strips, 18 mm
  2 pairs drawer-glide assemblies, 550 mm

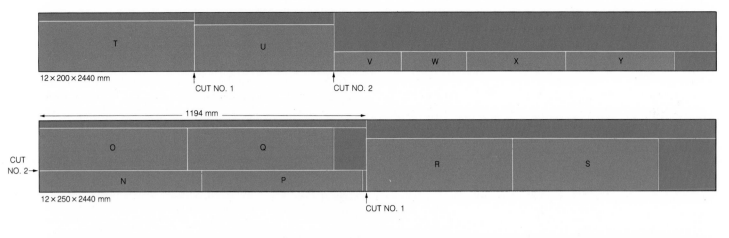

12 × 200 × 2440 mm

CUT NO. 1

CUT NO. 2

1194 mm

CUT
NO. 2→

12 × 250 × 2440 mm

CUT NO. 1

CUT
NO. 2

CUT
NO. 1→

12 × 250 × 2440 mm

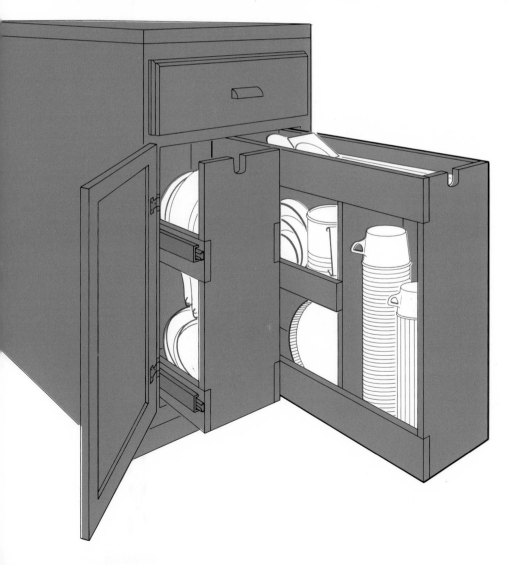

**Making the basic cuts.** To build both bins, cut three lengths of timber into pieces as shown in the diagrams above. As with any cutting diagram, the initial cuts are critical in minimizing waste and eliminating errors. The remaining cuts may be made in any sequence, but be sure to remeasure each piece before cutting, and allow for the saw kerf. The dark-shaded portions are not needed for the bins; save the larger off-cut pieces for other projects. Identify each piece with its name written on masking-tape labels. The name and dimensions of each piece, identified by letter in the diagrams, are given below.

A | left bin rail, 75 × 585 mm
B | right bin top, 138 × 573 mm
C | left bin rail, 75 × 585 mm
D | right bin bottom, 138 × 573 mm
E | left bin rail, 75 × 585 mm
F | right bin shelf, 138 × 380 mm
G | left bin rail, 75 × 585 mm
H | right bin partition, 132 × 459 mm
I | right bin middle rail, 50 × 392 mm
J | left bin short support, 50 × 166 mm
K | left bin short support, 50 × 166 mm
L | left bin ledge strip, 18 × 321 mm
M | left bin ledge strip, 18 × 321 mm
N | right bin rail, 75 × 585 mm
O | right bin front, 150 × 534 mm
P | right bin rail, 75 × 585 mm
Q | right bin back, 150 × 534 mm
R | left bin front, 190 × 534 mm
S | left bin back, 190 × 534 mm
T | left bin bottom, 178 × 573 mm
U | left bin partition, 166 × 516 mm
V | left bin support, 63 × 240 mm
W | left bin support, 63 × 240 mm
X | left bin middle rail, 63 × 345 mm
Y | left bin middle rail, 63 × 345 mm

## Cutting Channels and Notches

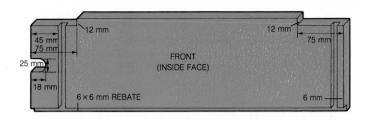

**Right-hand bin.** Housings, grooves and corner cutouts are most easily made with a router and a 12 mm double-fluted bit, though multiple cuts with a circular saw (*page 27*) will also accomplish the job. All housings and grooves are 12 mm wide (the finished thickness of the timber used) and 6 mm deep. Cutouts at the corners are 12 mm deep and 75 mm long. Rebates on the front and back pieces are 6 mm wide and 6 mm deep. They can be cut with a router and a 6 mm rebate bit or with a circular saw. Also make a cutout in the top edge of the front piece 25 mm wide and 18 mm deep, using the router or a jigsaw. The cutout will provide a finger-hold so that the finished bin can be pulled open.

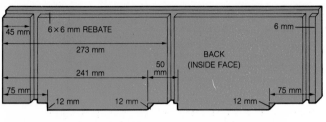

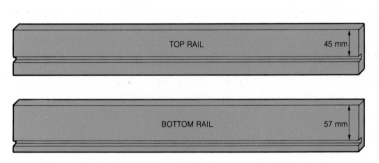

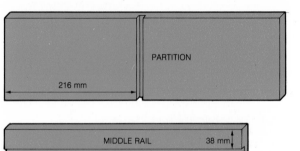

**Left-hand bin.** Make housings, grooves and cutouts for the left-hand bin, as shown in the diagram on the right and below, following the procedures described above. Take special care in positioning the middle housings on the front and back pieces of this bin precisely; otherwise the middle and top rails may not fit correctly.

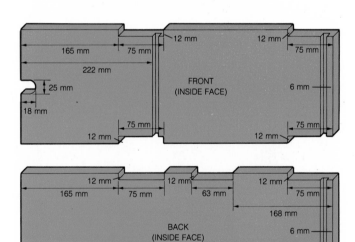

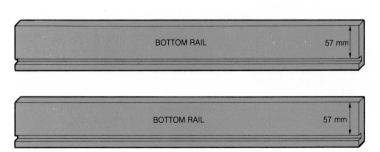

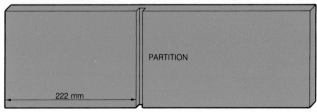

## How to Put the Bins Together

**1** **Assembling the right-hand bin.** Apply glue to both ends of the top and bottom, and slip them into the housings on the front and back. Position the top and bottom so that one edge of each piece extends 6 mm into the cutouts for the rails, and the other edge is flush with the rebates. Clamp all four pieces together with sash cramps and drive lost-head nails through the front and back into the top and bottom. When the glue has set, remove the cramps. Lay the bin on the side that will be next to the cabinet wall, and apply glue along the edges of the top and bottom, and to the corner cutouts on the front and back. Nail the top and bottom rails in place.

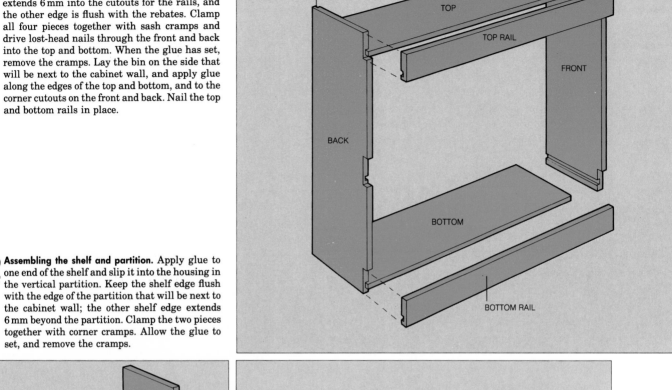

**2** **Assembling the shelf and partition.** Apply glue to one end of the shelf and slip it into the housing in the vertical partition. Keep the shelf edge flush with the edge of the partition that will be next to the cabinet wall; the other shelf edge extends 6 mm beyond the partition. Clamp the two pieces together with corner cramps. Allow the glue to set, and remove the cramps.

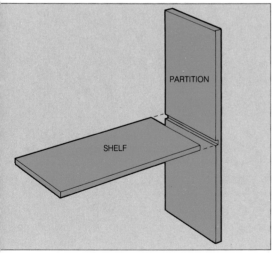

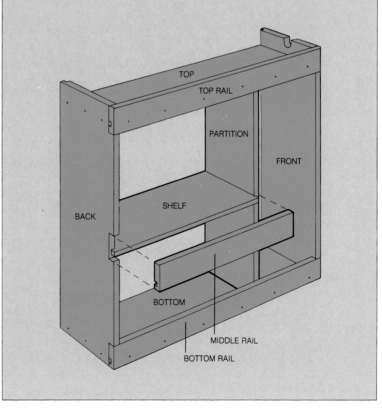

**3** **Installing the shelf.** Apply glue to the free end of the shelf and to the top and bottom edges of the partition. Set the assembly into the bin so that the shelf edge that projects beyond the edge of the partition extends 6 mm into the cutout for the middle rail, and the other shelf edge is flush with the rebate. Nail the top and bottom to the partition. Apply glue to the protruding edge of the shelf and nail the middle rail in place.

**4** **Attaching the side panel.** Place the bin so that the side that will fit against the wall of the cabinet faces upwards. Position the side panel over the bin. Lift the panel as far as you need to see the edges of the pieces underneath. Using a pencil, mark lines on the panel to indicate the centres of the pieces and to locate where the nails are to be driven. Remove the panel, apply glue to the edges and reposition the panel on the bin. Before the glue dries, drive nails through the corners and middle of the panel. Then hammer in more nails along the pencil lines, and recess all nails.

**5** **Positioning the glides.** Place both inner glide sections on the side panel, one at the top and the other at the bottom, so that the screw holes in the glides align precisely with the lines made in Step 4 and both glides are flush with the front of the bin. Drill pilot holes into the screw holes of the top glide, and attach the glide to the side panel. With a steel square, measure from the top glide to the bottom glide at both ends *(below)* to make sure the glides are parallel. Drill pilot holes and attach the bottom glide.

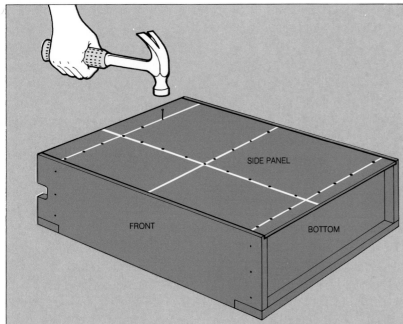

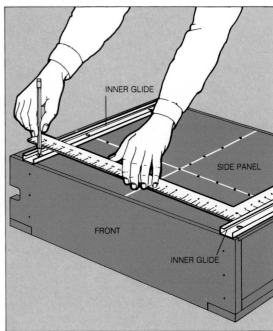

**6** **Attaching the outer casings.** For use as mounts, cut two pieces of wood 585 mm long and the same thickness as the space between the inside cabinet wall and the inside edge of the cabinet frame. Place the outer casings on the mounts, drill pilot holes through the casing screw holes and screw the casings to the mounts.

If you are modifying a free-standing cabinet, slip the mounted casings over the glides that are attached to the bins in Step 5 above. If the cabinet is not free-standing, do not insert the glides in the casings yet.

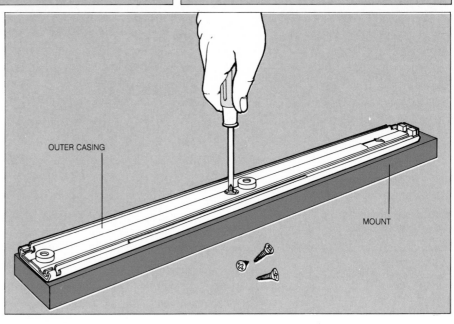

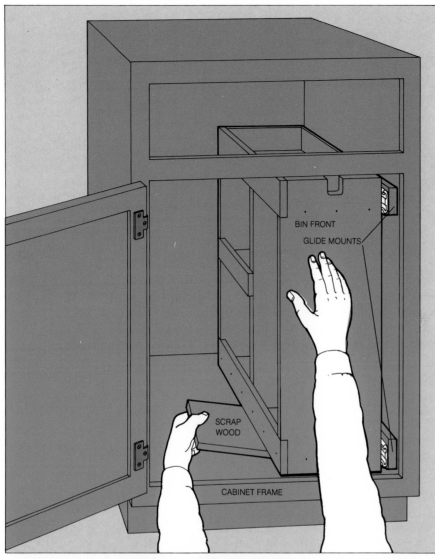

**7** **Positioning the right-hand bin.** Place the bin, with the completed drawer-glides attached, inside the cabinet so that the glide mounts are against the inside of the cabinet frame. Slip a piece of scrap wood under the bin to raise it temporarily, adjusting the height so that the bin clears the bottom of the cabinet frame when extended.

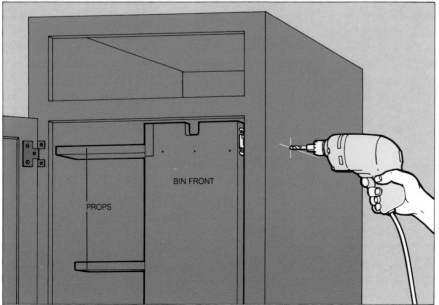

**8** **Installing the bin.** Wedge a few pieces of scrap wood between the bin and the opposite side of the cabinet to prop the bin firmly so that the glide mounts are flush against the inside of the cabinet. Using a steel square, mark lines on the outside of the cabinet wall to indicate where the centres of the glide mounts are located. Drill pilot holes on these lines through the cabinet wall and into the glide mounts *(left)*. Screw the mounts securely to the cabinet. Remove the wood props, then remove the bin from the cabinet by lifting the glides out of their casings.

If you want an unblemished outside surface, or your cabinet is not free-standing, install the glides from the inside. Position the bin as shown and mark locations for the glides on the front edge of the cabinet frame. Remove the bin, then extend the lines along the inside cabinet wall. Centre the wood mounts on these lines and screw them to the cabinet wall from the inside.

**9** **Assembling the left-hand bin.** Apply glue to the ends of the bottom piece and slip them into the housings in the front and back pieces. Position the bottom so that its edges extend 6 mm into the cutouts on both sides of the front and back. Clamp the pieces together with corner cramps and drive nails through the front and back into the bottom. After the glue has dried, remove the cramps and apply glue to the edges of the bottom piece and to the bottom cutouts on the front and back pieces. Position the bottom rails and nail them to the front, back and bottom.

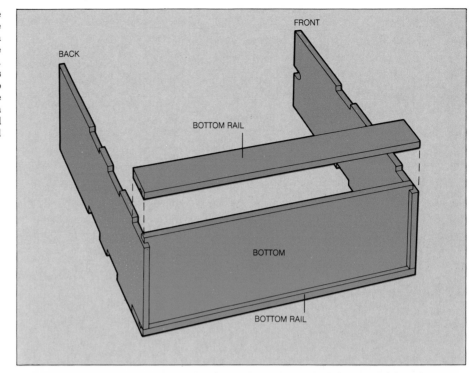

**10** **Installing partition and supports.** Apply glue to one end of each long support and slip the supports into the housing in the vertical partition. Position the supports so that their outer edges are flush with the edges of the partition. Clamp the pieces together with corner cramps and drive nails through the partition into the supports. Apply glue to the other ends of the supports and the bottom edge of the partition. Set the assembly into the bin so that the supports fit firmly in the housing on the front, and the edges are flush with the edges of the cutouts. Then drive nails through the front into the supports, and through the bottom into the partition.

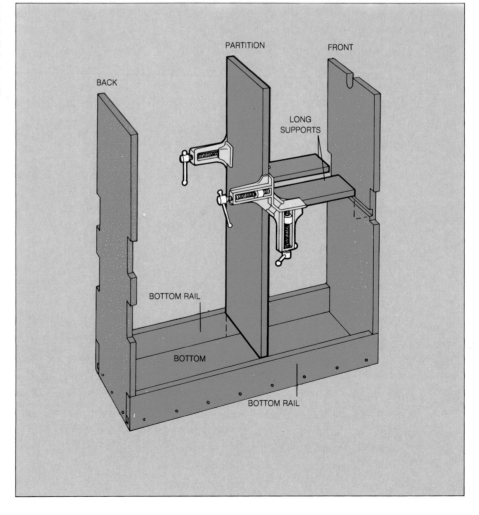

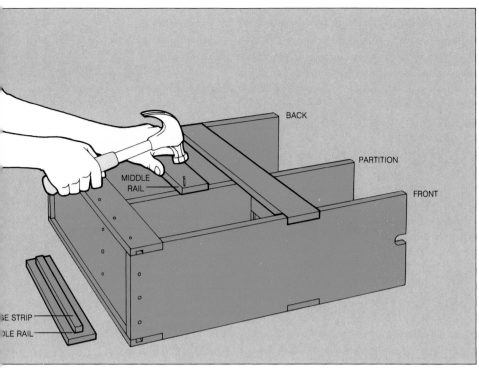

**11** **Installing the top and middle rails.** Glue and nail the top rails to the top cutouts on the front and back pieces. Glue and nail the ledge strips to the short middle rails, positioning the strips in the centre of the rails and parallel to the sides *(left)*. Use 20 mm nails. Apply glue to the middle cutouts on the back and set the middle rails into the cutouts with the ledge strips facing inwards. Nail the rails to the partition and the back.

**12** **Completing the left-hand bin.** Slip the short supports down inside the bin so that they rest on the ledge strips. (They may be glued in place or left loose to accommodate different-sized utensils.) Attach drawer-glide assemblies to the bottom and top rails of the bin and the cabinet wall, and install the bin following the instructions for the right-hand bin *(Steps 5–8)*.

If the cabinet you are modifying is not free-standing, follow the alternative procedure for mounting the glides given in Step 8, page 107.

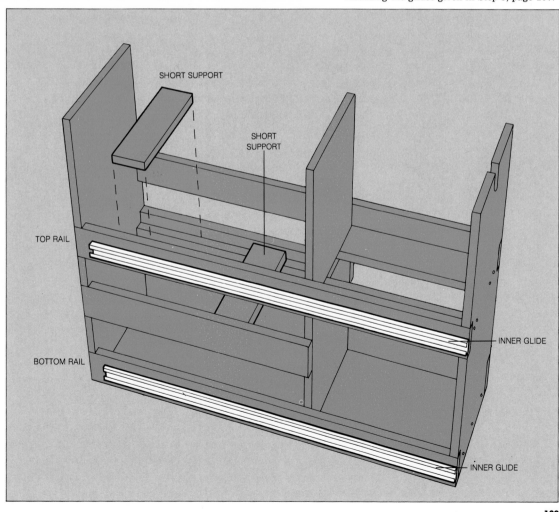

# Travelling Platforms for Unfinished Attics

An attic is far too valuable as storage space to be left unused merely because it has an unfinished floor or a roof so low as to make it little more than crawl space. Putting in flooring is an expensive, time-consuming, uncomfortable job that will solve your storage problem only if your attic is high enough for you to stand in. You can also lay down plywood panels round the trap door to provide a make-shift storage area.

However, a more efficient solution may be to put together trains of movable platforms, such as the ones shown below, which can give you access even to the space at the ends of the attic. The trains are ideal for use in long, low-roofed attics where the location of the trap-door opening permits them to be several platforms long.

Each plywood platform is really a small wagon that runs back and forth on castors along 50 by 100 mm wooden tracks laid at right angles across the joists—the horizontal structural beams in the attic. When you nail the tracks to the joists, be sure they are parallel so that the platforms will move smoothly. A clothesline pulley draws each platform past the trap door for loading and unloading. The wagons are hitched together with heavy-duty hooks and eyes. Rails round the platform edges keep the cargo from shifting out of place.

The width of the platform units will be largely determined by the spacing between the tracks. Do not set the tracks so wide apart that you will have difficulty in reaching the far side of a platform (a 400 to 500 mm spacing is usually advisable). Before building the platforms, measure the attic trap-door opening to be sure that the finished platforms will fit through it.

**Providing for maximum storage.** Usable attic space can be maximized by building two trains of storage platforms, one on each side of the trap door. For easy loading and unloading, you must be able to pull the platforms to within reach of the trap-door opening; therefore, for an attic with a central trap door, each train should be not much longer than half the length of the attic.

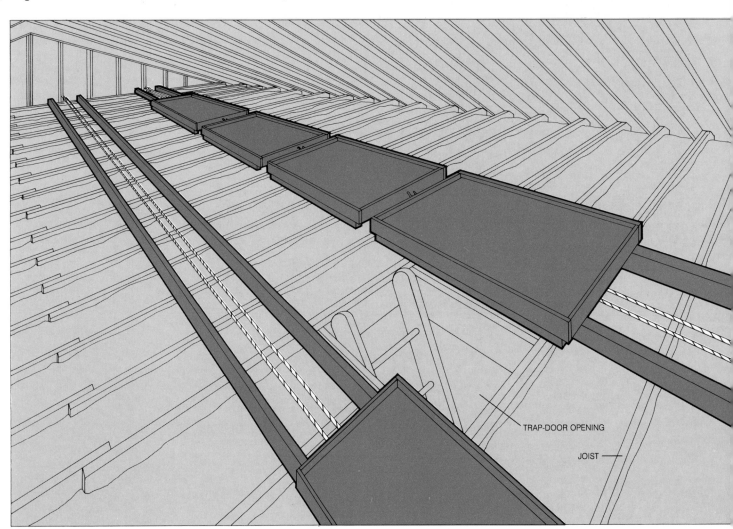

TRAP-DOOR OPENING

JOIST

**Constructing the platforms.** The positions of the parts that make up a platform and the sizes of wood recommended are shown in a head-on view *(below)* and from beneath *(right)*. Fixed-plate castors—not the swivelling type—are used for both the weight-bearing wheels attached to each platform bottom and for the rollers attached to the guide rails that stabilize the platform on its tracks. Remember to allow for the height of the castors when calculating measurements for the platforms. The pulley rope should be anchored securely to the platform bases of both the front and rear wagons of each train.

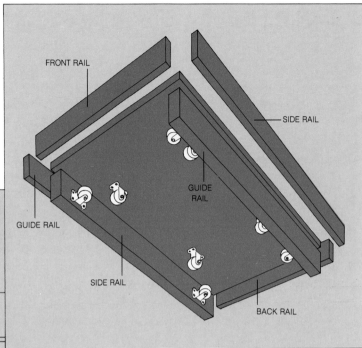

FRONT RAIL

SIDE RAIL

GUIDE RAIL

GUIDE RAIL

SIDE RAIL

BACK RAIL

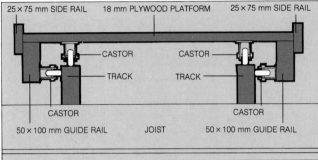

25 × 75 mm SIDE RAIL · 18 mm PLYWOOD PLATFORM · 25 × 75 mm SIDE RAIL

CASTOR · CASTOR

TRACK · TRACK

CASTOR · CASTOR

50 × 100 mm GUIDE RAIL · JOIST · 50 × 100 mm GUIDE RAIL

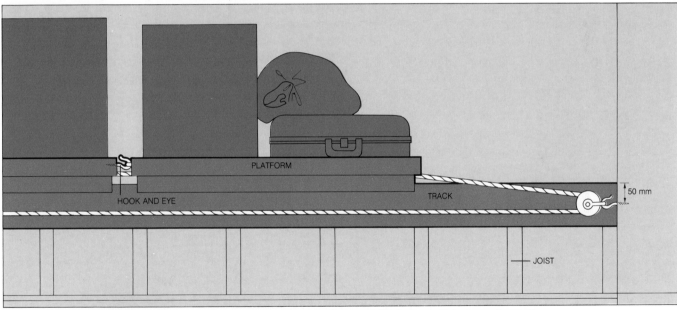

PLATFORM

HOOK AND EYE

TRACK

50 mm

JOIST

**Installing the pulleys.** For each storage train, pulleys should be screwed into beams at opposite ends of the attic, about 50 mm below the top level of the tracks. If there are no beams to which the pulleys can be conveniently attached, nail lengths of 50 by 100 mm beams between the track ends and screw the pulleys into them. Run a single length of clothesline through one of the pulleys and then through the other pulley; tie the ends to form a loop and leave the knot in the centre of the attic where it will be concealed under one of the platforms. If the knotted part of the rope is left too close to the pulley, it could become jammed when the train is moved. Put the first, fully assembled platform on the tracks and fasten the looped rope directly to the bottom of the platform with heavy-duty steel staples or nails. Link the middle wagons together with hooks and eyes; they need not be attached to the rope. Finish by fastening a second point on the pulley to the wagon at the other end of the train.

# Roll-Out Storage Bins to Fit under the Stairs

The awkward triangular space beneath open stairways does not lend itself readily to convenient use. But if storage space is at a premium in your house, installing three roll-out units like the ones shown below can turn the area under the stairs into an efficient repository.

The tallest unit slides into a framework of 50 by 100 mm timber beneath the higher end of the stairs; the unit is designed to store equipment such as brooms, mops and floor polishers. The middle unit is shorter but wider and provides shelves to hold cans, bottles, tools, linen or whatever. A small bin, for holding a vacuum cleaner, footwear, toys or sports equipment, completes the trio. All three pieces roll on 75 mm high fixed-plate castors. A strong handle should be attached to each one to help in pulling it out and manoeuvring it.

The storage units are made entirely of 18 mm plywood. The side pieces and the back are housed to hold the bottom; the side pieces are also rebated to hold the back. All of the shelves are held in position with wood cleats *(page 48, below)* cut from scrap pieces of plywood.

After assembly, the units can be faced with wood panelling to give them a well-finished look. If panelling is added, it should also be attached to the exposed areas of the frame that positions the tall storage unit. A small triangular panel at the lowest end of the under-the-stairs space will mask the remaining open section, which is too low to be of use.

The project was designed for an area where the stringers—the long beams supporting the stair treads—rise at a 35 degree angle. However, since staircases come in a variety of heights, widths, lengths and angles of ascent, you will have to measure the space available under the stairs before deciding how many units you can accommodate and what size they should be. In making your calculations, follow the steps on pages 52–57. To duplicate the angle of ascent of your stairs, stand a plywood sheet on its end flush against the stringer and draw a line on the plywood, using the stringer's bottom edge as a guideline.

If your stairs have treads but no risers (the upright boards behind the tread), you will have to seal the back of the staircase to keep dust and dirt from falling through into the storage units. The easiest way is to cover the back of the staircase with a sheet of 12 mm plywood, and nail it to the bottom of the stringers.

**Three types of roll-outs.** The amount of space beneath the stairs usually is large enough to accommodate versions of the three units pictured below. You should allow about 75 mm of lateral clearance between one unit and the next, so that they can be moved from under the stairs without scraping against one another. If the stairs rest on vertical supports, build your units to fit between them. The framework into which the tallest unit slides should include a pair of 50 by 100 mm studs and a pair of 50 by 100 mm guide rails running along the floor to the wall at the back of the space below the stairs. One of these rails also helps to steer the middle unit into position. A third 50 by 100 mm rail should be added as a guide for the small bin.

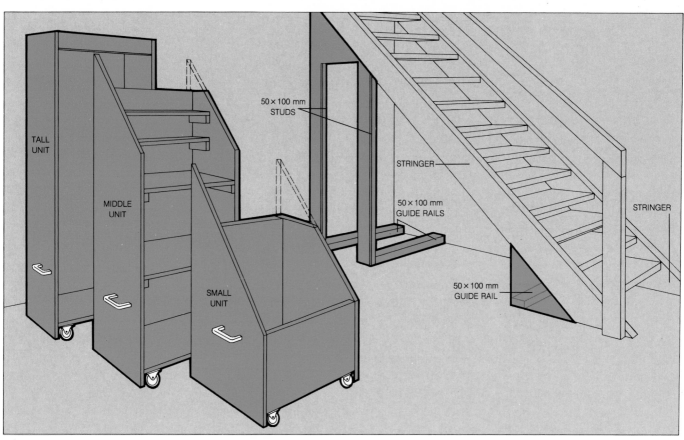

# Assembling the Units

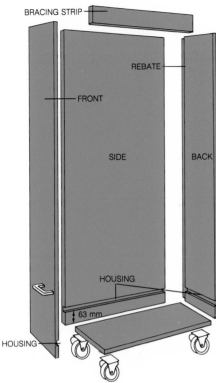

BRACING STRIP

REBATE

FRONT

SIDE

BACK

HOUSING

63 mm

HOUSING

**The tall unit.** This storage unit is merely a rectangular box with one side left open. Housings into which the unit's bottom is glued are 6 mm deep and 18 mm wide and are cut into the front, back and side pieces 63 mm above the bottom edges. This allows for 12 mm clearance between the unit and the floor when 75 mm high castors are attached to the bottom. Rebates 6 mm deep and 18 mm wide are cut along the inside edges of the front and back to hold the side more securely. The parts are then glued together. A strip of wood across the top of the open side braces the structure at that point. Metal hooks or clips can be added to hold a variety of tall objects.

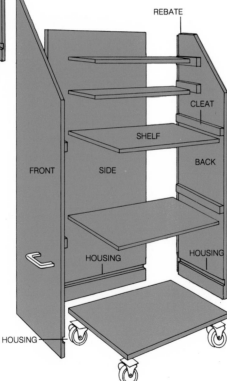

REBATE

CLEAT

SHELF

FRONT

SIDE

BACK

HOUSING

HOUSING

HOUSING

**The middle unit.** The front, side, back and bottom of this unit are joined using housings and rebates positioned in the same way as those in the tall unit, and cut to the same depth and width. All shelves are supported by 18 by 45 mm wood cleats cut from scrap plywood. A more complicated alternative would be to install adjustable shelves *(pages 46–48)*. To place shelves at a convenient height, measure the height of items you plan to store before securing the cleats.

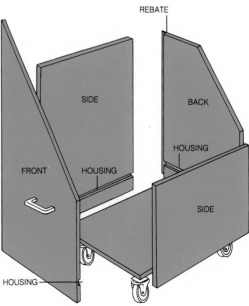

REBATE

SIDE

BACK

HOUSING

FRONT

HOUSING

SIDE

HOUSING

**The small unit.** This unit is essentially a smaller version of the middle unit, but with a closed side and no shelves. It is housed and rebated in the same way as the other units. If you require additional shelf space, the bin can be modified to take shelves like those in the middle unit.

# Reorganizing Cupboards

Cupboard clutter is often due less to an actual shortage of space than to wasteful design. The project on the following pages shows one way to reorganize a typical wide and shallow cupboard to make the most of space that goes unused at the moment or is utilized inadequately. The interior may be sufficiently spacious: a sliding-door cupboard can be 550 to 650 mm deep, 2000 to 2500 mm high and often 1500 or more millimetres wide; but the clothes rod, usually 1650 mm high, seems designed only for full-length coats and dresses, and 600 mm or more of valuable room underneath the shorter garments is left empty. The one shelf that is usually found above the clothes rod is often narrow and hard to reach, so that significant space is also wasted at the top of the cupboard. These unused areas can be put to work; by reorganizing facilities for hanging clothes and by installing a unit consisting of drawers and a set of adjustable shelves, you can increase the storage capacity of the cupboard by as much as 50 per cent.

The first step in remodelling a clothes cupboard is to group your garments according to length. The longer ones should still be hung on a 1650 mm high rod. The shorter garments—such as blouses, folded trousers and jackets—can be hung on two rods, one above the other. The space saved can be converted into a central drawer-and-shelf section for folded clothing, linen or shoes. Shelves for luggage or other rarely used items can be added to take advantage of the space above the clothes rods.

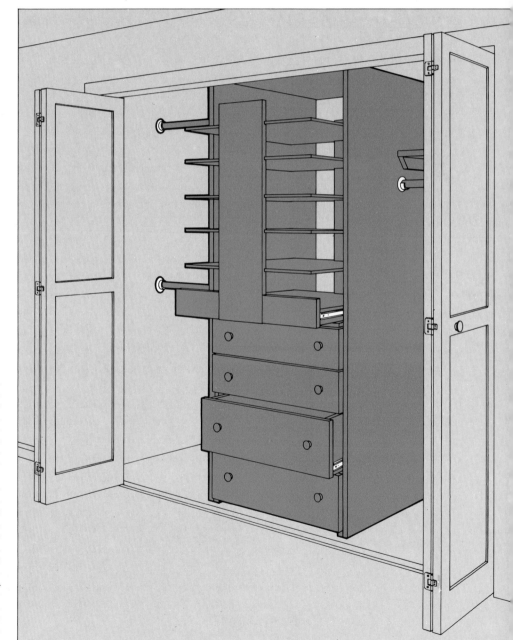

**A more efficient clothes cupboard.** The completed project shows how a wide, 610 mm deep cupboard can be efficiently redesigned by eliminating the typical long clothes rod and shelf fixtures, and adding new elements. The rod has been replaced with three shorter rods: one *(far right)* is at the standard height for dresses and other long clothing; and the other two are for the shorter garments, such as jackets and folded trousers.

A 610 mm wide central storage area, combining drawers and a series of shelves, extends from floor to door height and provides almost a cubic metre of additional storage. The lower unit, 915 mm high, has two shallow and two deep drawers. The upper unit, also 915 mm high, consists of six shelves; the entire shelf unit is mounted on fully extended glides so that it can be rolled out for easy access from the sides. Additional shelving for bulky or less frequently used items is provided on top of the central structure and over the right-hand clothes rod. To allow full access, sliding doors have been replaced with folding ones.

Many cupboards are fitted with sliding doors that overlap when opened, so that only half the cupboard is accessible at one time. By removing such doors and replacing them with concertina-type folding doors or with plain or louvred folding doors, the interior can be made completely accessible. The doors, which are available to fit all standardized cupboard openings, should be added before a drawer-and-shelf unit is built; otherwise it may be difficult to install the overhead glide necessary for folding doors.

The project described here can be varied to suit either a smaller cupboard or a smaller budget. The storage unit illustrated here, 610 mm wide, is designed for a cupboard 1830 mm in width, but smaller cupboards can be reorganized by building a narrower stack of drawers and shelves. As an alternative, you can simply divide the cupboard with a central panel, placing a 1650 mm high clothes rod on one side of the panel and two rods for short clothes, one above the other, on the other side.

The parts of the drawer-and-shelf unit that will be exposed to view can be built of hardwood plywood (such as birch) if you plan to apply a stain or oil finish, but a less expensive plywood or chipboard can be used throughout if you plan to paint the completed unit.

Using the techniques explained here and elsewhere in this volume, you can imaginatively redesign other cupboards for specialized uses. The office/hobby area below is just one alternative suggestion. However, by adding pegboard, shelves and other fittings, any utility, linen or food cupboard can be modified to accommodate more items in a more convenient and easily accessible manner.

## Shopping List for the Clothes Cupboard

| | |
|---|---|
| 2 sheets plywood, 18 × 1220 × 2440 mm | cut to appropriate cupboard width |
| 1 sheet plywood, 9 × 1220 × 2440 mm | 125 g lost-head nails, 40 mm |
| 1 sheet plywood, 6 × 1220 × 2440 mm | 250 g lost-head nails, 25 mm |
| 1 length softwood, 25 × 50 × 1830 mm | 50, 3.5 mm countersunk screws, 30 mm |
| 1 length softwood, 25 × 50 × 2440 mm | 15 metres 19 mm iron-on veneer |
| 2 lengths softwood, 12 × 141 × 2440 mm | to match plywood |
| 2 lengths softwood, 12 × 235 × 2440 mm | 5 sheets No. 120 grit abrasive paper |
| 4 pairs 550 mm fully extending drawer-glide | 2 sheets No. 280 grit abrasive paper |
| assemblies, 25 kg capacity | 1 pair folding doors and matching door glide |
| 1 pair 550 mm fully extending drawer-glide | (only to replace sliding doors) |
| assemblies, 50 kg capacity | PVA glue |
| 8 drawer pulls | contact adhesive |
| 3 pairs rod sockets, 25 mm diameter | wood filler |
| 3 lengths 25 mm chrome-steel tubing, | |

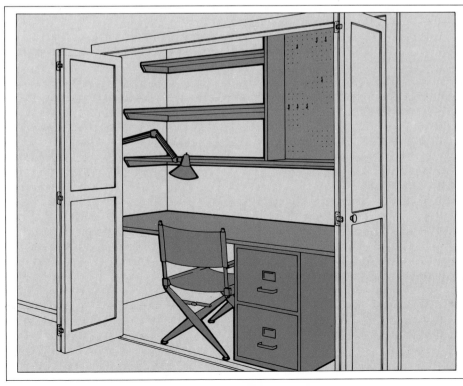

## An Alternative Design

A spare cupboard whose dimensions are similar to the one on the left can be readily converted into a home study, office or hobby area. The desk, which is 740 mm high, is made by cutting a sheet of plywood to size, covering the surface with laminated plastic *(page 94)* and mounting the plywood top on 25 by 150 mm wood cleats that are attached to the cupboard's back and side walls. A ready-made filing cabinet serves both for storage and as a brace for the desk top. Deep overhead shelves are mounted on 25 by 50 mm wood cleats (as shown) or with adjustable standards and brackets *(pages 46–47)*; the highest shelf is less deep to afford access. Pegboard, spaced away from the back of the cupboard by a frame of 18 mm square moulding, provides additional room to hang miscellaneous items. An adjustable reading lamp is mounted on the side wall.

# Cutting Diagrams

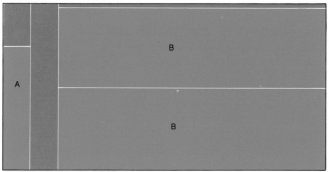

18 × 1220 × 2440 mm PLYWOOD

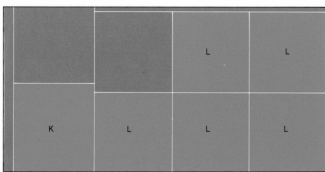

9 × 1220 × 2440 mm PLYWOOD

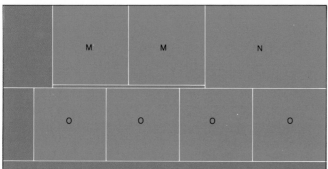

6 × 1220 × 2440 mm PLYWOOD

25 × 50 × 1830 mm SOFTWOOD

25 × 50 × 2440 mm SOFTWOOD

12 × 141 × 2440 mm SOFTWOOD (2 LENGTHS)

12 × 235 × 2440 mm SOFTWOOD (2 LENGTHS)

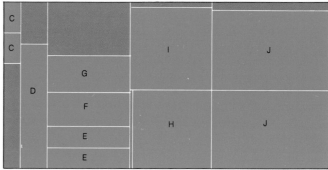

18 × 1220 × 2440 mm PLYWOOD

**Making the basic cuts.** Names and dimensions of all the plywood and timber parts are given in the key below, and are identified by corresponding letters on the cutting diagrams. As each piece is cut, attach masking tape to it and mark the tape with the letter designation of the piece. The scrap pieces, identified by dark shading in the cutting diagrams, can be used for extra shelving, and as guides for the circular saw and router.

A | back shelf support, 200 × 915 mm
B | side panels (two pieces), 592 × 2030 mm
C | shelf-unit false front (two pieces),
  100 × 223 mm
D | front shelf support, 200 × 915 mm
E | false drawer front (two pieces),
  157 × 610 mm
F | false drawer front, 251 × 610 mm
G | false drawer front, 271 × 610 mm
H | drawer-unit bottom, 592 × 586 mm
I | drawer-unit top, 610 × 603 mm
J | drawer-unit sides (two pieces),
  586 × 897 mm
K | central-structure top, 646 × 592 mm
L | shelf-unit shelves (five pieces),
  586 × 589 mm
M | top and bottom of shelf-unit base (two
  pieces), 586 × 571 mm
N | drawer-unit back, 610 × 915 mm
O | drawer bottoms (four pieces), 538 × 554 mm
P | side pieces for shelf-unit base (two pieces),
  25 × 50 × 571 mm
Q | brace for shelf supports, 25 × 50 × 571 mm
R | cross pieces for shelf-unit base (four pieces),
  25 × 50 × 546 mm
S | shallow-drawer fronts (two pieces)
  12 × 141 × 538 mm
T | shallow-drawer backs (two pieces),
  12 × 141 × 538 mm
U | shallow-drawer sides (four pieces),
  12 × 141 × 578 mm
V | deep-drawer fronts (two pieces),
  12 × 235 × 538 mm
W | deep-drawer backs (two pieces),
  12 × 235 × 538 mm
X | deep-drawer sides (four pieces),
  12 × 235 × 578 mm

# Routing Diagrams

**1 Routing the drawer parts.** Sort the drawer parts into fronts, backs and sides, and then separate the sides into left and right pieces. To avoid confusion while cutting, mark the inner surface of each part to indicate the top and bottom edge, and also mark the sides to indicate the front and back edges. Twelve mm from the bottom edge of each front, back and side piece, rout a groove 6 mm wide and 6 mm deep. (For routing techniques, see the instructions on pages 26 and 27.) Twelve mm from the back edge of each side piece, rout a housing 12 mm wide and 6 mm deep. At the front edge of each side piece, rout a rebate 12 mm wide and 6 mm deep.

**2 Routing the shelf supports.** Place the two shelf supports on the work surface, butted together side by side, with their inner surfaces upwards. Carefully align their top and bottom edges, and fix them to the work surface with G-cramps. To indicate where the housings will be cut, locate five points on the surface of each support; the distance of each point from the bottom edge is indicated in the drawing *(below)*. At each point, use a combination square and a pencil to mark lines across each shelf support. Rout a housing 9 mm wide and 9 mm deep, positioning the router so that the bottom edge of each housing is flush with each marker line.

**3 Routing the drawer-unit sides.** The bottom of the drawer unit should be positioned 50 mm above floor level so that the bottom drawer will clear the cupboard door sill when the drawer is opened. To mark positions for grooves in the drawer-unit bottom, place both drawer-unit sides on a flat surface, measure 50 mm from the bottom edge of each and make pencil marks across each side. Then rout a groove 18 mm wide and 9 mm deep along each mark.

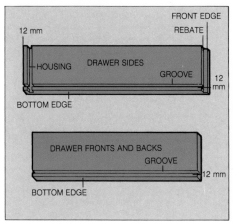

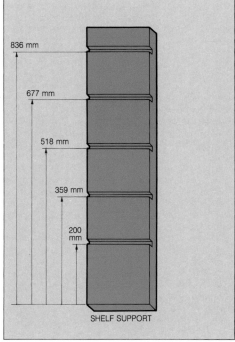

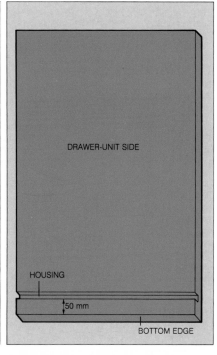

## Building the Drawer Unit

**1 Assembling the drawers.** Sort the drawer parts into two identical sets for the smaller two 141 mm deep drawers (left and right sides, fronts, backs and bottoms), and into two other sets for the two 235 mm deep drawers. Assemble the drawers, following the instructions in Steps 1–3 on pages 28 and 29. Glue the drawer bottoms in the grooves and use glue and 25 mm panel pins to strengthen the housing and rebate joints. Finally, attach a set of 25 kg capacity inner glides to the sides of each drawer *(page 30)*.

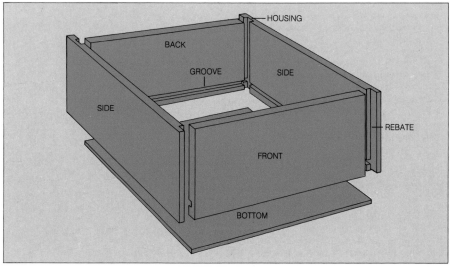

**2** **Measuring the glide assemblies.** Place the two drawer-unit sides on a flat surface with their inside surfaces up and their front edges butting. Align both sides exactly at the top and bottom and at the housing. Hook a steel tape measure in the housing and extend the tape measure along the butted edges. To locate the positions of the glide-assembly outer casings, make pencil lines across both butted edges *(right)* at the following measurements, starting from the housing: 7 mm, 261 mm, 515 mm and 675 mm. Lift one side piece and reposition it so that the back edges butt. Repeat the marking procedure. Finally, join all pencil marks across the sides.

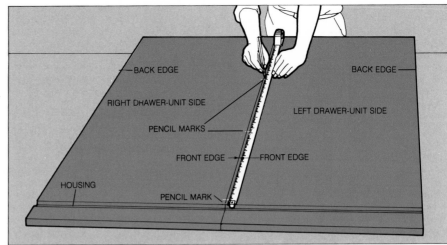

BACK EDGE
BACK EDGE
RIGHT DHAWER-UNIT SIDE
LEFT DRAWER-UNIT SIDE
PENCIL MARKS
FRONT EDGE
FRONT EDGE
HOUSING
PENCIL MARK

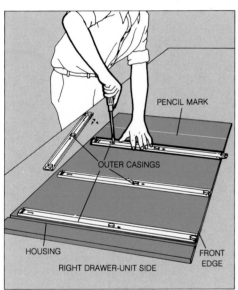

PENCIL MARK
OUTER CASINGS
HOUSING
FRONT EDGE
RIGHT DRAWER-UNIT SIDE

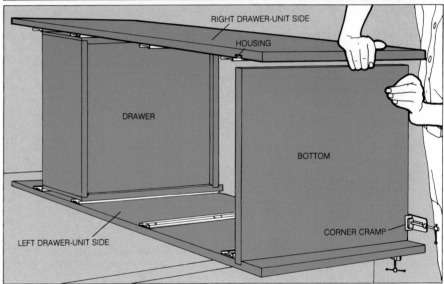

RIGHT DRAWER-UNIT SIDE
HOUSING
DRAWER
BOTTOM
LEFT DRAWER-UNIT SIDE
CORNER CRAMP

**3** **Attaching the outer casings.** Sort the outer casings of the 25 kg capacity drawer-glide assemblies into the left and right-hand units. Place a right-hand casing on the right side piece; the bottom edge of the casing should be flush with the 7 mm mark made in Step 2, and the front end of the casing should be flush with the front edge of the side piece. Place the casing in position; make starter holes for the mounting screws, and secure the casing with the screws. Repeat this procedure for the other right-hand casings, installing them at the locations previously marked *(above)*. Attach the left-hand casings in the same way.

**4** **Assembling the sides and bottom.** After dry-fitting, apply glue to the housings in both side pieces and to the side edges of the drawer-unit bottom. Insert the bottom into the housing in the left side pieces and place a corner cramp on the lower rear joint. Put the second drawer from the top in position by inserting the drawer's inner glide into the corresponding outer casing on the left side piece. With a helper to align the right-hand glide assembly, slide the right side piece into position on the corresponding inner glide. Using the drawer as a support, position the housing in the right side piece over the bottom and press the side into position *(above)*. Place another corner cramp on the upper rear joint.

**5** **Fastening the sides.** With the corner cramps and drawer still in place, make three bradawl marks for screw holes on the right side piece centred over the housing. Drill and countersink the pilot holes through the side and into the bottom, and fasten the side with three 30 mm countersunk screws. Turn the drawer unit over, taking care that the drawer does not slide out. Mark, drill and fasten the left side piece in the same way.

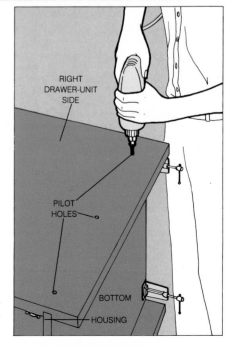

RIGHT DRAWER-UNIT SIDE
PILOT HOLES
BOTTOM
HOUSING

**6** **Attaching the top.** Stand the drawer unit upright and apply glue to the top edges of the side pieces. Place the top in position by aligning its back edge flush with the rear corners, but leaving an 18 mm overhang in front. Place cramps in the top rear corners. Mark and drill four evenly spaced pilot holes through the top and into the side pieces. Fasten the top with 30 mm countersunk screws. Fill all screw holes on the sides and top with wood filler and sand smooth *(page 16, Steps 11 and 12)*.

**7** **Adding the back.** Remove the drawer and all corner cramps. Place the drawer unit face down on the worktable as shown. Measure 59 mm from the bottom edge of the back piece and make a mark across the width of the back to locate the centre line of the bottom piece. Apply glue to the inner edges of the back piece and to the rear edges of the side, top and bottom pieces. Place the back in position and fasten it with 25 mm lost-head nails; nail the corners first, then add nails 135 mm apart round the edges.

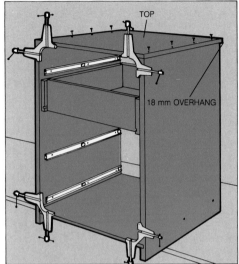

TOP

18 mm OVERHANG

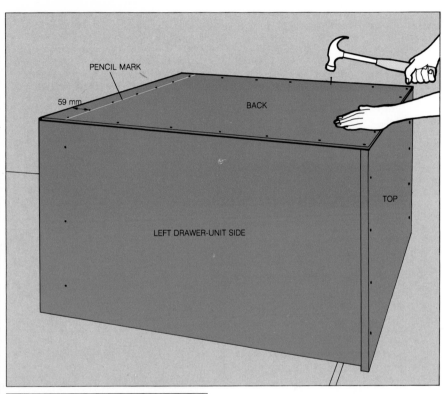

PENCIL MARK

59 mm

BACK

LEFT DRAWER-UNIT SIDE

TOP

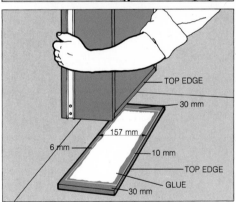

TOP EDGE

30 mm

157 mm

6 mm — 10 mm

TOP EDGE

GLUE

30 mm

**8** **Gluing the false fronts.** Place a 157 mm wide false drawer front face down and outline a rectangle on its back as follows: mark a line 30 mm in from each side edge, a line 10 mm in from the top edge and another line 6 mm in from the bottom edge. Mark the other three false fronts in the same manner but, for the line at the bottom edge of the 271 mm wide front piece, measure in 26 mm instead of 6 mm, so that when this front is attached to the lowest drawer it will extend down over the front edge of the cabinet bottom. Apply glue to the front of the top drawer and also to the area within the rectangle marked on the 157 mm wide false front. Place the drawer on the false front as shown in the drawing above, aligning it with all sides of the rectangle formed by the pencil marks. (Make sure that the top edge of the drawer is on the 10 mm line.)

**9** **Securing the false fronts.** When the glue has become just tacky enough to hold the false front in place on the top drawer, slide the drawer into the outer-glide casings previously attached to the side pieces. Make sure that the overlapping side edges of the false front are flush with the sides of the drawer unit and that there is a slight clearance between the false front and the top of the drawer unit. If necessary, adjust the alignment by sliding the false front on its film of glue *(left)*. Remove the drawer and fasten the front to it with screws *(page 32, Step 2)*.

Position and fasten the other false fronts as follows: the remaining 157 mm front on the second drawer from the top, the 251 mm front on the third drawer, and the 271 mm front on the bottom drawer. Check for a slight clearance between the top and bottom of each front before fastening it. Attach drawer pulls to all drawers *(page 32)*. Apply veneer edging *(page 76)* to the front edge of the cabinet top and to the side edges of the false fronts.

# Building the Shelf Unit

**1 Assembling the base.** To make the 571 by 586 mm frame for the base, butt the four 546 mm crosspieces against the 571 mm side pieces of the base at 163 mm intervals. Use glue, 40 mm lost-head nails and corner cramps to secure the joints, as shown in Steps 1–7 on pages 12–14. Next, position the 586 by 571 mm plywood bottom and top pieces *(right)* and attach them to the frame with glue and 25 mm lost-head nails. Then attach the inner glides of the 50 kg capacity assemblies to the 571 mm side pieces, as explained in Step 3 on page 30.

**2 Attaching the first shelf support.** In the lower front corners of the front shelf support, make pencil marks for the four screw holes at the locations shown. To centre the support on the base, measure in 193 mm from each corner of the base and mark with a pencil. Turn the base round and mark the other end in the same way. Apply glue between these marks, and to the corresponding area on the grooved side of the support. Place the support between the marks. To make certain that the shelves will be level when installed in the housings in both supports, you must ensure that the supports are perfectly square with the base; while the glue is still wet, check the front support with a combination square *(below)*. Hold the front shelf support firmly in the squared position, and drill pilot holes through the four marks in the support and into the base frame. Use 30 mm countersunk screws to fasten the support to the base.

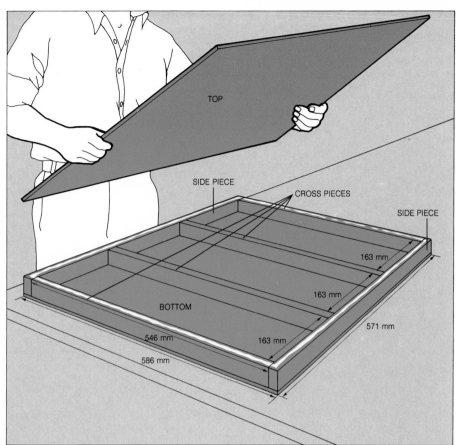

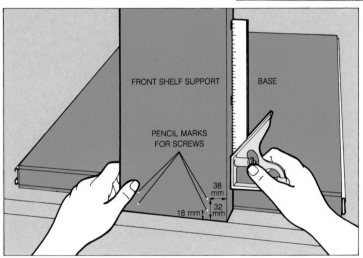

**3 Installing the shelves.** Stack together the five 586 by 589 mm shelves. On both of the 586 mm edges of the bottom shelf, make a pencil mark 193 mm in from each corner. Extend these marks down the edge of the other shelves. Place the attached front shelf support flat on the workbench and secure it with hand screws. Apply glue to the bottom housing joint of the front shelf support. Starting with the bottom shelf, apply glue between the pencil marks on one of its edges, and tap it into the bottom housing with a mallet. Use the same procedure for the remaining four shelves. Wipe off any excess glue while it is still wet.

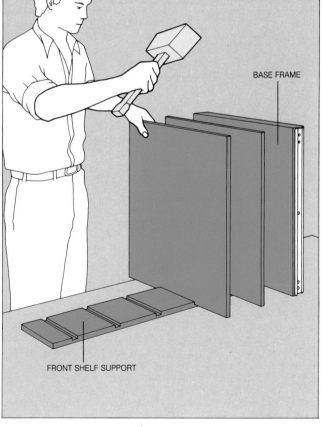

**4** **Securing the back shelf support.** Apply glue between the pencil marks on the other end of the shelves, and on the centre of the exposed side of the base frame. Glue each housing in the back shelf support, and use a piece of scrap wood and a hammer to tap the support on to the shelves. Measure and mark the screw holes *(Step 2)* for the back shelf support. Secure the support to the base frame with 30 mm countersunk screws.

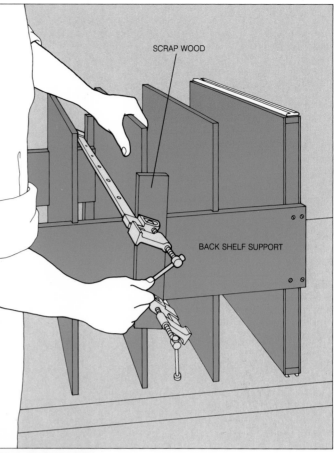

SCRAP WOOD

BACK SHELF SUPPORT

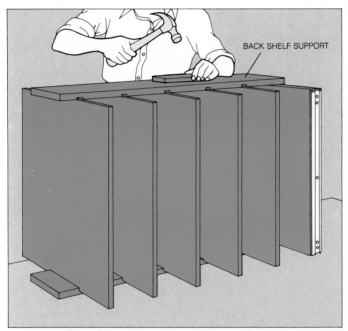

BACK SHELF SUPPORT

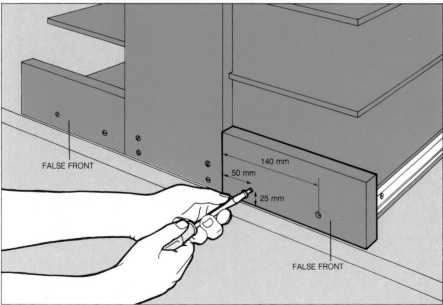

FALSE FRONT

140 mm

50 mm

25 mm

FALSE FRONT

**5** **Clamping the unit.** Loosen the front shelf support from the workbench, and then turn the unit 90 degrees so that both shelf supports are facing outwards. Starting with the bottom shelf, attach two sash or pipe cramps to the shelf supports to ensure that the joints are tight. Place blocks of scrap wood between the cramp faces and the supports to protect the unit. After several minutes, remove the cramps and attach them to the supports at the point where the top shelf is secured. Wait a few more minutes and remove the cramps. Use the same procedure for the second, the fourth, and then the third shelves.

Glue the 25 by 50 by 571 mm length of wood cut previously *(page 116)* to the underside of the fourth shelf to act as a brace for the unit.

**6** **Adding false fronts.** The two false-front pieces for the shelf unit serve as handles for pulling out the unit and as stops when it is pushed back in. With a pencil, mark each false-front piece for two screw holes at the points indicated. Butt the pieces against the front shelf support, with the bottom of each false front flush with the bottom of the base; check for a tight, even fit. Apply glue to the false fronts and base; allow the glue to become tacky so that it will help to hold the fronts in place. Drill pilot holes through the marked front pieces and into the base, and then countersink the holes. Attach each false front with two 30 mm countersunk screws. Fill the countersunk screw holes with wood filler, and sand the surface until it is smooth.

121

## Installing the Storage Unit

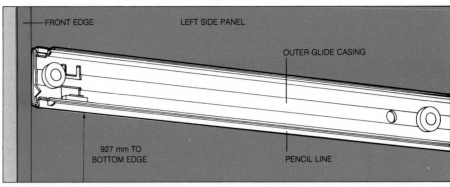

**1** **Preparing the side panels.** Apply veneer edging to the front edges of both side panels. Place both panels flat with their inner surfaces facing up. Measure 927 mm up from the bottom edge of each panel, and at that point make a pencil line across each panel. Position the 50 kg capacity outer-glide casings on the panels, with the bottom edges of the casings flush with the lines, and their front edges flush with the front edges of the panels *(right)*; screw the casings in place.

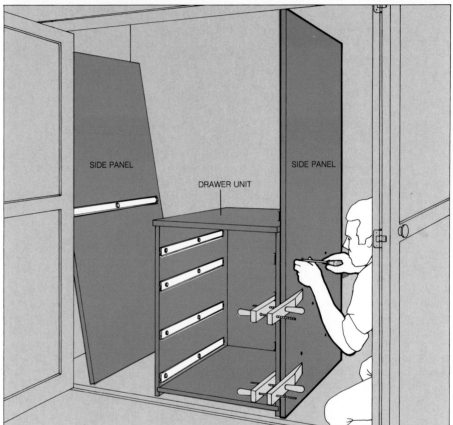

**2** **Fastening the panels.** On the outer surfaces of both side panels, mark the positions for screws as follows: two screws 230 mm from the bottom of each panel and 150 mm from each edge; one screw 460 mm from the bottom and centred in each panel; two screws 685 mm from the bottom of each panel and 150 mm from each edge.

Since it would be difficult to get the bulky panels into the cupboard after the cabinet is positioned, move the panels into the cupboard now, leaning them against the end walls. Install the drawer unit, centring it on the cupboard floor. Place the right panel against the right side of the drawer unit, aligning the front edge flush with the front edge of the unit's side. Clamp the two together with hand screws. Drill countersunk pilot holes at the points previously marked, and fasten the panel with five 30 mm screws *(right)*. Attach the left panel in the same way.

**3** **Attaching the top.** Standing on a chair or stepladder, apply glue to the top edges of the side panels of the storage section, and to the corresponding edges of the top. Place the top in position and fasten it with four 40 mm lost-head nails on each side *(right)*. Slide the drawers on to their outer casings. With a helper, complete the storage section by sliding the entire shelf unit on to its outer casings on the side panels.

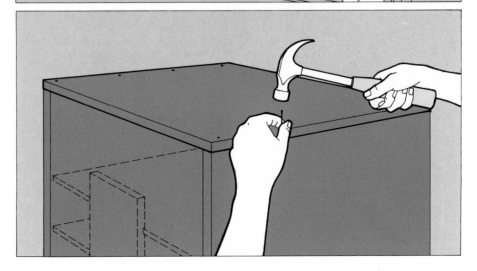

OPEN-END
SOCKET

1900 mm

OPEN-END
SOCKET

990 mm

SIDE
PANEL

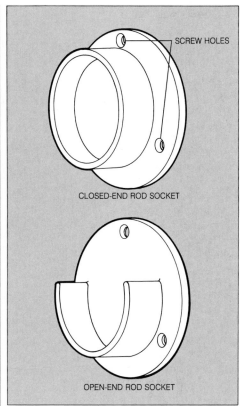

SCREW HOLES

CLOSED-END ROD SOCKET

OPEN-END ROD SOCKET

**4** **Installing clothes rods.** With a pencil, mark two points in the centre of the left side panel: make one mark 990 mm and the other 1900 mm from the floor. Mark the cupboard wall facing the panel in the same way. Screw two closed-end rod sockets to the wall at the points marked, and two open-end sockets to the panel *(left)*. Measure the distance between wall and panel, and cut two clothes rods of chrome-steel tubing, each 5 to 6 mm shorter than that measurement. Insert an end of each rod into a closed-end socket and drop the other end into the opposite open-end socket. Follow the same procedure to install the single clothes rod in the right side of the cupboard but position it at a height of 1650 mm.

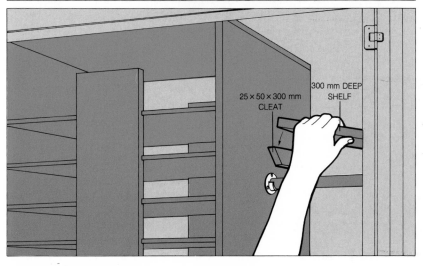

25 × 50 × 300 mm
CLEAT

300 mm DEEP
SHELF

**5** **Additional shelving.** An extra shelf mounted on cleats goes over the single clothes rod at the right of the central storage section. Remove the rod from its sockets and attach a 25 by 50 mm wood cleat 300 mm long to the cupboard wall (refer to the charts on pages 42 and 43 for the correct wall fixing), and about 50 mm above the sockets. Attach another cleat at the same height on the facing side panel. Cut the shelf from 18 mm plywood scrap; make it the same length as the clothes rod and 300 mm deep. Another shelf can be installed in the same way over the top rod on the left side of the central section.

## Picture Credits

*The sources for the illustrations in this book are shown below. Credits for the pictures from left to right are separated by semicolons, from top to bottom by dashes.*

Cover: Ken Kay. 6: Henry Groskinsky. 10: Photograph by Martin Brigdale—Photograph by Henry Groskinsky. 11: Photograph by Henry Groskinsky. 12: Drawing by Oxford Illustrators Ltd. 13: Drawing by Oxford Illustrators Ltd.—Drawings by Ron Jones. 14: Drawings by Ron Jones. 15: Drawing by Ron Jones—Drawing by Jackson Day Designs. 16: Drawing by Oxford Illustrators Ltd.—Drawings by Ron Jones. 17: Drawings by Fred Wolff. 18: Drawings by Fred Wolff, except top and bottom left: Drawings by Oxford Illustrators Ltd. 19: Drawing by Oxford Illustrators Ltd.—Drawings by Peter Trojan. 20: Drawings by Peter Trojan. 21: Drawing by Oxford Illustrators Ltd.—Drawings by Peter Trojan. 22: Drawings by Oxford Illustrators Ltd.; Drawing by Peter Trojan. 23, 24: Drawings by Peter Trojan. 25: Drawing by Oxford Illustrators Ltd.—Drawings by Gerry Contreras. 26: Drawings by Dale Gustafson, except top right: Drawing by Oxford Illustrators Ltd. 27: Drawings by Dale Gustafson. 28: Drawings by Ron Jones. 29: Drawings by Ron Jones, except top centre and right and lower middle: Drawings by Oxford Illustrators Ltd. 30: Drawings by Ron Jones—Drawing by Oxford Illustrators Ltd. 31: Drawing by Oxford Illustrators Ltd.—Drawings by Ron Jones. 32: Drawing by Oxford Illustrators Ltd.; Drawings by Ron Jones. 33, 34: Drawings by Adolph E. Brotman. 35: Drawings by Oxford Illustrators Ltd., except top and upper middle centre: Drawings by Adolph E. Brotman. 36: Drawings by Adolph E. Brotman—Drawing by Oxford Illustrators Ltd. 37 to 39: Drawings by Adolph E. Brotman. 40, 41: Drawings by Vantage Art, Inc. 42 to 46: Drawings by Dana Rasmussen. 47: Drawings by Oxford Illustrators Ltd. 48, 49: Drawings by Dana Rasmussen. 50: Henry Groskinsky. 52: Drawings by Dana Rasmussen. 55 to 57: Drawings by Vantage Art, Inc. 60: Drawings by Vantage Art, Inc. 62, 63: Drawings by Dale Gustafson. 64: Drawing by Oxford Illustrators Ltd.—Drawings by Dale Gustafson. 65: Drawings by Dale Gustafson, except lower middle: Drawing by Oxford Illustrators Ltd. 66: Ken Kay. 68 to 73: Drawings by Lennart Johnson Designs. 74, 75: Drawings by Dale Gustafson. 77 to 79: Drawings by Dale Gustafson. 80: Drawings by Dale Gustafson, except top left and bottom left: Drawings by Oxford Illustrators Ltd. 81: Drawings by Dale Gustafson, except top right and bottom right: Drawings by Oxford Illustrators Ltd. 82, 83: Drawings by Dale Gustafson. 84 to 89: Drawings by Vantage Art, Inc. 90 to 97: Drawings by Adolph E. Brotman. 98, 99: Drawings by John Massey. 100: Drawings by Oxford Illustrators Ltd. 101: Drawings by John Massey. 102, 103: Drawings by Vantage Art, Inc. 104, 105: Drawings by Dale Gustafson. 106, 107: Drawings by Whitman Studio, Inc. 108, 109: Drawings by Dale Gustafson. 110 to 113: Drawings by Kurt Ortell. 114 to 117: Drawings by Whitman Studio, Inc. 118: Drawing by Oxford Illustrators Ltd.—Drawings by Whitman Studio, Inc. 119: Drawings by Whitman Studio, Inc. 120: Drawings by Whitman Studio, Inc.—Drawing by Jackson Day Designs. 121: Drawings by Jackson Day Designs—Drawing by Whitman Studio, Inc. 122, 123: Drawings by Whitman Studio, Inc.

## Acknowledgements

The editors would like to extend special thanks to Susie Bicknell, Paris; Tim Fraser, Sydney; and Christel Wiemken, Hamburg. They also wish to thank the following: Association Française de Normalisation (AFNOR), Paris; Fa. Beese & Schmidt, Hamburg; M. Bichet, Centre Scientifique et Technique du Batiment, Syndicat National des Fabricant de Quincaillerie, Paris; Emily Brandt-Clarke, Hamburg; Centre Technique du Bois, Paris; English Abrasives, London; Finnish Plywood Development Association, London; Forestry Commission, Cambridge, Cambs; Neville Foster, The Timber Development Association (NSW) Ltd., Sydney; Furniture Industry Research Association, Stevenage, Herts; Philip Griffiths, London; Alan Hollingbery, London; Jackson Day Designs, London; Fa. Ernst Kruse, Hamburg; Fa. F. R. Musfeldt, Hamburg; Office de Diffusion des Applications du Contreplaqué (ODAC), Paris; Office de Diffusion des Panneaux de Particules (ODIP), Paris; John Tate, The Master Builders Association of New South Wales, Sydney; Timber Research and Development Association (TRADA), High Wycombe, Bucks; Patrick Wiemken, Hamburg.

## Index/Glossary

# Metric Conversion Chart

## Approximate equivalents—length

| Millimetres to inches | | Inches to millimetres | |
|---|---|---|---|
| 1 | 1/32 | 1/32 | 1 |
| 2 | 1/16 | 1/16 | 2 |
| 3 | 1/8 | 1/8 | 3 |
| 4 | 5/32 | 3/16 | 5 |
| 5 | 3/16 | 1/4 | 6 |
| 6 | 1/4 | 5/16 | 8 |
| 7 | 9/32 | 3/8 | 10 |
| 8 | 5/16 | 7/16 | 11 |
| 9 | 11/32 | 1/2 | 13 |
| 10 (1cm) | 3/8 | 9/16 | 14 |
| 11 | 7/16 | 5/8 | 16 |
| 12 | 15/32 | 11/16 | 17 |
| 13 | 1/2 | 3/4 | 19 |
| 14 | 9/16 | 13/16 | 21 |
| 15 | 19/32 | 7/8 | 22 |
| 16 | 5/8 | 15/16 | 24 |
| 17 | 11/16 | 1 | 25 |
| 18 | 23/32 | 2 | 51 |
| 19 | 3/4 | 3 | 76 |
| 20 | 25/32 | 4 | 102 |
| 25 | 1 | 5 | 127 |
| 30 | 1 3/16 | 6 | 152 |
| 40 | 1 9/16 | 7 | 178 |
| 50 | 1 15/16 | 8 | 203 |
| 60 | 2 3/8 | 9 | 229 |
| 70 | 2 3/4 | 10 | 254 |
| 80 | 3 1/8 | 11 | 279 |
| 90 | 3 9/16 | 12 (1ft) | 305 |
| 100 | 3 15/16 | 13 | 330 |
| 200 | 7 7/8 | 14 | 356 |
| 300 | 11 13/16 | 15 | 381 |
| 400 | 15 3/4 | 16 | 406 |
| 500 | 19 11/16 | 17 | 432 |
| 600 | 23 5/8 | 18 | 457 |
| 700 | 27 9/16 | 19 | 483 |
| 800 | 31 1/2 | 20 | 508 |
| 900 | 35 7/16 | 24 (2ft) | 610 |
| 1000 (1m) | 39 3/8 | | |

| Metres to feet/inches | | Yards to metres | |
|---|---|---|---|
| | | 1 | 0.914 |
| 2 | 6' 7" | 2 | 1.83 |
| 3 | 9' 10" | 3 | 2.74 |
| 4 | 13' 1" | 4 | 3.65 |
| 5 | 16' 5" | 5 | 4.57 |
| 6 | 19' 8" | 6 | 5.49 |
| 7 | 23' 0" | 7 | 6.40 |
| 8 | 26' 3" | 8 | 7.32 |
| 9 | 29' 6" | 9 | 8.23 |
| 10 | 32' 10" | 10 | 9.14 |
| 20 | 65' 7" | 20 | 18.29 |
| 50 | 164' 0" | 50 | 45.72 |
| 100 | 328' 7" | 100 | 91.44 |

## Conversion factors

| | | |
|---|---|---|
| **Length** | 1 millimetre (mm) | = 0.0394 in |
| | 1 centimetre (cm)/10 mm | = 0.3937 in |
| | 1 metre/100 cm | = 39.37 in/3.281 ft/1.094 yd |
| | 1 kilometre (km)/1000 metres | = 1093.6 yd/0.6214 mile |
| | 1 inch (in) | = 25.4 mm/2.54 cm |
| | 1 foot (ft)/12 in | = 304.8 mm/30.48 cm/0.3048 metre |
| | 1 yard (yd)/3 ft | = 914.4 mm/91.44 cm/0.9144 metre |
| | 1 mile/1760 yd | = 1609.344 metres/1.609 km |
| **Area** | 1 square centimetre (sq cm)/ 100 square millimetres (sq mm) | = 0.155 sq in |
| | 1 square metre (sq metre)/10,000 sq cm | = 10.764 sq ft/1.196 sq yd |
| | 1 are/100 sq metres | = 119.60 sq yd/0.0247 acre |
| | 1 hectare (ha)/100 ares | = 2.471 acres/0.00386 sq mile |
| | 1 square inch (sq in) | = 645.16 sq mm/6.4516 sq cm |
| | 1 square foot (sq ft)/144 sq in | = 929.03 sq cm |
| | 1 square yard (sq yd)/9 sq ft | = 8361.3 sq cm/0.8361 sq metre |
| | 1 acre/4840 sq yd | = 4046.9 sq metres/0.4047 ha |
| | 1 square mile/640 acres | = 259 ha/2.59 sq km |
| **Volume** | 1 cubic centimetre (cu cm)/ 1000 cubic millimetres (cu mm) | = 0.0610 cu in |
| | 1 cubic decimetre (cu dm)/1000 cu cm | = 61.024 cu in/0.0353 cu ft |
| | 1 cubic metre/1000 cu dm | = 35.3146 cu ft/1.308 cu yd |
| | 1 cu cm | = 1 millilitre (ml) |
| | 1 cu dm | = 1 litre  see **Capacity** |
| | 1 cubic inch (cu in) | = 16.3871 cu cm |
| | 1 cubic foot (cu ft)/1728 cu in | = 28.3168 cu cm/0·0283 cu metre |
| | 1 cubic yard (cu yd)/27 cu ft | = 0.7646 cu metre |
| **Capacity** | 1 litre | = 1.7598 pt/0.8799 qt/0.22 gal |
| | 1 pint (pt) | = 0.568 litre |
| | 1 quart (qt) | = 1.137 litres |
| | 1 gallon (gal) | = 4.546 litres |
| **Weight** | 1 gram (g) | = 0.035 oz |
| | 1 kilogram (kg)/1000 g | = 2.20 lb/35.2 oz |
| | 1 tonne/1000 kg | = 2204.6 lb/0.9842 ton |
| | 1 ounce (oz) | = 28.35 g |
| | 1 pound (lb) | = 0.4536 kg |
| | 1 ton | = 1016 kg |
| **Pressure** | 1 gram per square metre (g/metre$^2$) | = 0.0292 oz/sq yd |
| | 1 gram per square centimetre (g/cm$^2$) | = 0.226 oz/sq in |
| | 1 kilogram per square centimetre (kg/cm$^2$) | = 14.226 lb/sq in |
| | 1 kilogram per square metre (kg/metre$^2$) | = 0.205 lb/sq ft |
| | 1 pound per square foot (lb/ft$^2$) | = 4.882 kg/metre$^2$ |
| | 1 pound per square inch (lb/in$^2$) | = 703.07 kg/metre$^2$ |
| | 1 ounce per square yard (oz/yd$^2$) | = 33.91 g/metre$^2$ |
| | 1 ounce per square foot (oz/ft$^2$) | = 305.15 g/metre$^2$ |
| **Temperature** | To convert °F to °C, subtract 32, then divide by 9 and multiply by 5 | |
| | To convert °C to °F, divide by 5 and multiply by 9, then add 32 | |

Phototypeset by Tradespools Limited, Frome, Somerset
Printed in Spain by Artes Gráficas Toledo, S.A.
D. L. TO:163 -1984